MANAGING CONFLICT IN A NEGOTIATED WORLD

MANAGING CONFLICT IN A NEGOTIATED WORLD

A Narrative Approach to Achieving Dialogue and Change

Peter M. Kellett
Diana G. Dalton

Sage Publications
International Educational and Professional Publisher
Thousand Oaks ▪ London ▪ New Delhi

For information:

 Sage Publications, Inc.
2455 Teller Road
Thousand Oaks, California 91320
E-mail: order@sagepub.com

Sage Publications Ltd.
6 Bonhill Street
London EC2A 4PU
United Kingdom

Sage Publications India Pvt. Ltd.
M-32 Market
Greater Kailash I
New Delhi 110 048 India

Printed in the United States of America

Library of Congress Cataloging-in-Publication Data

Kellett, Peter M.
　　Managing conflict in a negotiated world: A narrative approach to achieving dialogue and change / by Peter M. Kellett and Diana G. Dalton
　　　　p.　cm.
　　Includes bibliographical references and index.
　　ISBN 0-7619-1888-4 (cloth)
　　ISBN 0-7619-1889-2 (pbk.)
　　1. Conflict management.　I. Dalton, Diana G.　II. Title.
HM1126.K45 2001
303.6′9–dc21　　　　　　　　　　　　　　　　　00-011091

01　02　03　04　05　10　9　8　7　6　5　4　3　2　1

Acquiring Editor:	Margaret H. Seawell
Production Editor:	Denise Santoyo
Editorial Assistant:	Candice Crosetti
Designer/Typesetter:	Siva Math Setters, Chennai, India
Indexer:	Teri Greenburg
Cover Designer:	Michelle Lee

Contents

Acknowledgments

My special thanks go to the late Professor Donald MacDonald for teaching me the importance of understanding conflict, and to Professor H. L. "Bud" Goodall Jr. for teaching me to understand the importance of a good story. I am also indebted to the students of CST 344: Negotiation and Conflict Management at UNCG whose stories and dialogues made this book possible. In particular, I would like to thank those students who allowed us to use their personal narratives to help us better understand conflict.

Peter Kellett

I would like to thank Ina Ames, whose interpersonal communication class changed the way I thought about communication forever; Dr. Bud Goodall, my professor and advisor, who always encouraged and challenged me; my loving family, Howard and Diana Dalton, Liz Sullivan, Matt Dalton, and Lesli Lindgren, whose love and support have always helped me achieve my goals. But most of all, I would like to thank Dr. Peter Kellett, a friend I greatly admire, for giving me this opportunity to work with him.

Diana Dalton

Introduction

Conflict is part of our everyday lives in relationships, families, and workplaces. It is also an enduring presence in the neighborhoods and the various communities we inhabit. Conflict is also an important communicative expression of the extraordinary and often explosive divisions, oppositions, and tensions in and around situations or relationships. Simply, it can be a useful clue that something deeper needs to be addressed. Similarly, conflict is a process by which divisions, opposition, and tensions are created and potentially resolved. That is, conflict can be useful in stimulating productive dialogue and necessary change in our everyday lives. How people manage the conflict process in the various contexts of their lives is the main question we address in this book.

How to manage conflict effectively is a simple question with an often highly complex and elusive answer. Some phrase this as a behavioral question, "How should I act when such and such situation occurs?" Sometimes, a bulleted list or steps in a formula can work. Managing conflict is, however, only partly a behavioral question, and therefore behavioral change is only part of the answer. Conflict and how it should be managed are also learned and have a cultural meaning and context, a historical significance and a rhetorical purpose, and a complexity and multiplicity of function that eludes simple behavioral or communication formulas. Managing conflict is, therefore, more about developing a deeper *understanding* than simply *doing* something differently.

To determine how conflict should be managed ideally requires an understanding of the meaning of conflict for those engaged in it. It requires an understanding of the underlying cultural and systemic tensions expressed by the conflict. It requires an understanding of how and why it occurs in and through communication. It requires an understanding of how conflict can indicate opportunities to improve dialogue in relationships.

The interpretive approach of this book makes asking these questions a central part of developing conflict communication skills. An interpretive approach is based partly on the idea that asking "why" is often far more revealing and productive in understanding conflict than just asking how to manage it. In short, interpreting the lived meaning of conflict—asking deeper questions about why it happens as it does—is a necessary precursor to determining how to act when you find yourself in a conflict situation. Simply, an interpretive approach to conflict management is timely and necessary. It is also based on a far more realistic appreciation of the often multiple meanings and complex dynamics of conflict than approaches based on simple behavioral formulas and abstract communication models.

Our main goal in writing this book is to help readers, as narrators (storytellers) and interpreters (audiences), become more aware of their own conflict experiences and the conflict processes in their communities, workplaces, families, relationships, and so on. Note that we focus on these contexts as exemplars of the conflict processes that affect people most often. Note also that we begin with the broadest context and continue to the most intimate and personal context. This organization is used so readers develop an understanding of the broadest context that structures most personal experiences of conflict to some degree. But we hope to do more than just develop awareness. We also invite readers of the personal conflict narratives on which we base this book to engage in an ongoing dialogue about real conflict experiences. If you follow the lead of these narratives, this ongoing dialogue will result in a deeper understanding of your own conflicts by learning to interpret the your experiences and those of others.

Dialogue always begins with an existential risk—a moment of transparency in which a seam in our everyday performance of being ourselves appears. This transparency, whether viewed as a moment in a clearing in the woods or a place where a narrow connecting ridge between differences becomes visible, drives our search for more clarity. The narrators whose stories are included in this book have risked the questions that such transparency invites. The reader is asked to do the same. Given this perspective, understanding *how to act* becomes grounded in understanding *what the conflict means, what can realistically change* given the context, and *what the participants want to achieve* psychologically, relationally, and rhetorically. This approach to understanding conflict is connected at each turn in the discussion to a dialogue model of communication through which the reader learns to appreciate the opportunities and realistic limits of improving communication as a way to manage conflicts.

In subsequent chapters we more fully define and apply these key concepts of interpretive theory and methodology, the dialogue approach to communication, and principles of negotiation. At this point, you learn to develop the ability to reflectively narrate conflict experiences and ask theoretically informed questions about the communication practices those narratives represent. You also learn to explore the choices made in a conflict. These communication skills are the very essence of our interpretive approach to managing conflict.

PART I

Understanding Conflict Narratives

Understanding why conflicts happen in your life is the key to well-reasoned action and productive change in how you handle conflicts. The level of understanding necessary to know why conflicts happen and how you can do them differently where appropriate does not come easy. Such insight comes through careful and constant reflection on your conflict experiences and how you account for those experiences. Careful reflection requires both a useful means of accessing, collecting, and studying your conflicts and a systematic process of inquiry into those conflicts. The following section of this book is designed to help you develop the ability to collect and reflect on your conflict experiences so you achieve deeper and more empowering levels of understanding about the choices you make in conflicts and the choices you could make.

More specifically, Chapter 1 presents you with a perspective on conflict as a necessary, even beneficial process, depending in large part on how it is managed. You acquire an understanding of the opportunities for improved dialogue that almost all conflicts represent.

Chapter 2 enables you to develop the ability to collect and reflect on conflict experiences through personal narrative accounts—stories—of conflict.

Chapter 3 enables you to develop an understanding of how to analyze conflict narratives for clues about ourselves and how we represent others in our conflicts. You also come to understand that the communicative contexts we create and that are created for us by our conflicts play an important role in our ability to fully understand the contextuality of conflicts.

Chapter 4 provides a detailed explanation of how to collect, write, and interpret conflicts through personal narratives.

Each of the four chapters in the first half of this book combine to equip you with the ability to collect, analyze, and learn from conflicts from the perspective of developing more dialogic relationships. At each step, others' stories are available for you to interpret. You learn how to ask good questions of these stories presented for your analysis. You also are challenged to ask yourself good questions about your own conflict experiences. By developing your ability to ask good questions and to synthesize the answers into coherent interpretations of narrative, you become prepared to collect and interpret your own conflict experiences as well as those of others. Part II of this book enables you to apply this interpretive process in several communication contexts.

Conflict and Dialogue in a Negotiated World

"[Peace is] the optimal outcome of conflict, and a necessary condition of civilization."

(Donohue, 1997, p. 65)

"Negotiation is a test of the self."

(Nierenberg, 1973, p. 87)

Typically, we all bring to a discussion about conflict a number of preconceptions representative of our lived experience. They are true for us, but sometimes they are quite limiting. Specifically, we often realize that conflict is a difficult, complex, and frequently mismanaged process in the world around us. We may also feel uncomfortable about and even afraid of conflict. For a variety of reasons, we are more likely to experience the results of avoidance, aggression, and compromise than we are to see the results of increased understanding through effective dialogue. We may realize that our approach to conflict management affects the health of our relationships and the quality of the social world that we help to create. However, cultural myths about conflict that structure our communication practices are also often deeply held. Besides showing how your conflicts affect your relationships, this chapter outlines some of the central assumptions that frame this text. You are challenged to examine cultural myths about conflict that often limit both your willingness to do conflict, and your understanding of conflict as a potentially positive experience. You are introduced to the concept of the negotiated world and how conflict can play beneficial or dangerous roles in that world, largely depending on how it is approached and managed. You are challenged and encouraged to start thinking about conflicts that occur in the communities, workplaces, families, and relationships that make up your life-world. You are also challenged to think about conflict processes that are important in all of these contexts. Finally, the importance of a dialogic approach to managing conflict and a narrative approach to studying conflict, are introduced.

Key Concepts, Terms, and Definitions to Learn in This Chapter

- Why conflict is inevitable and even necessary in human relationships

- How conflict can be beneficial or damaging to relationships depending partly on how it is managed

- The factors and choices that create productive and destructive conflicts

- Why truly negotiating conflicts is rare

- How to approach conflict as a peacemaker

- What some of the myths about conflict practices are and how they affect your conflicts

- How you negotiate and create your reality partly through conflict

- How to practice dialogue as a way of communicating

- How dialogue is different from arguing

- How to evaluate the quality of dialogue in a conflict by analyzing narrative accounts of the conflict

- How narratives provide a way in to understanding your conflicts

Key Definitions

- *Productive and destructive conflict.* Productive conflicts occur when a conflict moves toward resolution and where the psychological and relational health of the participants is maintained. Destructive conflict results in a worse situation and, sometimes, harm to the participants.

- *Negotiation.* Negotiation occurs when participants strive to collaboratively resolve conflicts.

- *Dialogue and argument.* Dialogue occurs when conflict participants engage themselves and the other(s) in the deep questioning that leads to mutual understanding and resolution of the conflict. Argument is polarized talk based on the demonstration of reasoned positions.
- *Peace.* Peace is the presence of habits of communication that promote both conciliation and reconciliation.
- *Narratives.* Narratives are more or less fully developed personal accounts or stories of a conflict.

THE NEED TO UNDERSTAND CONFLICT IN OUR WORLD

As humans, we have an innate need to make sense of and understand our experiences. This is a precursor to developing the intelligence to make choices about that experience. Language, specifically narrative, allows us to step away from the ongoing flow of action and talk about and reflect on that action so that we can rethink and sometimes reshape our actions. As we reflect on our conflict experiences, one of the curious paradoxes we face is the fact that most conflicts would be easy to resolve if the participants truly communicated, but they rarely do. Although communication is pervasive and largely instinctive, it is not easy to do well. The following story illustrates the fact that real life can be informed by applying theories and resolution principles, but that life does not necessarily fall neatly into simple formulae. This narrative also illustrates that conflicts in families can reappear and come out in interesting ways that may be only symbolically or tangentially related to the original conflict. This is one of the main reasons conflicts are often difficult to resolve. Note the ways that people become symbolic in the other party's construction of the conflict. Notice also the imagery used to describe the conflict and its "buildup," for example, and the "cycle" as an image of repeating patterns.

————◄○►————

Exemplar Narrative: The Never-Ending Conflict

—REINA

When I was three years old my mother decided to leave my father. He was an abusive husband and she feared him. My mother and I moved to New York until the divorce settlement was finalized. When I was about six years old, we moved back to Charlotte, NC. While we were in New York and even after we moved to NC, my mother always told me what an awful man my father was. After we moved to North Carolina, she had me escorted in and out and around school. She told me that my dad had threatened to kidnap me. My mom also nailed the windows down and had four locks on both the front and back doors. She did not want to encounter my dad.

From the time I was three years old to about twelve years old, I was not allowed to see or talk to my dad, with few exceptions. The exception was when my dad got a court order for visitation rights. I was about seven when this happened. I was able to go different places with my dad and stepmom. I spent the whole weekend with them every two weeks. However, my mom made me give a report of events every time I came home and she would write it down in a notebook. After the third visit with my father, I was not able to spend time with him again. From being around my father, I desired to have a relationship with him. I was becoming more of a daddy's little girl and my mother hated it. So, I was told that if I made contact with him, I would be punished.

I was in sixth grade and I wanted to go on a field trip for a week to Boone with my school. My mom didn't have the money, so she asked my dad for it. He gave her the money with the condition that he could start seeing me again. I got very close to my dad within a year, but I got more and more distant from my mother. My mother and I never had a great relationship, but at this time in my life it was very bad. She finally got mad enough to send me to live with my father. I was scared because my relationship with my father was based on random weekends spent together over my entire life of twelve years. My mom knew she had instilled fear of my father in me. She felt that this would punish me and straighten me up.

My mother's worst fear happened, I was daddy's little girl. I loved living with my father. I had never had such a stable life before. It was like going from rags to riches in all aspects. There was very little arguing, not because I was avoiding it, we just never had conflicts. I lived with my father for four years this way.

My dad did not like a guy I had been seeing, and tension was building. On this particular day, I was sick with food poisoning and had been sleeping all day. I made a phone call to a guy friend to cancel going out that night. My dad, step mom, and my little sister came home when I was making this phone call. My little sister picked up the phone and wouldn't hang it up. So, I went and told dad on her. Dad told me to get off the phone as I had been on it all day long. I made a smart remark, which I had never done before, and he came after me up the stairs. I ran to my room, locked the door, and got off the phone. I decided to open the door when my dad threatened to break the door down. When he came in he tore the phone out of the wall and threw me on the bed. I began screaming, "You're not going to hurt me like you did Mom, Peggy (my step mother), or David (my step brother)." This was, of course, mixed in with a lot of foul language. All my dad could do was hit me over and over again in my face, screaming, "SHUT UP." Finally, I stopped saying things and he stopped hitting me. He went downstairs and I cried in fear. I wanted out of the house so bad I couldn't stand it. He was in control with all the power, and I wanted to stand up to him to have power, but first I had to get out of the house. So, I called the guy friend I was supposed to go out with that night, and then I called my mother. By this time, my father had come back to see whom I was calling, to not allow me to do such a thing. When he found out it was my mom, he let me call her, but she wasn't home. So, I went downstairs to get some ice for my face. Somehow, my father and I got into it again. I don't remember what was said at this point, but I do remember going through two doors. There was a knock at the door. It was George, the guy I called. Of course my dad was not going to invite him in; instead he got the door slammed in his face. However, about ten minutes later, my mother showed up because of the message I had left her on the answering machine. I packed a bag and left with my mother. My mother called the police and convinced me to press charges for abuse.

At that time, in the state of North Carolina, a parent could not be legally prosecuted for abuse unless permanent damage was done. The left side of my face was swollen with broken blood vessels, but there was no permanent damage. The case was thrown out of court. Since that time, my father has refused to talk to me, and has cut off all communication. I tried for about two and a half years to talk to him and establish some kind of relationship, even if it was distant. I have had no reaction except from hearsay that he was slandering my name and using a lot of foul language. It has now been seven and a half years since this conflict has happened. Technically, there was no resolution to this conflict.

Initial dialogue questions include the following:

1. Was this conflict about her little sister being on the phone, or was it about her getting smart with her dad, or, was the conflict about some other deeper and more enduring issues?

2. How were symbolic issues important in this conflict? How did they each represent people and things to each other, and how were these issues involved in creating and maintaining the conflict?

3. How did the relationship of Reina's mother and father create and maintain the conditions for the conflict?

4. How were attributions and previous experiences important in generating this conflict?

5. How did the repeating pattern of conflict get established and maintained?

6. Why did Reina and her father not have any conflicts for the first couple of years and then a major eruption?

7. How did "hot buttons" or "trigger" words and phrases figure into the violent conflict?

8. Why was there so much verbal aggressiveness in this conflict?

9. Why did the relationship of Reina and her father end as it did?

10. How could they have thought differently and what might they have done differently?

Reina goes on to help us answer some of these questions through her own retrospective on the experience. Placing the conflict in a "big picture" helps her make sense of it as the inevitable expression of conditions she is part of, and that others are part of also. They all in some part create—negotiate—these conditions as their family reality of the experience Reina is responsible for but, more important, some of it she recognizes as beyond her control. This is an important realization in moving through the conflict existentially.

The Big Picture

The big picture is that I don't have a relationship with my father, regardless of what the conflict was really about. As I look at the conflict, I think, was this fate? Was this supposed to happen this way? My answer to this is yes. Families repeat dysfunction until the cycle is broken. My father was abused as a child and didn't speak to his father for many, many years. In fact, I met my grandfather only one time. They had conflicts when he was a young man. They didn't speak until after I moved in with my father. My dad was about 43 at the time. Do I want to break this cycle of dysfunction? Yes, but how do you do that when the other party wants to perpetuate it?

Additional dialogue questions include the following:

1. What would be your advice to Reina to help her answer this final question?

2. What is the piece of the puzzle that helps make sense of the whole experience for her and for us?

3. How can she break the cycle of dysfunction?

4. What does it take in reality to break such deeply ingrained patterns in relationships?

5. What are some ways that you have heard of or seen people use to break such cycles?

6. What are the constructive alternatives if breaking a cycle is unrealistic?

These are some useful questions through which you can learn from Reina's experience. We move on to examine the conflict issues and processes represented in this narrative in more detail.

THE REALITY OF A WORLD OF CONFLICT

Conflict Is Inevitable and Necessary

Moments and times of conflict are as inevitable as moments and times of cooperation. As Heisey (1991) explains, humankind is both individualistic and communal, we are similar and different, and the tension between these complementary but opposing forces results in conflict. Further, as Rapoport (1992) illustrates, conflict and cooperation are essential to each other's existence. They are complementary as a "union of opposites" (p. 87). Each, Rapoport argues, is a "cardinal principle of life" (p. 81). They stimulate each other, and at the same time, justify themselves by the existence of the other (p. 81). Conflict is, therefore, both natural and often beneficial. The key, according to Arnett (1986), is to allow these natural oppositions to exist in creative tension such that they generate ideas and new possibilities.

Not an easy thing to do, although managing this creative tension is possible through dialogue. In dialogue, conflict participants can move beyond a position-based conflict, characterized as "you versus me" to an issue- or interest-based conflict, characterized as "us versus this problem." Participants can learn to speak from a "we" perspective, as opposed to an "I versus you" position, and examine and negotiate mutual as well as opposing interests (Fisher & Ury, 1981; Rapoport, 1992; Troester & Dowlin, 1991).

In Reina's narrative, the sense of inevitability or fate is a powerful sense-making strategy for her. Of course, conflicts in family relationships are inevitable. Families experience all of the typical conflicts associated with developing and maintaining committed, long-term relationships, with raising children through adolescence, balancing the goals and satisfying the needs of several people, and so on. In the above narrative, there is a sense that the tensions of the individual and community/family stimulate each other, but the stimulation creates negative portrayals of the other. This maintains the conflict and its underlying conditions.

Consider how negatively Reina's mother characterizes her father. How do her actions create the image of the father as the destroyer of the family community? How is this image maintained through the symbolic power of actions, images, and representations? How might his portrayal of his wife have paralleled and opposed her own account? How do these early experiences create expectations about family communication and particularly conflict for the narrator? Such questions help you understand how conflicts inevitably arise.

Conflict Can Be Beneficial or Damaging

Conflict should not necessarily be viewed as a negative or dysfunctional form of communication (Cahn, 1997). Rather, conflict can be positive and constructive.

It is hard work for Reina to see positives in her family conflict experience, but she did learn some valuable lessons, and the conflict probably has had a greater impact on her life than she might imagine. Her family experiences might be partially the reason she graduated with a degree in communication, and is about to enter a master's program to ask deeper questions about conflict communication. Based on her difficult experiences, she can also develop some life goals and strategies that may prevent her from repeating the patterns she inherits. There can be useful learning from the experience.

Walton (1987) identifies three possible benefits of conflict. First, conflict can generate a certain level of energy and motivation. How did the conflict with her father create the energy that led her to seek him out as a teenager? How did the violent incident with her father create the energy that moved her into the next part of her story? Without these conflicts, she would not have the full story that she has at this point in her life.

Second, in bringing out varying viewpoints, conflict can increase levels of creativity and innovation. For example, Reina ends her narrative with the deeper realizations that she can engage in the conflict, but she also needs her father to participate. Her story tells her what it would take to be creative in engaging the conflict. It also leads to the realization that the sort of creativity and innovation Walton refers to is absent from Reina's and her father's current avoidance of the conflict. What would it take for them to engage in a healthy conflict process?

Third, people can gain deeper understanding of their conflicts and themselves from engaging in conflict. Reina has learned some valuable life lessons about conflict, the deep patterns that structure the present and the future, and what it takes to have a healthy family communication system. What are these main lessons she has learned?

However, Walton also shows us that conflict can be debilitating. It can rigidify the social and cultural system in which the conflict takes place, and it can lead to a host of other distortions, polarities, and additional conflicts. It is clear that Reina's father's early conflicts with his own father have created repeating patterns that have debilitated him in his family life. It is also clear that Reina inherits some deeply polar and distorted accounts of her father and family conflict. Only years later is she able to place those polar and positional elements of her mother's account in perspective.

The following four factors can make the difference between so-called productive and nonproductive conflicts.

• Learn to ask good questions about conflict experiences and the narrative representation of those experiences. As Reina asks useful questions that build her understanding of the family conflict, she is able to put the conflict in perspective, potentially forgive others, and avoid blaming herself for the conflict.

• Make understanding our conflicts a priority. Reina has attempted to piece together the clues and fragments of memories and experiences that help her to understand the conflict, how she is placed in it, and how she reifies it in her own communication. You can learn from engaging in the same process for your experiences.

• Learn from your own and other peoples' conflicts. Reina's understanding of her conflict leads her to take a perspective of learning. As she wrestles with the question of how she can end the negative conflict cycle in her family, she is also confronting the deeper question of how she can learn to change. If successful, she may not recreate the conditions in the next generation that created this type of conflict in her family.

• Learn to manage conflicts more effectively based on a lifestyle of inquiry. Although Reina cannot fulfill her desire to solve the conflicts that happened long ago, she can examine specifically how she will and will not think and act as she creates her own family. She can also decide how she will treat her family members and allow them to treat her. If she chooses to restart a relationship with her father, how could she manage the communication to achieve the relational goals that she has for her father and herself in terms of how they might discuss the past? How might forgiveness move their relationship in a new direction? If she were preparing to meet with her father, what would her main strategic choices be? What advice would you give her in approaching such an experience? What might be the next chapter of her conflict narrative? The ideal that you create as you imagine the answers to these questions helps you realize that such dialogue is all too rare.

The Rarity of Dialogue and Negotiation

Not only is the dialogic negotiation of relationships and their conflicts rare, it is also often unconsciously, and sometimes even consciously, avoided. Consider Reina's narrative and imagine all of the ways the participants create good reasons not to have dialogue. What are some of these conscious and unconscious avoidance strategies? How might the participants justify not talking with each other? The "truth" you come to is a freeing thing on which to base your reality because arriving at the truth of a conflict is the best place from which to change. It is also a frightening and difficult prospect as well because you confront the often stark reality of your conflict with the understanding that you need to change. The result is that we all tend to experience a world consisting of the results of compromises, avoidance, and aggressions that make up our shared social realities. Think, for example, about the ritualized way that conflicts in Reina's life reflect the patterns of avoidance and violence she inherited from her family. It is difficult, almost naive sounding, to suggest that she should strive for better quality dialogue in her relationships, particularly with her father. She can try, if that is important to her. She can also make a concerted effort to understand how in her conflicts she is recreating the patterns she learned from her family and how she also contributes to creating her conflicts. You can do the same by asking yourself the following questions:

1. How is my approach to conflict grounded in my early family experiences?

2. Why is it so difficult to envision a more dialogic world, or even a more dialogic family? What factors get in the way?

3. If I could point to a relationship, a conversation, or even a moment in a conversation when I truly negotiated something by using dialogue, how would I describe that communication experience?

4. What, if any, might be the moments of dialogue in the family portrayed in Reina's narrative?

CONFLICT MANAGEMENT, PEACE COMMUNICATION, AND RELATIONAL HEALTH

The Ideal of Peacemaking in a Complex World

Heisey (1991) argues convincingly that peacemaking is more important and certainly more realistic than the existence of a peaceful world. The world will likely never experience peace because competition and differences are always part of relationships. We often gain more as nations and as individuals by engaging in wars and other deeply symbolic conflicts, as in Reina's narrative of family "war."

Complete peace in any family is probably unrealistic, although striving for more peace—peacemaking—is a valuable pursuit. Wars are a good rhetorical opportunity to prove our own rightness and moral or technological superiority. They validate our way of life and all the decisions that brought it about. Focusing on common interests is a goal that, in the complexity of rhetorical and political processes globally, is beyond reach for most of us. Consider how Reina's mother and father both create and propagate perspectives in which the other is evil and they are victims of the actions of that evil person. However, you can strive to engage in creative, productive, and generative dialogue that helps produce conditions for more peaceful relationships.

Looking beneath and beyond the manifest reality of communication for opportunities to communicate more effectively, and taking those opportunities whenever possible, is peacemaking. Reina has chosen to pursue peacemaking, not necessarily in the conflict with her father but certainly because of it, in the rest of her life. Peace is conceptualized as both the process of *reconciliation* and the end state of *community* (Troester & Dowlin, 1991). Perhaps we can elaborate on this by adding that peace is also about conciliation, that is, creating the conditions that support peace and that minimize the need for reconciliation. Reconciliation is not impossible between Reina and her father and between her and her mother. It will take dialogue to move in that direction, but a better family community is possible through genuine efforts to reconcile. Reina can learn to recognize the conditions creating similar conflicts in her own life and change those patterns. This is the habit of conciliation.

Rather than an absence of war, a sort of energyless state, peace involves the redirection of energy into discovering new or hidden possibilities (Donohue, 1997; Kahn & Landau, 1988). As she asks herself where she wants the next phase of her conflict to go, Reina moves from the negative peace of silence to a more active place where she makes conscious choices. Peace is also not the absence of differences or struggle. As Keltner argues, "There is ample room for struggle in a peaceful world (1991, p. 77)." According to Keltner, peacemakers are "those who prevent, avoid, or eliminate the use of destructive violence in the settling of differences" (p. 78). This necessarily involves the strategic use of communication, such as negotiating and mediating. Simply, peacemaking requires communication as the tool or process of addressing conflicts. In striving to avoid the anger of previous conflicts and choosing to think about how she can break those negative and warlike family patterns, Reina is becoming a peacemaker.

Making a difference between the unattainable ideal of peace and the real possibility for peacemaking involves developing the ability to create peace, that is, to become a better peacemaker through communication and interpretation of others' communication. You can be better peacemakers in your communities, workplaces, families, and personal relationships by developing this ethos. Peace is the blessing associated with being a peacemaker. This is closely linked to what we might call healthy relationships. Reina has built the foundation of healthy future relationships—most important perhaps, within herself—by bringing a sense of peace to her past.

Understanding Myths About Conflict, Peace, and Communication

Myths, James (1996) points out, function to represent and reinforce our culture's deepest beliefs and perceptions about communication practices, including conflict. There are a number of common myths about conflict that are important to address.

First, there is the myth that *more communication always creates more clarity.* Clarity is a powerful metaphor in structuring how people think about and practice conflict (Kellett, 1987). The assumption that more talk increases the clarity of the issues in a conflict is a widely held belief. Moving from conflict defined as a "messy" or chaotic state to a less ambiguous, "clear" state is a useful visual metaphor for expressing changes in conflict processes and experiences. Maintaining diplomatic channels of communication—keeping in touch—is also a useful strategy that helps to prevent conflicts. This belief does, however, help propagate the myth that more talk moves a conflict from mess to clarity. In fact, it is the quality of thinking, understanding, and talk, as well as silence, that often moves a conflict forward. "Let's talk about this" is sometimes, but not always, the best strategy. Sometimes, as Reina does, we should begin with "let's *listen* to this and see where this came from, and what kind of talk we need from here."

The second myth says that *there is always an answer or solution to a conflict.* This myth is often grounded in cultural assumptions about our abilities to predict and control experiences that are namable and open to careful analytic study. Answering a question implies that a particular problem is solved and ended. Creating a solution implies that a problem is dissolved—made invisible by the catalytic actions of communication. Certainly, giving names to conflict processes opens them to our consciousness and our actions. Certainly, changing even small patterns of behavior can have significant effects on our lives. The whole self-help industry is based on this premise.

However, for many of life's conflicts there are no easy solutions. Problems such as that of Reina's family do not easily dissolve and go away. Life rarely falls into a simple format through which communication works to eliminate problems by creating solutions. Conflicts are almost always embedded in contexts and historical and cultural patterns and hierarchies. These conflicts are almost always more difficult to solve than they might appear because of this embeddedness. And they rarely disappear even if they are "solved." As Reina discovers through her narrative, conflicts often consist of echoes and convergences of other conflicts that have gone before. Often, in turn, these new conflicts create reverberations that pass through other contexts and generations. Understanding this may be a sort of solution, but it does not mean the conflict suddenly dissolves and disappears. It means that we know more about how and why conflict happens.

The third myth says that *managing conflict is primarily about doing things differently.* One of the first questions people often ask about conflict is "what can I do, or what should I do differently (to solve this conflict)?" If you take our earlier advice and focus on understanding and learning from conflicts, "doing" should be your last priority. Particularly in western cultures, people often learn to rely on doing things as a way of solving. In the United States, we have a pragmatic heritage that still filters into how people think about the world. We have also been somewhat conditioned to believe in behavioral formulas and programs that help us do things differently.

Doing things differently is a useful skill dimension in conflict communication. As Reina discovers, working to address and talk through conflicts in the future, rather than propagating the same patterns, is a useful form of "doing." However, doing should follow from, and be an expression of, understanding. In family conflict patterns, for example, to choose to do one thing differently from the previous generation—to break even one pattern—might be a realistic goal. To develop a deep understanding of how early patterns have shaped you and how you interconnect with other contexts because of those patterns, is also a very valuable goal.

The fourth myth says that *peace is the absence of conflict.* The absence of violence or war is what Rapoport (1992) calls "negative peace." As Donohue (1997) points out, the fact that people are not fighting does not mean cooperation is present (p. 67). Reina's family is not at peace even though they have not openly fought in a while. Theirs is a very thin version of peace.

We are culturally conditioned by the mass media to pay attention to extreme conflicts with powerful images of easily identifiable persons and simple oppositions (Galtung & Ruge, 1965). By the same token, we often assume that if we do not hear anything about a particular country or about a specific conflict, somehow that conflict has gone away, and peace is there now. Both assumptions are somewhat misleading and dangerous. If Reina had represented her father's violent outburst as the conflict, without developing the story before and after the conflict, the narrative would be of limited use. We would have captured only a moment in their relationship. Through her narrative, we gain a deeper sense of the source and ultimate destination of the conflict, as well as what is necessary for things to occur differently and, perhaps, lead to a different reality.

Some Final Reflective Questions on Reina's Narrative

1. Why is Reina's conflict inevitable and necessary in her family life?

2. How could this conflict be both beneficial and damaging to Reina in her relationships?

3. How productive is Reina's conflict, and how might she attempt to make it more productive?

4. What goals might Reina set for herself to promote more peace in her relationships?

5. What myths about conflict are important in describing how each participant acted in Reina's conflict?

THE NEGOTIATED WORLD

In the following conflict, Brian explores a life-changing past experience and asks several "why" questions. Specifically, he is trying to determine why this conflict happened within a broader picture of his life events and life narrative. Recast— renegotiated—as a gainful turning point, the conflict can become a useful part of his full life story.

————◄○►————

Exemplar Narrative: The Worst Job I Ever Learned From

—BRIAN

I felt as if my whole life was being crushed in one of those machines the junkyards use to reshape a whole automobile into one of those nice, neat three-foot square cubes for shipment to whoever buys such scrap metal. Every nerve seemed to be tearing loose from its origin and insertion point, only to have that experience magnified with each new encounter with JB. I was losing it and I didn't know what to do to stop the cycle.

Four years earlier, I had successfully traversed the formidable five-step interview process with one of our major utility companies to secure a position in their advertising department. My duties included evaluating customer advertising needs; designing, proposing, and selling to these needs; and preparing copy for our printer. JB began training 12 of us new recruits. The eight weeks of eating, sleeping, and drinking ad design, UDAC (universal directory advertising codes), customer objection rebuttals, and closing techniques had reduced our class to five. The company grapevine had labeled JB "the hatchet man." He was also known as a very capable trainer, and I came to believe that about him during my eight weeks. He knew the business.

I had consistently been one of the top producers with two other sales organizations, and my intent was to follow that same path with this company. To do so, I needed to learn as much as possible from JB during training. I was sent directly from training to DJ, a field sales manager on the Raleigh campaign. JB told me that he and DJ felt I could fill the recent vacancy on DJ's sales team. I thought this was an honor as the other four in my training class were sent to a very small rural campaign to what was called a "training book." Even JB said I was fortunate.

DJ was a great encourager. He also allowed me the freedom to discipline myself as long as I produced the numbers for the team. For four years, we had a great working relationship as we moved from city to city. Statewide, there averaged around 60 reps with whom I shared the same job title. Each of us competed against one another. My years under DJ's supervision were very successful. That first campaign in Raleigh with him set the stage for me. I finished in the top five against some seasoned reps. For the next four years, I managed to consistently be a top producer. I came within "spare change" of being the year's top producer in the entire state.

The next year brought numerous changes in the company structure. The state was split into two territories with new local offices in Greensboro and Raleigh. I chose the Greensboro office because it allowed me to be at home nights during all but four months of the year. Previously, I had been home only on weekends, and in many cases, every other weekend. I was considering marriage and the Greensboro locations would give me more time for this relationship.

During a two-week vacation in December, I received notice that my request for an assignment to the Greensboro office had been granted. JB was called out of his trainer's position in Charlotte, and he would be my new manager. I enjoyed

Christmas vacation with a number of pleasant thoughts. I had finished second in the state. I had made more money that year than ever before in my life. I was in love and scheduled to be married in August of the following year. My thoughts for the upcoming year were very positive. I could have more of a home life. I could begin to build on the ten acres I had bought that year. And I was comfortably familiar with my new sales manager, JB. Several of my coworkers had even commented on my good fortunes. What a success I thought I had become.

Two days after the new year began, I arrived in my new office in Greensboro. It was not hard to hold my head up among my new work crewmembers after the previous years. We spent the day organizing things so we could hit the streets the next day. JB arrived late in the afternoon and greeted us briefly, but he had his own things to organize. The next day, I felt as though he had knocked the breath out of me with one brief exchange. He came by my desk and remarked, "You did pretty well working for DJ." I said thanks. He continued, "Well, you're not working for him now. Let's see how well you perform doing things my way." Then he walked away.

Shock would scarcely describe my feelings. Surprise, amazement, discouragement, deflation, disappointment, maybe even insult were some of the feelings that raced through me. Why was I feeling such negative messages from JB? It got worse. No encouragement, no support, constant criticism, and growing resentments were my experiences. I no longer had the freedoms I had enjoyed with DJ. I felt like JB was constantly checking up on me for some unknown reason. I was required to give detailed activity plans that seemed unreasonable and unwarranted. The other duties of the job were stressful enough without all of this added pressure that I felt from JB. Attempts to address these issues with him failed miserably, and I got to the point where I didn't even try. I did try to avoid him.

At this point in the story I am back to where I began this narrative. The anxiety levels experienced in my relationship with JB were off the scale. Ulcers, panic attacks, and psychosomatic chest pains were the daily burdens. Months of this with no resolution or even understanding of the roots of this conflict led me to take a leave of absence from my work in September. The doctor's medications were not providing enough relief, so I began supplementing them with some of my own concoctions.

I never went back to work with this company, and the conflict continues as unresolved six years later.

———◄○►———

Communication and the Negotiated Reality of Conflict

Dialogue questions based on Brian's narrative include the following:

1. How did the organizational culture of hard-driving sales and competition contribute to the problem?

2. How did the change in Brian's power and place in the organizational culture contribute to the conflict?

3. How did the skill of knowing how to balance the cooperation of the team culture with the competition of the business figure into the conflict?

4. How did Brian's own expectations, character, and sense of self contribute to this chain of events?

5. How did Brian's avoidance and internalization of the conflict help create a downward spiral of communication?

6. How did attributing malicious intent to the other and pure intent to the self (as well as assumption of right and wrong) contribute to this conflict?

7. Why did cycles of demands, avoidance, demands, and confrontation occur?

8. How did the complex move of his family, and the fact that his commission relied on others, figure into JB's style?

9. How did the complexity of Brian's life figure in creating a climate that was primed for difficulty? (He married a woman with two children and was struggling to build relations with the children. He had new financial responsibilities. In the midst of this, his father died.)

10. How did assumptions of a continued pattern of success figure into Brian's reaction? (He used to say, "even my stamps fall sticky side up.")

11. How do Brian's choices of language and imagery help to support his narrative position?

In answering these questions, you begin to explore how Brian and the other participants consciously and unconsciously negotiated the reality of this conflict. Nierenberg (1973) offers the following as a useful definition of negotiation:

> "Whenever people exchange ideas with the intention of changing relationships, whenever they confer for agreement, they are negotiating."

Simply, negotiation involves the thoughtful, collaborative exchange of ideas with the intent, ideally, of creating agreements that all parties are happy with because they meet the needs of those parties (Fisher & Ertel, 1995). Given this definition, you can start asking useful questions about how the participants created their conflict and how they moved through—navigated—the conflict. You can examine the particular styles of negotiating, and how those styles connected to particular outcomes through the micro level of choosing particular strategies and tactics (Folger, Poole, & Stutman, 1997).

In a broader sense, the negotiation of reality occurs through the patterns of how people create agreements through conflict. If agreements are typically created through a collaborative process of examining parties' interests, then a social reality of collaboration pervades communication relationships in that context. Similarly, if agreements are achieved through manipulation or domination—technically not negotiation in the constructive sense, but in the sense of negotiation as navigation—then a more general communication climate of manipulation and domination endures. These cultural expectations, in turn, create the normative expectation that this is how communication is practiced and how it should be practiced in this context.

Characteristics and Guidelines for Dialogue

How much did dialogue, especially internal dialogue, figure into Brian's conflict? What were the personal and professional effects of approaching the conflict as he did? Were there any opportunities to approach this conflict more dialogically? What constrained the perception and choices of strategy? You can explore the characteristics of dialogue as they help you address these questions and understand Brian's narrative.

As Cissna and Anderson (1998) explain, *dialogue* derives from the Greek word *dialogos,* which combines the sense of "moving through" and "shared meaning." Simply, dialogue is a quality of communication, however fleeting, where people find themselves in communication that moves them to a shared meaning that they did not necessarily have before communicating. The phrase, "find themselves" is used because often we recognize moments of dialogue only in retrospect, when we have just had such a moment and we feel its effects on our understanding of and relationship to others.

This phrase is also used to describe dialogue in that we often find ourselves carried along—moved through—by our talk such that, while we are living it, it is all we are living for that moment. We blend with the other, and the context often disappears. As a result, we are *really talking together.* Brian has been working on the psychological and emotional effects of this conflict for a number of years. He seems to need to move through the conflict outside of it. This enduring sense of failing to resolve the conflict internally usually clearly signals a failure to engage the conflict externally through communication. At the same time, dialogue involves a strategic intent

1. to take the perspective of the other

2. to genuinely engage the other

3. to embrace the possibilities created in communicating with others (Cissna & Anderson, 1998).

This duality of dialogic communication as strategic ideal and prereflective reality and as thoughtful and ego-less existential talk points to some of the core paradoxes involved with handling conflict dialogically. First, you should prepare for dialogue and make all of the right decisions about how you will communicate.

However, the ethos—the spirit of dialogue—gives the talk a life of its own that cannot be micromanaged. You can organize your talk, but dialogue to some extent takes you where it will. Dialogue is lived as moments of good talk that finds its place in your ongoing conversation.

How did Brian prepare for his talks with JB? In what ways did his perceptions of himself and of JB's intent mean that he took a reactive and defensive approach to communicating with JB? Were there any opportunities for more open talk to take them through to a better working relationship? What got in the way of this need to both prepare and allow dialogue to lead?

Second, although we typically engage in conflict to meet our own outcome and process goals, dialogue necessarily means we have to fully engage the other to achieve what we want for ourselves. You begin dialogue with a genuine concern for the other to create the possibility that you will get what you want. Dialogic communication is about planning to talk about specific issues and living with the direction the talk actually takes. What you plan and where the dialogue actually goes are likely to be different in some ways. Dialogue also implies that you need to value the participation of the other to achieve your own goals. Because of these paradoxes, dialogue is simultaneously the riskiest and the safest and most naturally satisfying form of communication. Risking nothing does not create safety for either party. Risking everything might create safety for both.

In Brian's narrative, it appears that JB "won" the conflict. He was able to evoke a hard-driving and competitive organizational culture to create his own style of leadership. In his style, there is no need to engage the other. Dictating, in the sense of telling without listening (Senge et al., 1994), becomes the communication mechanism in the workplace. Reality is imposed rather than negotiated. How does Brian respond to this style of communication? How does the lack of risk in openly communicating affect Brian and JB's relative experiences of safety in the workplace?

Walton (1987) identifies the main distinctive features of a dialogue approach to conflict as when "parties directly engage each other and focus on the conflict between them, including aspects of the relationship itself" (p. 5). The first key issue is that the parties engage each other as people with valid, if conflicting, interests. How would you characterize the level of engagement between Brian and JB? Second, the parties focus on the conflict between them. That is, they recognize that they have constructed the conflict together. How well do Brian and JB focus on the conflict between them? How much do they recognize that they both actively constructed the conflict? Third, the parties to a conflict show a willingness to examine the systemic connection of current conflicts to underlying relational dynamics and to explore that relationship for change possibilities. This is how patterns are explicated, discussed, and changed. How well do Brian and JB discuss their relationship? How well did they develop a shared understanding of why they have such a conflict within that organizational context?

This dialogic approach to conflict can be further elaborated through explicating the seven main characteristics or necessary features of dialogic talk (Kellett, 1999). For the following exercise, imagine that Brian and JB go back to their working relationship to engage the conflict through these essential features of dialogue and related questions:

- Dialogue is a spatial container in which the time necessary for collective thinking to emerge is taken (Senge et al., 1994).
    1. What would Brian and JB need to do to create a context in which they can address and renegotiate their working relationship?

- Reflective thinking is an ongoing and thoughtful exchange about the issues people need to discuss to learn (Brown, 1995).
    2. How could Brian and JB communicate regularly about their work relationship?
    3. What specific issues would you advise Brian and JB to address?

- The purpose of dialogic exchange is to create mutual understanding and action (Brown, 1995).
    4. What do they need to develop a mutual understanding about?
    5. How might their dialogue be paralleled with changes in how they behave?

- This collaborative sense-making involves reflective questioning leading to explicit reasoning, assumptions, and possibilities (Putnam, 1996).
    6. On what specific questions would you have Brian and JB focus their dialogue?
    7. What assumptions need to come out in their dialogue?
    8. What possibilities for change would you like to see them explore?

- This focus on questioning relies on our ability to listen, value others, and address deep issues (Brown, 1995).
    9. How could Brian and JB make sure they listen to and value each other more?
    10. What deeper personal, organizational, and cultural issues are possibly expressed through this specific conflict?
    11. Which of these issues should Brian and JB become more aware of and discuss?

- This spirit of inquiry is central to dialogue, and involves focusing on connections and embracing diverse perspectives.
    12. What are some of the "why" questions you would want the participants to think about either separately or together?
    13. What important lessons could Brian and JB learn from exploring each other's perspectives and experiences?

- We should allow this shared understanding in the discursive "container" that dialogue creates to transform us (Bennett & Brown, 1995).

14. In what direction might Brian and JB's dialogue take them?

15. What is realistic given their contextual constraints?

Dialogue, Conflict, and the Negotiated World

As you have seen, dialogue is an ideal that creates a template through and from which you can compare everyday realities. This is not intended to imply that people's experiences are somehow inferior. Their narratives are their reality. Rather, dialogue is first a process by which you can ask valuable comparative and systemic questions and through which you can understand patterns, styles, and approaches to conflict. If dialogue is the ideal form of negotiation in which each party's concerns and interests figure into the process and solution, then you can gain a valuable account of conflicts that are and are not effectively negotiated. You have a deeper sense of why Brian and JB's conflict was not effectively negotiated, and what it would take to change that reality.

Second, dialogue enables you to examine the patterns of practices and social conventions that systemically and systematically facilitate and impinge upon how you create and navigate—negotiate—everyday life. The constraints affecting your ability in and expectations of conflict communication in the various contexts we explore in this book can be explicated. Taking a dialogic approach enables us to ask why the participants in the narratives negotiated their reality as they did.

Third, dialogue represents those moments of ideal existential communication to which you can strive (Cissna & Anderson, 1998). Hence, dialogue represents the form of negotiation that participants can implement in their specific relational context where such changes are possible.

Fourth, dialogue enables participants to develop concrete communicative practices and strategies through which they can change nonproductive conflict patterns. Hence, dialogue is a goal but it is also, reflexively, how you achieve that goal. Dialogue gives you a set of practices and guidelines for effectively constructing and navigating—negotiating—reality.

Dialogue and Argumentation

Dialogue is quite different from argumentation as a model of conflict management. Specifically, as Hyde and Bineham (2000) illustrate in referring to argumentation as "polarized discourse," dialogue emphasizes connections and collaborative approaches to communication. Argumentation or debate focuses on differences. Examine Brian's narrative for clues about how differences and oppositions are important in shaping the conflict. In dialogue, ideas may be collaboratively nurtured and developed, but in argumentation ideas tend to be challenged or rebutted because the context in which we argue through a conflict suggests that strong opposition works. Of course, explicating differences is often important to moving through differentiation to integration (Folger, Poole, and Stuttman, 1997), and is also a key part of stimulating dialogue. This key difference separates the dialogue and argument approaches to conflict. As Tannen (1998) illustrates, "... Opposition does not lead to truth when an issue is not composed of two opposing sides but is a crystal of many facets. Often the truth is in the complex middle, not the oversimplified extremes" (p. 10). The narratives included in this book are almost all examples of this complex middle. Conflict narratives rarely represent simple positions and goals. Human experience does not simply have a front and a back, a left and a right, a right and a wrong, or even a good and an evil. It is, as Tannen shows us, multifaceted. It is also embedded or, to follow the gem analogy further, "set" in particular ways by the wearer for particular rhetorical effect, depending on the context or occasion when it is worn. Simply, conflicts are complex in and of themselves, but are also further complicated by the context and perspective captured in the experience and in the telling of the story to create a particular account of that experience.

A second relevant difference between dialogue and argument deals with the accessibility to and representation of personal experience in the process of moving through dialogues or arguments. Argument has value in promoting logical debate and reasoned discourse, but it also tends to relegate personal experience to anecdotes (Arnett, 1986; 1997; Hyde & Bineham, 2000). Hyde and Bineham argue that few places in formal academic debate consider personal experience, despite the importance of such experiences in shaping our daily actions and decisions. Understanding this complexity and lived reality is essential to accurately describing, representing, and working through conflict. We have probably all experienced looking at an abstract conflict process model and thinking that, while it shows how the main moves of a conflict fit together, it may or may not closely capture what conflict is really like.

By way of illustration, an argumentation approach to Brian's narrative would involve explicating the positions of the stakeholders and looking for the best possible solution for both—a rational enough enterprise at first glance. A dialogue approach recognizes the contextual, cultural, historical, and lived reality—facets, as Tannen (1998) would say—of the complex crystalline character of conflicts. From this understanding, participants can make informed choices that affect the underlying generative structures of conflict in their lives.

Dialogue, Conflict, and Personal Narratives

Based on our discussion of conflict, dialogue, and negotiation so far, you may recognize the dangers and opportunities associated with conflict in your lives and our world. Conflict can lead to greater division such that a father and daughter never speak again, or a coworker harbors hateful and destructive feelings for years. Conflicts can lead to greater acts of oppression and even violence such that to maintain power, a father violently attacks a child, or a supervisor dictates a workplace culture that undermines the wellness of others. Conflicts can lead to repression such that conflict experiences in one life context flow through and affect other contexts and relationships often distantly removed from the original. A father might take his family conflicts to work with him, and a frustrated employee might bring them home and seek a solution in substance abuse. Conflicts may repeat themselves throughout generations such that a daughter who experiences traumatic conflicts at home is drawn to a life partner who helps her recreate the same feeling in their marriage and family. A daughter is often drawn to feel what her mother felt at a certain traumatic moment. An employee who creates a narrative account of a conflict in which he or she is a victim might tend to look for the same characteristics in future supervisors and, often unwittingly, recreate the same tensions they experienced earlier. An effectively managed dialogue can bring more options to the surface. Negotiating conflicts through dialogue can bring closure, renewal, and other creative possibilities for change, possibilities that do not tend to emerge in the polarized and personalized heat of arguments.

Beyond these relational narratives, the stakes associated with how we handle conflict as people and tribes within nations and for international relations are clearly very high. Recently, news reports described the case of a father who shot his teenage son, apparently for not refilling the ice trays in the freezer. Cases of violence and even mass murder and suicide in schools have steadily risen. We wonder what narratives could justify and rationalize such acts. Criminal court systems are glutted with cases of conflicts that, for whatever reason, the participants are unable to effectively resolve without intervention. Paralleling and responding to these trends have been efforts to increase understanding and negotiating skills among people who are inevitably in conflict with one another. There are now mediation or alternative dispute resolution (ADR) programs in most states to lessen costly burdens on the court system. There are peer counseling and conflict management programs in many school systems to increase awareness among young people and lessen violence in schools. There are numerous conflict-training seminars and audiotapes that deal with managing conflict with coworkers, difficult customers, and others. These innovations all indicate how important searching for ways to understand and manage conflict is.

Changing conflict takes a great deal of communication. Often, small changes make the biggest differences. A gesture or invitation to talk more deeply, a graceful act of forgiveness and reconciliation, a choice to renew efforts to engage the other, or an effort to rethink and rewrite the past, can lead a conflict in a productive direction. A father and daughter reunite in a tearful moment of openness. An employee lets go of an episode that has haunted him for years. These events may be unrealistic, but they are communicatively possible. Your personal narratives can be central in more fully understanding your conflicts so such choices become probable and not simply possible.

Personal conflict narratives—to further develop Tannen's crystal image—can help you examine the communicative practices and social contexts and constraints that affect your ability and willingness to understand the multifaceted complex middles of conflicts. Conflicts can also represent valuable clues to the quality of your relational world and valuable learning experiences through which you can improve your quality of life. Dialogue and negotiation provide you with a qualitative point of comparison through which to understand, critique, learn from, and reframe the everyday conflict communication represented in those narratives. Personal narratives are also a point of departure, a good place to start to develop dialogue as a sort of metanarrative about the lived experience and representational issues associated with our own conflict experiences and those of others. Dialogue is both the critical framework through which you can "evaluate" your conflict experiences and the process by which you conduct that evaluation. So, conflict narratives are an important communicative artifact through which you can understand your experiences and go beyond them to rethink and reshape your thoughts, actions, reactions, and interactions that in turn improve your conflict dialogues.

Some Final Reflective Questions for Brian's Narrative

1. How did the participants in Brian's conflict create or negotiate the reality of their relationships?

2. What, if any, elements of dialogue and/or argumentation were evident in this story?

3. What would dialogue enable the participants to do?

4. What understanding do you gain from Brian's narrative about his conflict?

CONCLUSION

We live in a world that we partly negotiate through our communication. As Reina discovers, the world is also partly negotiated for us by our predecessors and contemporaries. These patterns of negotiation and conflict are quite enduring, mostly invisible, and often limiting. As you have seen through the narratives in this chapter, understanding conflict in our world is often the first step to developing strategies for changing how you negotiate. If, as Donohue's quote at the beginning of this chapter suggests, you want to have more peaceful relationships, then you need to connect this understanding to communication practices that can make a difference. This chapter challenges you to recognize the constructive and destructive roles that conflict can play in our world. You are also challenged to think about ways to improve your dialogue in conflict processes. Finally, you are challenged to test yourself by striving to negotiate a more peaceful world around you through these communication skills and competencies.

2

Conflict Narratives as a Good Place to Start

"[Narrative is] the primary form by which human experience is made meaningful."

(Polkinghorne, 1988, p. 1)

"Storytelling works to build a continuous life of experience, linking the past to the future from the standpoint of the present."

(Bochner, 1997, p. 418)

"[We create our sense of self partly] by telling our stories and consuming the stories of others."

(Langellier, 1999, p. 125)

We are all familiar with the importance of talking about our experiences for the health and development of relationships of all kinds. We are, however, often less familiar with the implications of what (and how) stories are told and not told, and how conflict stories necessarily represent particular versions of a conflict episode or process. We often tend to assume that the story simply reports reality—the story "just is." This chapter challenges you to tell conflict stories not as an end in itself, but as a place to start deepening your interpretive understanding of your own and others' conflict processes and experiences. You learn the role of various narratives in your life and why your narrative accounts of conflict—your conflict stories—are crucial mediating points of interpretation between conflict events and your understanding of and actions in those events.

We discuss conflict narratives within the context of a narrative approach to communication and, more generally, within the context of interpretive social science. Also, we explore how a narrative approach enables you to learn about and potentially change your conflicts. The important benefits, limits, and ethical issues of this narrative approach to conflict are also examined.

Key Concepts, Terms, and Definitions to Learn in This Chapter

- How your narrative accounts of conflict help you to look more deeply into the processes and meaning of conflict

- Why taking an interpretive approach to studying conflict gives you insight into your conflicts

- Why recollecting your own narratives and collecting those of others leads to insight, understanding, and possible changes in how you practice conflict

- Why you need to be careful about the limitations of studying the story accounts of events

- How you need to be ethical in your storytelling and in your research practices related to collecting and interpreting conflict narratives

Key Definitions

- *The Narrative Paradigm.* The approach to studying human experience through the fundamentally human practice of storytelling

- *Interpretive Social Science.* The approach to studying human experience through explication rather than explanation, and through involvement with, rather than objective detachment from, the processes being studied

- *Personal Narratives.* Accounts of experiences written or told by those actually involved in those experiences

- *Aha! moments.* Moments of clarity when we see the deeper connections between things and the meaning of those connections (as in, "Aha! So that's what that meant!")

- *Oughts.* Guidelines for ethical narrative research

NARRATIVE AND INTERPRETATION
IN COMMUNICATING CONFLICT EXPERIENCE

We use the following story to illustrate the main assumptions and practices of an interpretive approach to conflict narratives.

———◄○►———

Exemplar Narrative: This Time, I'm the One That Got Away

—JILL

When I was 20, my relationship of three years with Craig took a drastic change of direction. He told me there was something we needed to discuss…some news he needed to share with me.

"Jill," he said, "I'm going to be a father in six months."

A feeling of nausea instantly gripped me. There were no words I could say. I was in complete shock, as I knew I wasn't carrying his baby… He had cheated on me.

He tried to explain. "There was only that one time," he said. My disgust was too great to hear the words of apology and explanations for why he could hurt me this way. Weeks later, when all the bad news and horrific images had soaked in, we met to talk.

Because I loved him so, I wanted to forgive him. He wanted to remain together and to put the "slip-up" out of our minds for a while, especially mine, if possible. Being my naive self, I let him charm me, but it didn't last for long.

The gossip and humiliation of this conflict had spread all over my hometown. People were telling me the stories they had heard, things they had seen, and what I should do. The truth came out that Craig had been seeing another girl—the mother of his now six-year-old daughter—for some time. He denied these claims, but the humiliation I felt was too profound to "live and let live."

I went to college the next fall. Craig had begged me to stay. He had wanted me to go to the local community college so we'd be close. His thoughts were that hope was still in the air and that this conflict would just blow over. My thoughts were to get as far from my hometown as possible so that Craig wouldn't be able to stop by and harass me to forgive him.

I went to ECU [East Carolina University] and one year later met Jason. We've been together for four years, and are planning our life together. A bad conflict definitely made an improvement in my life.

I still see Craig once in a while when I'm at home. He's dating still. He hasn't found that special someone yet. "Jill," he says, "I lost my special someone when I lost you."

———◄○►———

The Narrative Paradigm and Conflict Communication

What does it mean to approach the above narrative as a way to understand conflict and communication and as the basic unit of analysis—a paradigm exemplar of communication? To answer this, we explore two of the main assumptions of the narrative paradigm and examine how it orients us to stories such as Jill's. According to Walter Fisher, people are essentially story-telling animals; hence, his term "Homo Narrans" (1987, p. 62). We recount (telling through biography, history, and autobiography) and account for (theoretical explanations or arguments) human choices and actions. Therefore, our first assumption is that narrative is a pervasive and important means of communication in conflict and for understanding conflict. In other words, communication is necessary for conflict.

Our second assumption is that narrative is where conflict, as the cultural practice of sharing meaning, that is, as communication, can be discovered. The historical, biographical, cultural, and social contexts providing the reasons you handle conflict in certain ways can be examined. The moral and ethical reasoning we make when narrating conflict—in other words, how you organize narratives to represent conflict strategically, how people and things are depicted and characterized, why you act as you do, and so on—can be explicated and understood through narrative. In short, the stories you collect and analyze are one way to interpret conflict.

Taking each of these interpretive possibilities in turn illustrates how you might approach the Jill's narrative as a paradigm exemplar of human communication by asking the following questions:

1. What is the historical, biographical, cultural, and social context in which Jill's narrative works as communication?

This question helps you to reflect on the place and time in Jill's life that structures her viewpoint in telling her story. Simply, you are asked to consider where in her life Jill is writing from and how this perspective permeates the narrative. Of course, examining her viewpoint as a narrator suggests that you also ask about your perspective as a listener and interpreter of her narrative.

2. What is the moral and ethical reasoning that apparently guides the actions of those involved in the conflict?

This question examines the purpose of the story in representing and resolving the underlying moral and ethical issues of the conflict. What is the basic moral that drives the story and gives it a meaningful structure? What are the ethical or moral issues that create the conflict presented in this story? What is resolved relationally and morally as the conflict is resolved? Why, for example, is Jill's experience of "winning" and his of "losing" justified through the narrative choices she makes?

3. How would you describe the strategic organization or plot structure of the narrative and how people and things are represented so the result is a meaningful story?

This question examines how people, places, and things are organized in a dramatic story structure by which the moral discussed above is established. What are the key actions and reactions, twists and turns, and archetypes of, for example, right and wrong, through which this story unfolds? What lessons are you supposed to learn from Jill and Craig's experiences? This narrative illustrates the power of retrospective sense-making in creating a story of a past conflict. This narrative also shows how sense can be made even of something as traumatic as the ending of a relationship. The ending becomes a device or event moving the drama—life—forward in a very useful way. What started out as Jill's loss and Craig's gain leads to significant gains for her and a big loss for him. This is a central narrative archetype in making sense of this conflict experience. They both learn a valuable lesson—her about winning, and him about losing.

4. What underlying beliefs, attitudes, actions, and ideology are supported or challenged by the narrative?

This question examines the cultural and ideological grounding of the beliefs, attitudes, actions, myths, and so on, that are important in the story. For example, what beliefs about relationships, such as fidelity, truth, and forgiveness, are important? What is the attitude of the narrator toward infidelity, and how does she draw us into sharing that attitude? What myths of gender and family structures are invoked? How do these create a sense of the values and practices that should be part of intimate relationships currently in your culture?

This valuable framework for your interpretation of narrative has subsequently become more politically grounded and sophisticated through the personal narrative ethnography movement. We explain these developments after placing the narrative paradigm within its broader context of interpretive methodology and human science.

The Interpretive Approach to Conflict Narratives

The narrative paradigm is more broadly contextualized within an interpretive approach to communication. This broader context helps you to understand your approach to conflict narratives as a mode of inquiry within a research tradition. The important methodological and epistemological issues concern understanding the meaning of communication practices through engagement with people and their practices.

This interpretive approach implies that you are, as researchers, engaged with the texts you study and the people who write those texts. Simply, you are always humans studying humans, rather than objective scientists studying human subjects. You want to show the "interpretive schemes used by those studied, while recognizing the researchers' own influence on the situation." (Jones, 1983, p. 151). Morgan (1983) shows how science is a process of "engagement," in which the observation and conclusion are results of the interaction between observer and object through their frames of reference. You are concerned with understanding the frames of reference that the narrators and you, as interpreters of those narratives, bring to the object and process of study (p. 13). "Science" should be viewed from within its contingencies and the contexts of language and historical and cultural interests (Denzin, 1997). At the same time, you should not valorize neutrality. Taking the notion of engagement further into subjectivity, you can even interpret your own communication practices. As Bochner illustrates, scholarly inquiry can begin at the "site of one's own experience" (Bochner, 1997, p. 424).

   The interpretive approach also implies that you are studying the meaning of communication practices (Jones, 1983). It is in the subjective and intersubjective meaning of narratives that they make sense. As Rosenwald and Ochberg (1992) show, personal stories are "the means by which identities may be fashioned" (p. 1). That is, they are self-formative. The omissions, portrayals, and relationship to the audience all shape the account of life that you partly choose to create. Narratives also need to be read as histories through which you "read the more or less abiding concerns and constraints of the individual and his or her community" (Rosenwald and Ochberg, p. 4). Conflict is the competitive context and set of practices through which these processes of self-expression and contextual concerns are brought into stark relief and consciousness. This happens when communication ruptures the everyday and allows these dialectical concerns to be acted on. For example, you may find yourself in a conflict that forces you to ask deeper questions about a relationship. As such, conflict represents points or moments of possible dialogue where the self in a relationship has the opportunity to change or to struggle for sameness.

   Narratives do not just record, mirror, or report facts; they reflect our creative search for "life plots" (Josselson, 1995, p. 33) that serve our human needs (Denzin, 1997). Through narrative, we reason to create sense and representations (Richardson, 1995). The two are inextricably linked through the rhetorical and communicative function of narrative. Stories are important to us in talking about success (Benoit, 1997), as are stories of justification of actions (Wetherell & Potter, 1989; Kellett, 1995); performing resistance (Goodall, 1995); achieving recovery (Ochberg, 1992); expressing passion (Whyte, 1994); passing on values and life lessons (Krizek, 1998); humanizing time (Richardson, 1995), and so on. Stories are intimately tied to our purposeful relationships with others. According to Banks and Banks, narratives actively represent, create understanding, make us vulnerable, and express suspicion and desire (1995). In this sense, stories do not just show or represent things; they *do* things communicatively. They are speech acts that give us a window into our own world of meaning and of our intersubjective reality in Jackson's sense of how stories negotiate and reflect the metamorphic tensions and struggles between personal and public—self and other (Jackson, 1998).

Thus, interpreting conflict narratives is a way into the intersection of self-expression—subjectivity—and cultural constraint and expectations—inter-subjectivity. Hence, you create your world partly through conflict expression, but this is mediated by a "network of typifications that endow a particular culture with a coherent rationality…" (Rosenwald & Ochberg, p. 148). You are exploring the cultural context of handling conflict, including mythology, typifications, and social conventions. You are also concerned with the "everyday common-sense world, and in the constructions and explanations members of that world use to describe their reality and actions." (p. 149). Hence, because narratives are at the core of human meaning, this necessitates an interpretive approach where you are interested in "elucidating meaning rather than determining causality" (p. 150).

Because narratives are so pervasive and reflect the intersections of self, others, and social contexts, they are our richest sources of information about human cultures and human experience (Polkinghorne, 1983, 1988). Stories are pervasive in that they are how we talk about events, how we represent ourselves, create coherent histories, and inform and justify our decisions (Polkinghorne, 1988). However, one tendency you need to watch for in working with such narratives is that they "turn lives and experiences into texts and concepts" (Jackson, 1995), that is, into case studies for theories and their categorizing and colonizing tendencies. You must recognize that in storytelling, your narrators become vulnerable and open to your "authority" (Chase, 1996). Remember, you are using Jill's experience not as a case study to build a grand theory or prove that our perspective has truth-finding capabilities. Rather, you are using interpretive methodology to better understand the lived reality of conflict. You are taking what Josselson calls "the empathic stance" (1995, p. 32). That is, as narrative researchers, you are concerned with understanding your and other people's experiences and meaning-making, represented in narratives. You are also taking a relative stance to our inquiry in that you are concerned with how theory and practice are mutually useful, rather than how narratives or your interpretation of narratives are "true" (Bochner, 1994; Ellis & Bochner, 1996).

Interpreting Personal Conflict Experience Narratives

We are focusing on illustrating these themes of narrative, interpretation, and human science through explicating personal experience narratives. Personal narratives are a "boundary phenomenon" (Langellier, 1989, pp. 223-224). This means that personal narratives are somewhere between or a combination of the following:

- Literary and social discourse. This means that personal narratives are shaped partly by the fact that they are written or recounted as complete texts. They are also accounts of real communication practices within real social contexts.

   1. In what ways does Jill's narrative reflect both the need to present in an appealing literary style and to represent her personal and social reality?

- Written and oral models of communication. This means personal narratives reflect both written conventions of style and structure and oral histories.

   2. In what ways does Jill create a text that sounds like a naturalistic story recounted orally, and how does the it appear to be composed as written text?

- Public and private spheres of interaction. This means that personal narratives reflect the inner thoughts and feelings of the narrator as well as more publicly recognizable formulas or archetypes.

   3. How does the story provide insight into both personal feelings and experiences as well as appeal to broader social and cultural archetypes?

- Ritual performance and incidental conversation.

   4. In what ways is this narrative similar to an impromptu story shared in a conversation?

   5. In what ways does it seem like a formulaic tale that might be told and retold for its central moral?

- Fact and fiction. This means that personal narratives usually contain elements of both direct reporting and more creative, embellished, or fanciful storytelling.

   6. In what ways does Jill's story appear to blend or blur the boundary between the factual and the more imaginative or fanciful?

Langellier's (1989) five theoretical positions on personal narrative help explicate a personal narrative approach to conflict. First, narratives are "story-texts" (p. 248). Narratives should be interpreted from the context of social and political discourse and interpretation by us as researchers.

1. What are Jill's goals in creating this narrative?

2. What does this narrative tell you about the social and political context of her conflict experience?

3. What schema do you bring to your interpretation of this story? How would you paraphrase the story? What is the essential moral of the story?

Second, narratives are storytelling performances. Specifically, personal narratives are meant to have a specific impact on audiences through the live performance of the text. As such, they embody structural and linguistic appeals that mark them as narratives. The total storytelling performance is the unit of analysis because to understand a text, we must examine text, performers, and audience in their social and cultural situations. This context creates the rules and norms of appropriate storytelling and marks the event as a story. Important also is the distinction between the "narrative event" as the performance of the story, and the "narrated event" as the event being narrated. These are interdependent (Bauman, 1986).

1. What opportunities for understanding emerge when the narrative is examined as a live and dramatic performance?

2. How does reflecting on the rules and norms of storytelling change your interpretation?

3. How might reflection on the audience's perceptions of a performance of this narrative enrich our understanding of Jill's conflict?

Third, narratives are part of conversational interactions. Narratives are woven into the fabric of everyday conversation. Also, as participants share stories, they create social constraints and boundaries that define and maintain the relationship.

1. In what kind of conversation and with what people might sharing Jill's story make most sense and be most appropriate?

2. What social constraints and boundaries are affirmed in this story?

Fourth, narratives are social processes. Narratives are embedded within broader contexts of social and cultural values and reflect those contexts. You need to examine the multiple contexts of narratives within the speech communities in which they have meaning and particular uses. For example narrative can be viewed as therapy, as blame, as catharsis, as coping, and as making sense of being poor, being women, being men, and so on.

1. What is the primary social function(s) of this narrative?

2. How does Jill's story reflect your social and cultural values?

Fifth, Langellier asks us to recognize narratives as political praxis. As Mumby (1987) argues, storytelling produces "certain ways of perceiving the world which privileges certain interests over others" (p. 114). As praxis, narratives involve issues of "power, knowledge, ideology, and identity" (p. 266). This means you need to be concerned with the politics of relationship between the text and context. This is particularly important in stories of domination, empowerment, and resistance, or the struggles of muted individuals and groups in families, organizations, and cultures (Conquergood, 1983).

1. How can Jill's narrative be viewed as a political praxis? What, for example, represents her resistance, struggle, and self-empowerment in living as a young woman?

2. How does being self-reflexive about the politics involved open up new opportunities for interpretation?

We have focused on personal conflict narratives because they are valuable descriptions of an individual's experience of conflict. Conflict themes and issues can also be found by studying conflict interaction or conversational narratives as well as fictional, literary, musical, and other artistic expressions of conflict (Banks & Banks, 1998).

Some Final Reflective Questions for Jill's Narrative

1. If you were in Jill's position in your life, how would your approach to the conflict have been similar or different from Jill's? Why?

2. Do you have a story similar to Jill's? If so, when and where would you share the story, and for what purpose?

3. How might either Craig's or Jill's parents' account of this conflict be different or similar to Jill's? Why would you think these similarities and differences would occur?

4. As praxis, narratives are concerned with issues of "power, knowledge, ideology, and identity" (Mumby, 1987, p. 266). This means that you are concerned with the politics of the text/context relationship, for example, in stories of domination, empowerment, and resistance, or the struggles of muted individuals and groups within families, organizations, cultures (Conquergood, 1983). If you were collecting Craig's account of the story, what questions would you ask to get at his experience of their conflict? What questions, if any, would you stay away from?

5. What are some key stories from your life that you use to create your more general "life-plot" and view of yourself?

THE OPPORTUNITIES OF UNDERSTANDING CONFLICT NARRATIVES

> *"Behind the story I tell is the one I don't. Behind the story you hear is the one I wish I could make you hear."*
>
> (Allison, 1996, p. 39)

When we consider how to capture an experience poetically, this reflective and creative thinking has some valuable payoffs. Specifically, as Michael's narrative (below) suggests, the creation of narratives enables the narrators/poets to rethink their experiences. By casting the story in a new format—a poem—poets learn more about how they feel about their experiences. From that exploration, poets may deepen their personal understanding and increase opportunities for learning how to manage conflicts more effectively.

———◄○►———

Exemplar Narrative: This Story of Mine

—MICHAEL

This story of mine is but a part of my life
About a job done well, of toil and strife
My dreams of success that didn't come true
Listen closely my friend this could happen to you
I begin at the end with conflicted worker and boss
Over responsibility, results, profit, and loss
You see, I was hired to make money, and I had, is true
But in a new role I struggled, knew not what to do
So I did what I was best at and pressed harder each day
And believed that my boss would soon come to say
You've done well, now rest, and then we'll talk more
About the wheres and the whens of opening the next door
But it never came to be, instead matters turned worse
And I truly began to feel as if I were cursed
It seems fate took control and affected my part
Too much worry and stress, health problems did start
And one day my boss said, it's sad but you must go
And I replied, what me, not true, how can this be so
For I've done what was asked and given my best
Sure you have, was his reply, but you still failed the test
Of being invincible, like machine, upon which we depend
To make more and more money, and so, it must end
After all I'm the boss and I say it must be done
My life in shambles, my career a setting sun
And so it's come to be a different path I now tread
Searching new meaning in life, I've heard it's been said
That's what's truly important is not what you do
Instead it's peace, love, and happiness and I wish them for you

———◄○►———

Narratives Are Good Starting Points

Interpretation begins with the artifact or text, but this is never the complete object for study. As we have shown, to gain a complete experience from the artifact, you need to examine the text in the contexts of its construction, performance, and interpretation by the narrator and the audience (Langellier, 1989). Michael's poetic narrative represents the crystallization of much careful thought about the experience he describes and the intended effect of the narrative on the audience.

The story is an interpretive account of a conflicted life event. Specifically, it tells about a conflict that leads to a major change in Michael's life. This account also enables to him represent the experience in particular ways for himself and the intended audience through his imagery and other structural devices. Simply, this narrative can be viewed as a starting point for his understanding of the conflict and for your understanding of how the conflict is represented through the poetic narrative. In terms of the context of performance, the text is the starting point for understanding how the intended message connects with the audience and brings the experience to life. That is, by reflecting on the construction of the text and the context of the performance of sharing conflicted life experiences that others can learn from, you understand the narrative as a relationship of message construction to interpretation, that is, as communication. In terms of the context of interpretation, this text is also a good starting point for understanding your own interpretive reactions and responses to the poem as participants in that communication.

Engage the following dialogue questions to explicate this poem as an interpretive starting point:

1. What meaning or purpose does the poem have from Michael's point of reference?

2. What are the main lessons he is communicating to himself and to you to fulfill that purpose?

3. What are the main narrative choices (oppositions, imagery, archetypes, and so on) Michael has made to represent the event in this way?

4. What are some of the myths about work and success he confronts and resolves?

5. What poetic imagery evokes the feeling of being in the conflict versus looking back on it?

6. What are some of your interpretations of the poem from the basis of your perspectives or viewpoints?

7. How does Michael draw the audience into his experience and make those experiences real?

8. In what ways are your life experiences similar to and different from his?

9. How does your viewpoint influence your interpretation of the poem?

Aha! Moments in Telling Your Story

You have probably all had conflict experiences that did not make complete sense to you as they were occurring. As you retrace and recreate the narrative account of those events, you may reframe or reinterpret the experience (Weick, 1979, 1995). This is partly how you form your perspective from the present back into the past. Sometimes the greatest learning or aha! (or Ah-ha!) moments happen because you are the subject, observer, and author of the text. Writing about your experience and being conscious of yourself in writing can be a valuable form of self-reflexivity. A narrative approach can foster in you what Richardson calls a "sociological imagination" through which constraints, opportunities, and change possibilities become real (1995, p. 216).

As Michael writes about his experience, it is certainly his life he is narrating, but he is also part subject and part observer of the events. Simply, you look at a conflict differently when you have the benefits of both distance from it and close involvement—engagement—in its reconstruction. This concurrent distance and closeness occurring in writing about an experience helps you rethink, reevaluate, and retell the experience in valuable ways. As Kirkwood (1992) illustrates, "Revealing unsuspected possibilities of the human condition is an important purpose of symbolic activity." That is, communication about conflicts can "open up the mind to creative possibilities" (p. 31).

The following questions may help you understand these aha! Moments, that is, when creative possibilities became real through retelling the story:

1. How do you think Michael would have told the story while he was actually experiencing the conflict?

2. How might the imagery used to evoke the experience at the time of the conflict have been different from the imagery used in the poem to recapture the experience?

3. How might his perspective on the meaning and function of conflict be different from when he was living through the experience?

4. What might have been the aha! experiences he had while rethinking and retelling the story?

These moments of learning create a particular understanding of the event and of conflict more generally.

Performing Narratives Leads to Understanding

Stories are meant to be told and retold; poems are meant to be performed; and conversations are meant to be lived with others (Langellier, 1989). In fact, when a narrative is performed, it can take on a life rarely found in a static text on a page. It is in the performance that the full meaning of the message takes shape and is complete as a communicative event (Peterson & Langellier, 1997). In this sense, performance can be a way of knowing and understanding both the self and the other (Pelias & VanOosting, 1987; Welker & Goodall, 1997). It can become a source of bodily as well as cognitive learning. Trujillo (1998) also shows how texts can lead to "autocritique" (p. 346). In other words, when story texts are examined, certain images and ideologies are privileged and even reinforced. Stories can reveal the ideological underpinnings of conflict in particular ways. The purpose of narrative analysis is for you to explore the "taken for granted cultural processes embedded in the everyday practices of storytelling" (Chase, 1996, p. 55).

1. How might Michael better understand how it feels to put an experience behind him, as well as know what it means to reframe the event as a valuable turning-point?

2. How might he better understand how it feels to give an audience advice about work and corporate life based on such a personal and emotional message?

3. How do these bodily experiences influence how Michael actually performs the poem?

4. How might his live performance of the poem influence how he and the audience understand the experience?

5. How might he complete the following sentences in light of the understanding that comes through constructing and performing the text?

   – Now I understand that....

   – Now I know more about....

   – Now I understand that conflict is....

Understanding Can Lead to Choices About Change

Understanding experience is a valuable goal in and of itself. Greater understanding usually leads to more choices for changing your ways of thinking, behaving, and communicating. In other words, better choices become more probable for you. Thus, through narrative analysis, it is possible to explore the struggle to "improve" or emancipate from restricted narrative accounts and, through understanding, begin to recognize constraints, opportunities, and possibilities for change (Earnest, 1992; Kohler-Riessman, 1992; Ochberg, 1992). Examine the following questions about change in light of Michael's poem:

1. What do you think Michael learned from writing and performing his conflict narrative?

2. How might that learning affect his memory of that period of his life?

3. How might it change the anxiety that was real to him at that time?

4. How might Michael develop perspective on other aspects of his life through this creative exercise?

5. What more do you know about this experience through this narrative?

6. What are you more conscious of after experiencing the poem?

7. What choices of experience and representation might be added to your own dialogue and understanding because of this expanded consciousness?

8. What are the possible ways of narrating periods of turbulence, failure, and loss in your own lives that you can take from Michael's narrative?

9. How might Michael's communication and particularly his conflicts change as a result of this?

Reflection Exercise

Complete the following sentences individually and then discuss them as a group or class to explicate the relationship of narrative and change.

- Understanding this poem helped me recognize that I can....
- Understanding this poem means that Michael can....
- Understanding this poem helped me recognize that I ought to....
- Understanding this poem means that Michael ought to....
- Understanding this poem helped me recognize that I can change...in my life.
- Understanding this poem means that Michael can change...in his life.

Change Can Lead to Stories You Want to Tell

The choices you make in thinking about conflict, behaving in conflict, and communicating about experiences affect your daily reality, including constituting and negotiating with others. Simply, your communicative choices partly create the context of your own and others' subsequent and ongoing communicative choices. Examine Michael's poem for opportunities to change conflicts by answering the following questions:

1. As this poem is shared with you, how does it create a particular version of reality and an approach to conflict for Michael and for those who share his life?

2. How would you handle a conflict with someone who views conflict as Michael does now?

3. How might you rethink some of your experiences, even current ones, in light of this poem's message?

4. Would taking a more retrospective viewpoint of some events in your lives, as Michael has in his, benefit you?

5. Are there conflicts in your lives currently that might lead to valuable turning points for you, as Michael's experience did for him? What would those issues be and how are they important stories in your lives?

6. Are there events that you react to differently when they happen in your own lives, as opposed to someone else's?

7. How might this difference in our communication affect the choices that others involved in our conflicts make?

Learning to apply the main themes a narrative brings to life and learning to make choices about changing your life are valuable aspects of the narrative approach.

THE LIMITS AND CHALLENGES OF CONFLICT NARRATIVES

Exploring the construction and interpretation of narratives as the paradigm unit of analysis for studying conflict also entails challenges. The poem *I'm Right* illustrates these challenges. They involve skills and choices in the construction of the story and levels of willingness and skill in interpreting and discussing the issues presented. Other challenges are suggested by the broader relationship of narratives to the social and cultural worlds they represent and evoke. The main challenge here is to recognize how your stories limit and are limited by the experiences they represent and, wherever possible, to make these opportunities and constraints explicit. This is a dialogic ethic.

——◄○►——

Exemplar Narrative: I'm Right

—LEIGH

Makes no difference when we fight
Which one of us is wrong or right
It makes no difference for you see
The one that's right is always me

And for that butthead I call Chris,
One of these days he'll get my fist
Goes out with the guys, forgets to phone
Leaves me sitting home alone

When the problem is discussed
He thinks I only want to fuss
I try so hard to make my point
But he just wants to leave the joint

Standing here upon the hearth
Always trying to play the part
And what I want him most to see
Is he should spend some time with me

At night when calling him at home
He lies in bed on the phone
Talking to me in his sleep
While I'm yelling, "you're such a creep"

I know that when we disagree
He wishes I would let things be
I try talking nice and polite
While he chants "I'm always right"

You'd think by now he'd understand
There's hell to pay when you're a man
The things you do aren't always right
But women know men aren't too bright

We take them all under our wing
And try to teach them everything
When you're wrong, bring us flowers
Otherwise we'll fight for hours

I'm sure he knows how sweet I am
Sweet and gentle as a lamb
And soon I think that he will see
The one that's right is always me.

Narrative Can Limit Dialogue

If questions open up dialogue, then answers tend to close it down. Narratives can be used as definitive answers when they are treated as fully enclosed and complete texts, that is, when they create "discursive closure" (Mumby, 1987, p. 113). When experience is put into narrative form, it can take on a sort of truth value that limits learning because narratives produce and reproduce particular power relations. This is more like monologue. For example, without further questioning and reflection, the poem might reify a view of communication as simply a strategy for achieving one's goals. It might also elicit the oppositional response, "No, you're wrong," at which point dialogue also ends. The manipulative strategies Leigh engages that help establish her consistent "rightness" show the impact of such competitive power on relationships. Note also how Leigh's boyfriend reacts by ritually agreeing to concede. The following questions may help you to open your own dialogue about conflicted intimate relationships.

1. What is communication like in such a competitive relationship? Notice the lack of exclamation points that might indicate playfulness in the poem.

2. Why do Leigh and Chris seem to avoid dialogue, or even good argumentation?

3. Why would Chris agree to cocreate such an unbalanced or unequal relationship when the costs appear to outweigh the rewards?

4. How do both parties appear to be complicit in creating this relationships style?

5. How can they "argue" more effectively?

6. Why do they both seem unable to discus the issues?

7. How might we imagine them pointing fingers, saying they tried to discuss their conflict but the other person is always unreasonable?

8. How many times have you used finger-pointing as a tactic to prove your rightness and effectively end dialogue?

9. Would Chris describe Leigh as a "lamb"?

10. How does Chris contribute to Leigh's style of doing conflict?

11. How can Leigh expect to always win and be "sweet"? Is this possible? If so, how?

This poem raises many useful questions. Without your willingness to interpret and learn from your narratives, they simply prove to you that you are right and that there is little need to negotiate your communicative reality with others. You maintain your heroic roles in your narratives, minimize your ability to learn from experiences, and probably reinforce dysfunctional relational cycles in the process. Alternatively, you can use narratives to help you to open up dialogue.

Narratives Are Inherently Political

Hart argues that "... whatever we say, there is a political dimension to it" (1985, p. 162). Our knowledge of ourselves and the world is socially constructed in Richardson's sense that narratives—language, generally—always creates a particular version of reality (1995). Simply, narratives are inherently political acts because they reflect, reproduce, and sometimes, as in the case of resistance narratives, challenge, social and cultural constraints. Eisenberg and Goodall (1997) offer a useful framework for examining the political nature of narratives. First, they argue, narratives are *partial* because they are based on only parts of an event. In creating your accounts of conflicts, you notice only certain aspects of the conflict. You also unconsciously as well as consciously select the parts of the event that fit your story. Although you often convince yourselves that you have included all the important information, you nevertheless have a viewpoint from which you create your account of those events. Interpretive theory challenges you to recognize the contextual and personal constraints by which certain parts are included, marginalized, or ignored. Given that accounts have a cultural and personal context suggesting how stories are constructed and told, examine the following questions to help you understand the politics of Leigh's narrative.

1. How might cultural issues of power, gender, age, race, and class all have a role in shaping the parts of the relationships that are described to you?

2. How might Leigh's perspective be shaped by her cultural assumptions and those she assumes you have?

3. What assumptions held by the audience might the poem be designed to challenge?

4. How do both the poetic structure and humorous intent limit the content of the narrative?

5. What cultural archetypes, scripts, and myths about men and women would you have to believe for you to find the narrative convincing?

6. Which of these are important in your own conflicts?

7. What excluded parts or perspectives of this conflict would be useful to fully understanding the narrative?

Second, Eisenberg and Goodall say that narratives are also *partisan* in that we selectively represent an experience to portray the conflict participants in particular ways. You naturally want to remain the hero and/or victim in your stories. You tend to organize your account around that narrative constraint, even though the accounts of others might be radically different, that is, they may represent themselves as the hero/victim and you as the villain. This means your viewpoint is never neutral; rather, it is always political. Interpretive theory challenges you to make explicit the power interests that create partisanship. For example engage the following questions in relation to Leigh's poem:

1. Why does Leigh assume that appearing to dominate the relationship is a good thing?

2. Why is it good to always appear to be right?

3. Why is it usually the other people in relationships who tend to be wrong and need to change their understanding and behavior?

4. How do these interests then structure how Leigh and Chris talk about their relationship, that is, what aspects of their relationship are revealed and which are ignored?

5. How does Leigh's poem work as a humorous tale of relationships, and how does the intent to be humorous allow her to say things that might otherwise be regarded as unreasonable?

Third, Eisenberg and Goodall say that narratives are *problematic* in that they suggest more questions than they answer, and the answers generated are based on current theory and opinion. Interpretive theory challenges you to accept the incompleteness of narratives, both because you cannot completely describe every aspect of an event and you can never fully explain why a conflict occurs. Explanations are also contextual narratives, albeit perhaps more "scientifically" rigorous.

You can, however, increase your understanding of a conflict. For example, we have generated some questions for Leigh and Chris in helping them and you better understand their relationship. You also can turn those questions on yourselves and reflect on your own place in this story. You can offer some theories and principles to give Leigh and Chris the vocabulary and practices to resolve or work through their conflict. But, this is always problematical. How objective or expert an observer can you claim to be even though you are armed with the latest communication and conflict theories? Perhaps Geertz's (1998) notion of the "enabling conversation" is a more realistic goal. In this case, you might ask Leigh and Chris questions that enable them to enrich their conversations about relational communication. Consider how the following questions might work in that way.

1. What additional questions would you have for Leigh and Chris?

2. What central questions about communication, relationships, and conflict would you like to see them ask themselves and each other?

3. What other communication theories and principles would you like to see them learn more about?

4. What specific thoughts, judgments, and questions ran through your mind as you read or listened to this poem?

5. How did you filter or even change those private thoughts as you publicly discussed or wrote about the poem?

6. How do your values and perspectives embodied in those private thoughts and in your silence about those thoughts "problematize" your own interpretation of the poem?

7. How might your desire to represent yourself and your approach to conflict and relationships affect your interpretation of Leigh's poem?

8. What specific constraints and freedoms affected your account of the poem?

These political issues of viewpoint, intent, constraint, and selection are further developed in the next section, in which you are challenged to remember your dialogic ethics as you narrate and interpret conflict experiences.

The Ethical Challenges of Conflict Narratives

The interpretive approach to narratives combined with the peacemaking and dialogue perspective from the previous chapter suggests some important ethical boundaries (Benhabib & Dallmayr, 1990; Jensen, 1997). Specifically, you ought to carefully analyze conflict narratives and address the issues your analyses reveal. You ought to examine the ways your conflicts represent the interactions of many people and factors as they interconnect in creating social reality. Finally, you ought to ask questions about your conflicts to understand and possibly change yourselves and the world around you. For this valuable interpretation to happen, you must take what Johannesen (1981) calls the "attitude of dialogue." This means you should approach interpretation with a spirit of empathic understanding, authenticity, regard for the other, and supportiveness. You should also be aware of ethical dilemmas that sometimes result in misrepresentation and misuse of data and manipulation or coercion of narrators. You also need to be aware of how your values and goals affect how you tell and interpret narratives, which are in many ways inherently subjective accounts (White & Wooten, 1986).

As you examine Leigh's poem, or any conflict narrative, you should be very careful to apply these ethics to the questions you ask and to the thoughts, values, and judgments that underlie those questions. Being reflexive in your approach to the narratives of others is very important. Reflexivity stops you from judging others and appropriating their narratives into your own superior or expert meta-narrative. This also ensures that you engage texts with the awareness that your interpretations are historically, politically, intellectually, culturally, and textually constrained. Leigh's poem may have been created to open dialogue about relational issues, although to you, the poem may not seem to do that. Remember that you are somewhat distanced as readers of her text. Taking this ethos or spirit of dialogue into your interpretive conversations about the text—our inquiry—is important in making you tolerant listeners and interpreters of the world.

Given these broad ethical guidelines, consider the following questions as you think and talk about your own experiences through narrative and as you interpret and dialogue about them. As you work through these questions, ask yourselves what you can do about the habits and tendencies that limit dialogue and how you can be even better at generating dialogue. The following questions may further help you understand your conflicts.

1. In what ways do your own conflict stories mystify as well as clarify our experiences of the social, cultural, and relational worlds represented by the stories?

2. What can you do about this tendency toward ambiguity?

3. In what ways do your stories make your experiences and their contexts more explicit and open to interpretation and the scrutiny of questions?

4. In what ways do your narratives degrade, blame, or demonize you, others, or the context in their versions of conflict experiences?

5. In what ways do you honestly and empathically represent the actions, intentions, and motives of the conflict participants and contextual factors as coconstructors of that conflict?

6. In what ways do you limit the questions and learning possibilities that your narratives offer?

7. In what ways do your narratives invite further questioning, open dialogue, and even lead to the renegotiation of your reality?

8. How do your answers to these questions influence your recollection of conflicts and how you see the conflicts of others?

These questions are based on important issues of representation and intent. It is crucial that narratives generate dialogue. It is also crucial that the political realities of narratives are understood and engaged in interpretation. Finally, it is important for us as the authors of this book to approach the narratives of others as opportunities for dialogue. To do this, we carefully apply the questions above to our own discussion of others' narratives, and we invite you as the reader to become part of a dialogic conversation about conflict. This is how we want you to read this book.

**Some Final Reflective Questions
on Poetic Conflict Narratives**

1. Is there a poem or song particularly important to you during times of conflict? If so, why does that narrative capture the experience of conflict for you?

2. Why are poetic narratives, such as songs, so powerful in helping us to think about and feel our way through conflicts?

3. If particular poetic narratives capture some aspects of our conflicts, what aspects do they not capture or voice?

4. As you write poetic narrative accounts of your own conflicts, what language choices do you make?

CONCLUSION

You have seen in this chapter that conflict narratives do not merely report reality. Rather, they represent and shape your experiences of conflict. Narratives also give you a window into how you do conflict and how you give those actions meaning when you put them in narrative form. Simply, you have learned that conflict narratives are a good place to begin your understanding of conflict and think about changing your conflicts in strategic ways. You must, of course, recognize the limits of your ability to change the world around you. However, it is possible to move toward ethically grounded changes that result in conflict stories you are proud to share with others as examples of effective conflict management. In the stories you currently tell and do not tell are learning opportunities through which you can change your conflict communication.

3

Representing Self, Other, and Context

To create stories that adequately represent our experience, we typically determine the concrete set of actions and places around which the story revolves and through which the story moves. To do this, we make representational choices about ourselves, others, and the context of the conflict we are describing. This chapter explores the representations and experiences of self and others in conflict narratives. Understanding the social, cultural, and historical dimensions of those experiences and representations of self and others provides the context in which narratives make sense. This chapter explores life experiences embodied in your narrative representations. Understanding that the others in a conflict are performing similar interpretive representations of their experiences—perspective-taking—is explored as a starting point for dialogue.

Conflict can be understood partly as the negotiation of the reality of self in relation to others through tangible and symbolic disputes occurring in particular communicative contexts. Conflict narratives, therefore, are representations of those performances of self and others as they take place in conflict communication. Developing this interpretive perspective prepares you to examine narratives for how they reflect and shape your actions and experience of conflict. Questioning who you are in your conflicts, and what you assume about others, is a crucial reflective learning experience developed in this chapter. Learning to examine the representative nature of conflict narratives is also presented as essential to developing the ability to effectively manage conflict in different relationships.

Beyond representing your selves and others, your narratives represent the ways you create contexts for communication and how contextual factors shape how you do conflict communication. Simply, context is created by you and also partly creates you. This chapter explores the contextual factors that typically underlie conflict experiences. Intercultural, historical, religious, socioeconomic, gender, age, race, and other factors, as they impinge on your subjective and intersubjective experience of conflict, are all considered. You also learn to interpret conflict experiences for underlying power dimensions of context. The ability to interpret the influence of power, as well as make choices about the contexts and climate you create for your own and others' subsequent communicative choices, are the interpretive skills described in this chapter.

Key Concepts, Terms, and Definitions to Learn in This Chapter

- How you can better understand how your life experiences influence your conflicts

- How negative and positive experiences create patterns in our lives that we often perpetuate

- How your underlying views of life, often captured in metaphors, structure how you communicate

- How your internal (intrapersonal) and external (interpersonal) forms of expression are related

- How important dimensions of context, such as race, class, and gender, are important in conflicts

Key Definitions

- *Self, other, and context.* The relationship of you (self) to those with whom you are in conflict (others) within specific spatial, temporal, and historical locations (context)

- *Life metaphors.* More or less enduring ways we approach life that can be captured in a metaphor, such as "life is a game"

- *Perspective-taking.* The ability to acknowledge and engage the position and experience of others involved in the conflict

- *Representation.* The sometimes controversial way that events and experiences are accounted for, particularly through narrative

UNDERSTANDING THE SELF THROUGH CONFLICT NARRATIVES

"Why do I do conflict this way?" This is a common question, and the individual asking the question would like to better understand his or her experiences of conflict. To do this, it is necessary to examine the approach to conflict from within the complex interplay of relationships with others and the contexts that shape your experience of conflict. Self, other, and context make little sense individually. Neither you, nor others, nor your life circumstances very often completely determine your experiences. Taken together, however, these three can help you understand why you experience and narrate your conflicts as you do. You have an important impact on others' experiences of conflict, just as others affect your experiences in important ways.

To illustrate, the following narrative takes its author back to an early childhood experience through which she is able to explicate and understand her current, repeating patterns of behavior. It is a turning point of sorts for her to think systemically about the possible origins of current challenges in her personal relationships and contexts of conflict.

——◄○►——

Exemplar Narrative: Peace

—SUSAN

An unusual silence filled the house and the little girl wondered how long it would last. Maybe tonight will be all right, maybe he won't come home. She hoped not. She heard her mother hurriedly making dinner in the kitchen while her brother played on the floor, oblivious to what would probably occur. The peacefulness ended suddenly with the slam of a door and a bellowing voice yelling about whose tricycle is left outside.

"Is dinner ready yet?"

"Uh, almost," her mother answered quickly.

He tightly grabbed her mother's arm, making her wince in pain and asked why she did not have it yet. The little girl knew that tonight would not be different from any other night. After the usual tense dinner, her mother tucked her and her brother into bed, smiled bravely, and closed the door.

It started all over again, that horrible nightly ritual. She lay in her bed. Her tears falling continuously, 'til her green eyes burned red. She, unable to breathe, tried to suffocate her sobs in her tear-soaked pillow. Pulling it closer to her ears, she tried to block out the screaming, sobbing, and hitting. With her eyes clenched shut, light-headed from holding her breath, she felt the knot pulling tighter and tighter in her stomach. She thought she might explode. She wished she would explode, or at least fade away in a dark corner away from it all. Her mother's shrill frightened cries. The thuds of her mother's body being tossed against the wall and the sound of flesh hitting flesh.

She lay there paralyzed. A helpless child with such desire to help. The door slammed for a second time tonight. He was leaving. The screeching of tires confirmed this. The only sound throughout the house now was the sound of her mother's muffled sobs. It was over. They had survived another night. The peacefulness had returned, until tomorrow.

—◄○►—

Recognizing the Life Experiences We Bring to Conflicts

Handling conflict is far more complex and existentially meaningful than following a problem-solution process. We engage in conflict as people—selves— who are shaped by life experiences with others, and consciously or unconsciously, we bring those experiences to the process to recreate them in the present. Understanding how your talk about your conflicts reflects and represents your selves and your experiences with others is crucial to interpreting your narratives.

Recognizing how Negatives Create Negatives

It is important to recognize how you allow negative patterns to perpetuate themselves by creating conditions for similar negative patterns. First, conflicts can be created when you project your own feelings, particularly ones of fear and guilt, onto other people. These projections can often lead you to accuse others of what you actually feel about yourself. Hence, the truism that we tend to accuse others of what we feel most guilty of ourselves.

For example, one day a female student in her mid-20s (Susan) told me a story illustrating the destructive capability of this type of conflict. She had recently moved in with her boyfriend of a few years. He was apparently good to her, and she knew he cared deeply for her. Through college they had been planning on finally being together when they both graduated. However, after moving in together, she began having obsessive thoughts of jealousy and suspicion that he was cheating on her. She would go through his things when he was not there. She even started combing his car for evidence, such as hairs, that would prove his infidelity. One day, she was going through his sock drawer just in case he was hiding something from her. She came across a sealed envelope with his name written on the front in someone else's—apparently a woman's—handwriting. Her mind was racing with the possibilities. Had she finally found the conclusive proof that he was cheating? Could this be a love letter from his other girlfriend? She knew she couldn't open the letter, as he would know that she had been through his things. She steamed the letter open, careful not to damage the envelope. Inside she found the engagement ring that he was about to give her, along with the bill from the jeweler whose handwriting was on the envelope. He had been hiding the ring, waiting for the right romantic moment to present it to her. Her obsession had ruined the priceless moment he was planning, as well as the mystery of wondering how much it cost. She was devastated. She knew this wasn't *the* evidence, but perhaps she still might find it if she continued to look. She told me that her suspicions were driving him away and also driving her "nuts."

I told her the theory about projecting guilt onto others, and somehow it did lead to a moment of insight for her. At least, she began to question what personal experiences or feelings she was projecting onto her boyfriend so as to reduce her own feelings of guilt—How might I be constructing him as the guilty "other" to maintain my sense of self as moral and ethical? This question would be a good place for her to begin thinking about the relationship of self and other in her conflict.

Second, inherited, historical patterns of conflict behavior—baggage, if you will—can, to follow the image through, weigh you down later in life. It might not surprise you to know that the two stories above are from the same person. Often, people such as Susan seem lured into taking themselves back to their emotionally charged, early childhoods. Whether it is to relive what her mother lived and somehow make it right, or whether it is just to feel what her mother felt so that she better understands her mother's life experience, it is difficult to say. Susan does not really know the answer herself. The attraction to the same old flame is, nevertheless, quite a consistent experience associated with traumatic conflicts.

Third, negatives create negatives when you rely on past habits and trained incapacities to structure current choices. For example, many people choose to avoid conflict whenever possible. They are, for whatever reason, avoidance-oriented. Susan's close association between conflict and family violence and discord have shaped how she understands the role of conflict, and how she uses conflict to achieve particular relational goals. Susan's mother's apparent habit of minimizing the conditions that created violence in her husband worked well to ensure her daily survival. This would be particularly true when domestic violence was not a well-established concept in our culture and legal system. Simply, Susan's mother had few choices in her context for ensuring her survival. However, if this style of avoiding and minimizing conflict is applied to other contexts where broader opportunities for doing conflict exist, then her conflict habits would have been a further constraint to her. Thus, she continues to be constrained by the patterns set for her in her traumatic experience.

Fourth, it is possible to undermine the other and your self by making value judgments in conflict that limit ways of thinking and often diminish your experience of communication with others more generally. One of the principal benefits of dialogue is that communication can create more options than might first have appeared on the surface of a conflict. Communication is a creative process and not just the reporting of facts. Judgments of self and others can limit creative possibilities. For example, in her early experiences, Susan might have developed relatively enduring and negative ways of categorizing and valuing concepts such as marriage, wife, husband, father, daughter, family communication, and so on. Such categorical images can be quite difficult to overcome.

Understanding Negative and Positive Patterns

Recognizing patterns is crucial to both thinking systemically about your conflicts and making it possible to change those patterns. The following dialogue questions about repetitive patterns may help you explicate Susan's negative patterns.

1. How are Susan's current relational troubles possibly connected to the early experiences she narrates?

2. How did her parents' choices create the context for her adult choices of communication?

3. Why might she be suspicious and jealous of her boyfriend?

4. What relational pattern appears to be repeating itself in her adult life?

5. How might her actions be recreating and sustaining these patterns?

6. How might the feelings and the results of this current incident parallel her feelings as a child?

7. What conflict patterns established in your childhood create problems for you now?

8. How do you typically represent yourself in conflicts (for example as victim or hero, powerful or powerless, martyr, prosecutor, abuser, etc.)?

9. How are your personal histories important in understanding how you do conflict?

10. How might your own personal histories be important in structuring how you interpret Susan's story?

Recognizing how Positives Create Positives

Not all of your life experiences are bad. It can seem that way because you are dealing specifically with conflict experiences. Many of you remember ways early experiences have created dialogue skills and specific conflict competencies that determine how you conduct and narrate your conflicts. It may be possible for Susan to overcome some of the constraints that others created for her through her early experiences. That is, it is possible to turn a negative into a positive account—through a personal triumph narrative, for example. It is possible for Susan and her mother to go back to those early experiences and learn from the patterns that those experiences set for both of them. It is also possible for Susan and her current boyfriend to examine this experience and break the negative patterns that will almost certainly haunt their relationship. When small changes to patterns are made, they can often create significant changes as they affect other aspects of our self and our communication.

The following dialogue questions about positive patterns may help you examine constructive patterns in your own experiences with others.

1. How did your early experiences of conflict create positive patterns in your life?

2. What are the central features of the productive or positive conflicts of others that have influenced you the most?

3. How do positives create positives in your conflict?

4. What changes in your conflict habits and style, however small, might make big differences in your current relationships?

5. What one example, role model, or even piece of advice relating to conflict are you most grateful for as it has impacted your life?

6. How would you explain these positive patterns to Susan so she might learn from your experience?

Exploring Life Metaphors We Bring to Conflict

One of the most important factors related to how you approach conflict and communication relationships generally has to do with your basic approach to life. Life metaphors are one way you can understand where your views of life come from and how they affect your conflicts (Lakoff & Johnson, 1980; McCorkle & Mills, 1992; Hocker & Wilmot, 1995). Viewed through the lenses of different life metaphors, conflicts can become very different communicative realities, with different goals and expectations about the process and the desirable outcomes. The following statements are examples rather than an exhaustive list of all possible approaches to life. In reality, these examples may be combined or variously applied to different contexts and relationships.

• Life as the story of an adventurous journey.

People who tend to look at their lives as an unfolding adventurous journey typically approach conflict with a healthy sense of inevitability and perspective. These people often see conflicts along life's journey as inevitable turning points in the hands of fate and as experiences that orient them to the right direction. Conflicts move the plot of their life stories forward. Conflicts are inevitable in the complex twists and turns of life, but they rarely take on an overwhelming sense of disaster or danger. These people are most often capable of letting go of bad experiences and moving on their way, regardless of what happened. "When one door closes, another one opens" might be a familiar phrase. Conflicts remain an important, if sometimes painful, part of the journey.

• Life as a learning process.

"Well, that was a tough experience, but I learned a lot from it." This might be a familiar phrase for someone who views life as a continuous learning process. These people tend to look deeply at conflict experiences for lessons about themselves, about people, and about life in general. Conflicts may be traumatic, but some lesson can always be drawn from them. People who use conflicts to draw inspiration for poems, songs, paintings, and other artistic expressions also tend to view life as a learning process. Cast as learning experiences, conflicts can be kept in perspective as a useful source of life energy and valuable knowledge.

- Life as a cycle of give and take.

"You have to give a little to get a little," and "you win some and you lose some," are typical phrases that spring from the give-and-take view of life. These people typically are willing to bargain and negotiate to create a solution that, ideally, all participants are happy with. They are oriented toward collaboration in the process of conflict and integrative or win-win solutions as outcomes (Walton, 1969). They usually maintain a perspective that the long-term life of any relationship involves knowing when to push for what they want and when to let something go for the greater good of the relationship. Conflicts are viewed from within the bigger and more enduring picture of a "good" relationship.

- Life as a conspiracy.

People who have inherited and developed a view of life as "dog eat dog, eat or be eaten," or "get them before they get you" tend to see conspiracies in others' actions. These people often quickly portray themselves as the victims of the premeditated, purposeful, and overly competitive actions of others. The self is often in conflict with others. These people see strategies where there are none and the need to be competitive or proactively aggressive to get a fair piece of the pie. A conspiracy-based approach to life most readily lends itself to aggression and even violence in conflict. These people are usually the least likely to be open to dialogue, as disclosure often makes them feel too vulnerable.

- Life as a game.

The game metaphor has been developed as an explanatory model of how people act in conflicts with others (e.g., Hocker & Wilmot, 1995). Viewed as a game, conflicts consist of moves and countermoves based on largely rational calculations of possible and probable costs versus possible and probable rewards. Conflict is often viewed as the strategic process of outplaying the opponent to win as many "points" as possible. Game players in conflicts often bluff and use other strategies to outsmart and ultimately beat their opponents. These people, naturally, tend to be the most competitive participants in conflicts.

Exploring the life metaphor(s) in your conflict practices and styles is an important source of self-understanding. As Lakoff and Johnson (1980) explain, metaphors "structure how we perceive, how we think, and what we do" (p. 4). Conflict styles are often characterized by the categories of avoidance, accommodation, competition, compromise, and collaboration (Blake & Mouton, 1970; Thomas, 1976; Conrad, 1990; Hocker & Wilmot, 1995). These are good general categories that can initiate discussion about your particular styles. The main limitation with this list however, is that reality is more complex and existentially and historically grounded than such a framework explicitly encourages you to consider. Your conflict style is a manifestation of your self, especially in the sense of what it means to be in the world of others. For example, in Susan's narrative, what might be the life metaphor of each member of her family? How might the participants' metaphoric views of life have provided a basis for how they treated each other? In the second narrative we shared about Susan, how does her life metaphor influence how she relates to her boyfriend? Examine the following dialogue questions on life metaphors and conflict to look into your life metaphors and the impact that they have on your conflicts.

1. What metaphor or image best describes how you view life in general?

2. How do your everyday behavior and communication with others reflect this metaphor?

3. How is your everyday behavior and communication inconsistent with this metaphor?

4. Where do you think you learned to look at life this way?

5. How does this affect how you view and portray others in conflicts?

6. How do other people relate to you as a result of this approach to life?

7. How do your close friends and family view life?

8. What impacts do their life metaphors have on your relationships with them?

9. If you could make a change the life metaphor that most characterizes your everyday actions and communication, what would that be and how might you begin such a change?

The Bodily Experience of Conflict

The body is our instrument of communication. As such, we also use it to do conflict. Hope, fear, love, hate, anger, jealousy, rage, and even excitement are often intimately connected with conflict. These emotions give rise to conflict and let us know we are about to experience conflict, that we are in a conflict, or that conflict is over. These are all emotions that we might see as important to Susan's bodily experience of conflict. Go back through her story and our story about her and look for clues about how her conflict felt and the emotions that were most important in her realization that she was in a conflict situation. Also, look for ways the participants' actions created the emotional climate around them and how others responded to these emotions. How do the emotions of Susan's conflict provide a structural map of how a conflict arises, progresses, and finally, how it ends? This is the bodily experience of conflict that manifests itself repeatedly in conflict behavior. Work through the following questions in relation to your own conflict experiences to examine your bodily and emotional experience of conflict.

1. Describe how complex emotions really feel in a conflict and throughout the stages of a specific conflict episode.

2. How do these feelings drive or influence you? How do these feelings and emotions stimulate and energize you to be more creative or destructive?

3. Which emotions tend to recur when you personally feel a conflict starting, when you are in the middle of it, and when you know it is resolved?

4. How and why do different people who you interact with seem to draw out particular emotions when you are in conflict with them?

5. What climate or emotional feelings are you consciously or unconsciously recreating when you have conflicts with certain people?

6. How do your bodily experiences of a conflict mirror and influence those of the others you are conflicting with?

7. How are face-to-face conflicts different from those done at a distance, for example, by letters, phone, or email?

Some Final Reflective Questions on Susan's Narrative

1. How did Susan's story make you feel about your life and parental and family relationships?

2. What are the most important negative and/or positive experiences that shaped how you relate to people, particularly in conflicts?

3. What cycles and patterns have characterized your life so far, and where do those cycles and patterns come from?

4. What specific aspects of a conflict do you enjoy and/or dread physically or emotionally?

As we have shown, your understanding of yourself in conflict necessarily invokes your relationships with others. We move on to more closely explicate the role of others in your conflicts.

UNDERSTANDING OTHERS IN YOUR CONFLICTS

One of the most important practices in developing a dialogic approach to conflicts is to learn to understand the relationship between oneself and the other(s) in a conflict. This involves recognizing that the other is, like you, also a self—a real person—and not just an opponent or obstacle. Ideally, it also involves those others recognizing you as a self as well as their other (partner or opponent, for example) in the conflict. This realization is a good starting point for dialogue.

The following poem illustrates the opportunities for understanding the relationship between self and other in conflict. The poem describes the poet's bodily experience of a new career challenge as a graduate teaching assistant. The fear of this difficult and sometimes disaffirming experience of change can create major internal tensions. This poem explores the relationship of public and private performances of self in relation to her students—the others in the poem. The poet is also playing with the experience of otherness, that is, of becoming a stranger to herself—the person she is forced to become in the public performance of her profession. As the poem illustrates, these internal tensions interconnect with one's external presentation of self in important ways.

—◁○▷—

Exemplar Narrative: Between Dreams and Reality

—SHAKIRA

Dreaming about class
Over and over, again and again
I go through the text
Puzzled faces peer at me
Over and over, again and again
They won't let me sleep

I cannot sleep
I go back over it~3am
Puzzled faces~4am
The clock keeps ticking
Over and over, again and again
I cannot sleep

Dreams, the same ones, haunt me still
I feel naked, so disclosed and somewhat ill
"I graded those quizzes"
"I planned that class"
And what do you mean you "don't understand?"
"Kiss my ass" I want to say but I cannot!

Instead I dream most every night
When my fears from the classroom, then come to life
Over and over, again and again
Reality wakes me at 6 am
Class at eight, can't be late
I've gotta go, to do my dog and pony show

I leave my fright there in my dreams
All those fears don't come to class
Like they're at home enclosed in glass
When the night breaks, the glass breaks too
My fears resurface
Over and over, again and again

Intrapersonal and Interpersonal Conflict

Systems theory teaches us that we seek balance or equilibrium between change and sameness (Bateson, 1972, 1980; Johnson, 1977; Weick, 1979). We know we cannot keep things the same all of the time, and we know we cannot change all of the time. Much of our sense-making activity in times of conflict between these dialectics is concerned with working through the tensions and reducing the equivocality of the experience (Weick, 1979, 1995). The equivocality that Shakira is experiencing comes from the apparent contrast between her efforts to explain and illustrate the principles she is teaching and the fact that her students look at her with puzzled faces and claim they "don't understand." How could this contrast happen? How does she think the contrast reflects on them? How does she think the contrast might reflect on her? How is she struggling with the fact that she cannot decide whether this apparent failure of communication is her fault or theirs? It seems that she is unable to resolve this ambiguity in the reasons for this failure. She wants to blame them—the other—but she struggles with thinking that it might be her fault. The harder she pushes the blame onto the students, the deeper is her own anxiety that it might be her fault. She wants to delineate clearly between self and other in her experience but finds the reality of the conflict implies a shared responsibility. Self and other are rarely entirely divisible in a conflict.

The bodily feel of her conflict provides feedback that, if she listens to it, can be an important form of understanding. Her body tells her that she is out of equilibrium; she is out of her comfort zone, experiencing new things, and is taking the lack of complete success with her students personally. She experiences anxiety, fear, and self-doubt. These create the sleepless nights in which she struggles to make sense out of the teaching experience. This resolution or clarity does not occur. In turn, this generates more internal conflict and appears to create the heightened possibility for conflict with students. She gives you clues to this when she says, "kiss my ass" and so on, things she would like to say but cannot. These statements are usually clues that the energy of the conflict is displaced and may manifest itself somewhere else and in some other form that may or may not be related to the origins of the energy (Coser, 1956).

To make sense of the conflict, Shakira creates a narrative in which she tries hard to explain things clearly but her students just do not seem to get it. To recreate her sense of self as a competent communicator in this new situation, she finds herself characterizing the others in ways that allow her to create narrative closure on the experience. In Shakira's poem, the students are reduced from wholes to parts, from people to "puzzled faces." It is these puzzled faces that keep her awake at night, as "they" won't let her sleep. Their actions make her feel "naked" and therefore vulnerable. They seem to be choosing not to understand her. She tells herself that she has made every effort to explain things clearly and to fulfill her professional duties, such as grading papers, effectively. All of this is evidence to her that she has done all that she can for them. She remains competent while they appear not to be trying.

Yet, she has difficulty fully believing her own story. The nagging self-doubt remains. This sort of victim narrative relies on the characterization of the others as the victimizers—the creators of the conflict. This form of objectification in extreme cases provides the narrative space to demonize the others as evil or inherently bad.

As Shakira's poem illustrates, the amount of energy surrounding a conflict, created by a conflict, or drawn from you in a conflict, can be enormous. The tensions of living with these conflicting accounts of self and other—with trying to blame the other while feeling guilty yourself, with trying to reduce the ambiguity of the situation—all redirect energy in important ways. This conflict appears to be draining Shakira's energy away from enjoying the new challenge. The conflict is also taking energy away from building her teaching skills. Instead, her energy is redirected into creating the oppositions between self and other. She focuses on blaming them rather than resolving the conflict. Perhaps, she does not want to face the fearful fact that it may be partly her fault, and she also needs to change. Her energy goes into maintaining an inauthentic relationship she does not want to have with students—hence, the feeling of putting on a "dog and pony show." Clearly, Shakira's emotional and narrative energy is going into maintaining the conflict with an incompetent and belligerent other because this affords her some sense of partial closure. Ironically, this means that for all of her claims to present and explain things effectively, the broader classroom communication lacks effective dialogue. She assumes that putting on a good dog and pony show should be enough. In so many situations similar to this one, good conversation, or even a few good questions, can clear up all the misunderstandings. So many times, such conversations and questions do not happen because our sense of self and our characterizations of others, through which we create our narrative accounts, often keep us from the questioning and creation of possibilities offered by dialogue.

Perspective-Taking in Conflict

As we have shown, Shakira's poem illustrates some of ways conflicts escalate and are maintained through mutually supporting and opposing constructions of self and other. You probably have the impression Shakira and her students have little understanding of what the other is experiencing. Perhaps Shakira is more effective than she thinks she is, and as a new teacher easily takes minor comments very seriously. It does seem, however, that Shakira has no real sense of why the students are puzzled and claiming not to understand the lectures. Perhaps they really do not understand the issues. Perhaps they are not working hard enough and she is afraid to tell them this. Her students probably have little or no idea from her dog and pony shows that she is upset and angry with them. Perhaps they think all is fine. Perhaps they are concerned about the tension in the classroom, and this is decreasing their attentiveness. As readers, you cannot fully know Shakira's reality, as represented by the poem. You do get an impression of some things she would like to say in anger. But what conversations are missing in this relationship? Why do you think that self and other have become such archetypes of good and bad? What might the students' narrative account of the class say? We do not propose that people should always publicly discuss their feelings. If Shakira talked about how she felt with the class, it might make her even more vulnerable. You must recognize that this conflict is embedded in an organizational context carrying certain communicative constraints. Being honest about how you feel is not always appropriate or wise. However, for the sake of illustration, it might be useful to examine how this poem might be a good starting point leading Shakira and her students to more effectively address and resolve the conflict through dialogue.

For this to be a good starting point for dialogue rests on the skill of perspective-taking (Applegate & Delia, 1980). Perspective-taking, as it relates to Shakira's poem, and the lived reality that it represents, involves explicating the relationships between the self and the other. In Shakira's case, it involves her reflectively working through the following questions. As you review these questions, try to imagine how Shakira might answer them.

1. Why do I portray myself in the poem as I do?

2. Why do I portray the others in the poem the way I do?

3. How does my poem represent how I think they see me as a teacher and as a person?

4. How are my portrayals of myself and the students related to the deeper process of developing a new professional role with all the emotional and personal challenges that entails?

5. How are my portrayals of myself and the students based on suppositions related to my own need for a narrative that makes sense and affirms me?

6. How does my account of the conflicted working relationship influence our ongoing working relationship?

7. What specific changes need to occur for me to feel more comfortable that my teaching is effective?

The best way to generate perspective-taking is to engage the students in examining their perspective on the conflict. Imagine that Shakira shared the poem with the class after carefully preparing them for the dialogue and learning opportunities the poem might generate. The students would probably take the oppositional perspective, that is, it is Shakira's fault and not theirs. In some ways, her portrayals of self and other create this context of defensiveness. However, it is possible that the students would be surprised and even relieved that the topic was brought up for discussion. The following questions help determine the possible benefits from this perspective-sharing exercise.

1. How might Shakira's students be surprised, relieved, disappointed, and so on, at her perspective?

2. What learning moments would you expect Shakira and her students to experience as they share perspectives?

3. How might sharing perspectives lead to more mutual understanding?

4. What could they learn about conflict generally from sharing each other's perspectives?

5. What might they learn about recognizing differences and oppositions between self and others that create and maintain conflicts?

6. What nonverbal clues (including the role of silence) might be important in understanding this conflict in terms of how it started and continued?

7. How might Shakira and her students create a shared narrative account of their conflict, including their multiple, opposing, and often parallel voices?

8. What might they learn from the relationships of voices in such a text?

9. How might the dialogue change their assumptions about the motives and intents of self and other and their conflict and interaction more generally?

10. How can the framework of self and other help you make sense of and learn from the complexity of representation in a conflict?

11. How might this dialogue renew a sense of mutual needs, tolerance, and shared goals in the teaching and learning relationship between Shakira and her students?

12. What might they learn about the dangers and limitations of one-sided or self-oriented thinking about conflict and the need to value selves as others, and others as selves?

Representations of self and other in conflicts are often oppositional. In a divisive conflict, the participants normally maintain their self-image, and this is often done by portraying the other negatively. Negative portrayals are also used to justify and rationalize hurtful or even violent acts against that other. Hence, a conflict can easily escalate to a point where the other is objectified as an antagonistic barrier to personal goals, and the self is justified in whatever he or she does (Baron, 1984; Deutsch, 1973; Folger & Poole, 1984; Hocker & Wilmot, 1995).

This works both ways; despite the fact that representations of self and other are oppositional, they are also, ironically, mutually supportive. Until the narratives intersect or the participants make an effort to make them intersect, the participants in the conflict often have no idea they are actively maintaining the conflict. Each individual party usually is more concerned with being "right," while the other party appears to cause all the escalating. It is possible that perspective-taking and the dialogue it generates can create changes in this context of communication.

Some Final Reflective Questions on Shakira's Narrative

1. How would you describe your internal feelings when you know you are beginning to engage in conflict with someone?

2. How are your internal thoughts similar or different from your external expression during a conflict? What do you think but not say, or say but not take time to think about?

3. Have any of your conflicts became part of your dreams? Which ones? Why?

4. How would you feel and act if you were Shakira?

5. Have you been in a conflict where your self-concept was challenged? How did you react?

6. How might you improve your understanding of both yourself and others in conflicts?

To more fully understand how to change the relationship of self and other, it is important to examine the role of communication in creating contexts and the role of contexts in structuring communication. We next discuss the importance of understanding the contexts of conflicts.

READING CONTEXT FOR CLUES ABOUT SELF AND OTHER

The following narrative illustrates the cultural background context of assumptions, myths, and values as it plays out in what appears to be primarily a family and generational conflict.

———◄○►———

Exemplar Narrative: You're Doing WHAT With Him?

—ALEX

A year ago, my stepmother's (Donna) father (Willy) passed away. Hazel (Donna's mother and Willy's widow), recently began dating again. Hazel is 70 years old and the kids are having a hard time with this new information. Willy has not been deceased that long, and the kids believe that Hazel is making a big mistake.

One Sunday, I went to visit my father and Donna. Hazel came over that day as well. Donna asks Hazel, "What's going on with you and James?"

Hazel proceeds to tell Donna, "James wants me to pay off his mortgage and come live with him for six months to see if the relationship works. If the relationship can last for six months, then we will get married. If the relationship does not work, then we will part company."

Hazel told Donna that she does not want to do this and feels that she is being pressured to follow through with this act. Donna got very mad and told her mother, "This would not happen as it goes against our family beliefs and this is what you have always preached to your own kids." Donna attacked by saying, "We're not brought up this way and James should know better than to ask you to do something like this. How could you consider such a thing when you are a respectable member of the church, and Daddy was even the deacon there. Could you handle everybody in town talking about you?"

Donna is a very assertive person and Hazel tries to avoid most conflicts. Hazel cried and tried to give excuses for her actions. Hazel is lonely and regrets the reasons for her actions. Everybody wants to have someone to hold, and even more so when a loved one passes away. Donna did most of the talking because Hazel was so emotional. I could see that it is hard for Hazel to tell Donna these things. The other kids do not know what is going on, and I believe it will raise even more conflict.

The next day Donna went to see her mother when she got off work. Donna felt bad about the outcome of the conflict because nothing was settled in her mind. Hazel left crying, and Donna could not handle not getting any respect from James. Donna knew that her mother did not want to live with James without marriage and Donna was going to see to it that this did not happen. Donna told Hazel, "You know in your heart that this is not right. If you want to marry James and pay off the mortgage, that's fine. I will not like it but I can deal with it. I cannot let you disgrace yourself by living with this man."

Donna told Hazel that if they decided to live together, then James is not welcome in her home at all. Hazel again was crying but knew that Donna was speaking the truth.

A day later, Hazel told Donna that they had decided to get married in January. Donna is happy that James is finally going to respect her mother. Our family believes that you do not shack up with someone. In this day and time it happens all the time. But, for our family, a man respects a woman and takes her hand in marriage before they live together. It is old fashioned but ties need to be there for our family. Some say that you can learn a lot about someone if you move in together first, but this is just a man's way of holding off marrying that woman. He can get comfortable about this living arrangement, and then the woman never gets married, and he can leave at any time. Donna is afraid that her mother will get hurt and is also worried about what others would say. Donna accepts this marriage and she still communicates with her mother. James never comes over to Donna's anymore, but what matters to Donna is the relationship with her mother.

——————◄o►——————

The Where and Why of Conflict Contexts

Communication partly involves choosing contexts. Simply, when you communicate, you create reality as a reflection of those choices and as the context created for subsequent choices (Lanigan, 1988). For example, if you approach a conflict competitively, then that is the reality of conflict you experience. Communication can be understood as making choices in context. Simply, your communication is shaped and constrained by the social, historical, and situational conventions of the context in which you communicate (Lanigan, 1988). For example, for a variety of reasons, such as the choices my conflict "opponent" just made or the conventions of a situation, I may feel that a competitive strategy is appropriate or even necessary. This interplay of context and communication in conflict is important in understanding why you do conflict as you do and why you represent the relationship of contexts and choices as you do in your narratives.

Participants in a conflict partly choose the contexts for their own and others' actions. This fact sensitizes you to the ways participants create their own lived experience of a conflict through the strategies and tactics they choose and how these choices build into the turn-taking sequences that create a conflict episode.

The context of choice in a conflict refers to where a conflict occurs and how the physical, social, cultural, historical, and geographic context help to shape the conflict.

The first and simplest question is, Where did this conflict occur? We know that the part of this conflict retold by Alex occurred in a small town in North Carolina in 1999. The main scenes occurred in the homes of Hazel and her immediate family. The town, the family, and the place in life that the participants find themselves are also parts of the story's context represented or portrayed in particular ways.

The second important "where" question has to do with understanding these contexts as representational choices as well as factual reporting. The second important question is, what role do these specific contexts play in the representation of narrative themes and the stages of conflict? When you understand why this conflict happened in this particular context, the answers become more socially and culturally grounded. You can choose to include details of context that make the narrative effective. You may even be largely unconscious of the assumptions behind your representations of conflict. Narratives tell us about the social, cultural, and communicative context creating the conditions for generating, maintaining, escalating, and resolving conflict. The following questions may help in explicating the role of context in shaping and being shaped by conflict.

1. Why does Hazel's decision to start dating soon after her husband died create the context for the conflict? What community value is invoked by representing this as an important contextual detail?

2. Why do Hazel's children's attitudes about her dating help to create the foundation for the conflict?

3. Why are the contextual details of paying off a man's mortgage and moving in with him without being married important in generating the conflict? Why are these details persuasive choices in Alex's representation of the moral foundation of the conflict?

4. Why does Donna's assertively stating her objections to Hazel and James moving in together have an impact on the progress of the conflict? Why is the "truth" portrayed as such a clear-cut answer?

5. Why do Donna's appeals to family and church values, as well as the pressure of sanctions by the community, provide a persuasive context for the argument against their plan to move in together?

6. Why did this conflict resolution go so smoothly in terms of the speed of the decision and the lack of negative escalation? Why did the contexts of the actions that Donna evoked so clearly define what was "right" and what was "wrong"?

7. Why did the resolution of the conflict affirm or reify the particular moral and behavioral standards of the community where these people live?

8. Why does James not visit Donna's house anymore, even though the story seemed to work out well for all of the participants? In what ways might he not "fit" the contextual standards and values of these peoples' lives?

Answering these questions provides a clearer sense of how participants' communication creates context and how context structures their communication. In Alex's story of Hazel and James, the values and beliefs of the community are represented as a dynamic part of the unfolding story, providing the energy through which it takes on its particular meaning and message as the resolution of a moral dilemma. This conflict also reestablishes and reifies some of the shared values and practices of the community. Specifically, it is reestablished that a woman should wait to be married before moving in with a man or taking any financial responsibility for him. Religious, economic, family, and community voices all intersect to confirm this fact in the community context. These institutional voices are simultaneously affirmed as they help to resolve the conflict.

In the next sections, we explicate additional dimensions of context important in constructing and interpreting conflict narratives.

Questions and Issues for Explicating Important Dimensions of Context

It is unlikely we can ever fully account for all the contextual variables important in a conflict. However, the following dimensions provide enough insight for you to more fully understand the relationship between our conflicts and the world they both occur in and partly shape.

Climate and Conflict

Climate is an important characteristic of context. Climate can be defined as the general feel of a situation; it helps you partly explain why participants do what they do (Poole, 1985).

1. What emotional appeals create a climate in which Hazel feels encouraged to explain her actions and eventually conform?

2. What threats, promises, and other tactics create the climate of pressure to conform to social, religious, and family conventions?

3. What choices by any of the participants might have changed the climate and escalated the interaction?

4. In what ways is this still a fragile or changeable communication climate? What could be said or done to easily open up old wounds?

5. What lessons about creating a positive climate for discussing conflict does the story present?

Cultural and Intercultural Dimensions of Conflict

The conflict recounted by Alex took place in a small southern town in the United States in 1999 among participants in their 40s and 70s. This particular cultural context has an impact on how a conflict takes place (Gudykunst & Ting-Toomey, 1988; Hocker & Wilmot, 1995). Conflict is a cultural phenomenon (Fry & Bjorkqvist, 1997) in that it reflects a society's norms, practices, and institutions. These provide a framework for people's perception of conflict. Culture defines both the values and interests at the heart of conflicts, shaping perceptions and alternatives and defining outcomes as positive or negative. Communication about conflict is without a doubt culturally mediated (Pedersen & Jandt, 1996). How mothers and daughters talk to each other, how men and women are supposed to act, how elderly people should act, what power is given to local customs and community mores, and so on, are all encoded into the action and characters of the story.

1. What specific dimensions of how people acted, how they talked to each other, and what they assumed about appropriate relationships were encoded into the story?

2. What deeper cultural values and beliefs were at stake in this specific conflict?

3. How did cultural differences provide the oppositions creating the conflict?

4. How might Hazel's conflict have been different or similar in specific Latin, Asian, European, African, or Middle Eastern cultures?

Historical Dimensions of Conflict

Conflicts usually have historical dimensions because they are often created by previous conflicts, and are often about values and beliefs privileged as historical facts. Specific community values are reestablished as the moral of this story. Things are done in certain ways, and not done in other ways. The culture of a community usually embodies examples that illustrate right and wrong choices. Stories of heroes, villains, and fools usually serve this historical-cultural function (Morgan, 1989). Both choices are used to reconstitute a particular order in Alex's family and community so the social order is reestablished and particular historical facts or truths are reaffirmed.

1. In what ways does Alex's narrative illustrate how the past provides a context for present conflict?

2. What historical "truths" about this family's way of life are challenged and reaffirmed through this conflict?

3. What possible future conflicts might arise from how this conflict was handled?

Religious Dimensions of Conflict

Religious rhetoric is often used in conflicts to evoke deeper, spiritual dimensions of ethics and morality in terms of differentiating between good and bad actions and right and wrong.

1. How are religious values used persuasively in this narrative to guide right and wrong behavior and to influence the feelings of the participants?

2. What might you assume about the religious convictions of the participants of this story?

3. How does the behavior of the participants reflect religious values and beliefs?

4. How is religion used to connect economic and social practices into a coherent argument that for Donna is morally, economically, and socially appropriate?

5. What "truth" do all of the participants arrive at in this story?

Mass Media and Conflict

From newspapers to television, media interact with cultural images of conflict and individual perceptions in three ways. First, media reflect dominant cultural values and ideals of conflict. They portray conflict in ways that mirror your shared understandings. Second, media reproduce cultural views of conflict in individuals. By defining what is normal, media suggest how you should act when engaged in conflict. Third, media function as gatekeepers of information and images. By selectively regulating what you see, media influence how you perceive conflict.

It is difficult to imagine a story such as Alex's in a newspaper or news broadcast. It lacks the highly dramatic, negative, and violent qualities that define something as newsworthy. Perhaps it might have made a good plot for an episode of *The Andy Griffith Show.* The media can be significant in helping you understand the images and portrayals of conflict in family and small town life.

1. What small town and family conflicts are most often portrayed by the mass media?

2. What would have to happen in Hazel's family for their story to be newsworthy?

3. What important dimensions of conflict in family and community life do you think should be more readily reported by the mass media?

4. What effects do the mass media have on everyday conflicts?

5. What cultural images and myths of conflict do the media propagate as part of the context of doing conflict in society?

Racial Dimensions of Conflict

Diversity education and gradual changes in laws in the United States have changed many peoples' attitudes about race. However, it is still clear that race generates many conflicts in the United States. Race can also be present in the context or as an explanatory category in interpreting events. No apparent racial issues are evident in Hazel's conflict; both she and James are white southerners. However, race would probably be an issue if this were an interracial relationship.

1. What are some important racial conflicts that have shaped relationships in your culture?

2. How were these key racial conflicts started, and where do they manifest themselves in everyday communication?

3. Why is race an important difference that can generate conflicts in your culture?

4. How is race interconnected with, for example, class in your culture?

5. How do different races in your culture maintain conflicts through their race-specific narrative accounts of those conflicts?

Gender Dimensions of Conflict

Sensitivity to gender issues, and especially gender inequity as it is expressed and maintained through language, has become a valuable skill in the field of communication and other social science disciplines (Tannen, 1990; Wood, 1992). As Alex's narrative portrays the relationship between a man and a woman as well as between two females, there are gender dynamics occurring important to your understanding of the account of the conflict.

1. In what ways might so-called feminine and masculine conflict styles have had an impact on this conflict?

2. How is the conflict between Hazel and James typical or atypical of male and female conflicts?

3. How would you characterize the communication relationship between Hazel and Donna?

4. How might this narrative be different if the narrator were male?

5. How might the narrative be different if the story were told from the perspective of James and his son, rather than Hazel and her daughter?

6. In what ways would you regard the values and beliefs underlying the narrative to be sexist? How are men and women valued and treated differently in the religious, social, and family contexts of the narrative?

Age and Conflict

As the U.S. population ages, issues associated with aging and discrimination associated with age—ageism—have become important. As a whole, the United States is a culture that focuses on and privileges youth. Clearly Alex's conflict has some unusual dimensions that are related to the ages of Hazel and James. A 70-year-old woman begins dating again. The children have no easy formula for dealing with this reality. There is conflict between generations of the family. The younger generations, ironically enough, are taking on the responsibility for reinforcing community values and standards. Certainly age differences, along with gender and religious issues, account for part of the underlying dynamics of this conflict.

1. How do conflict between generations and generation-based attitudes contribute to this conflict?

2. How does the conflict tell you important things about Hazel's stage in life?

3. How does age influence the perspectives of each participant in the conflict?

4. Would this conflict have been different if Hazel and James were younger?

5. What are the community standards for behavior associated with age reaffirmed through this story?

All of these (and more) dimensions of context are important in structuring conflicts. In narratives, you also actively shape the portrayal of the relationship between self, other, and context to achieve your narrative and communicate goals. Next, we discuss narrative representation.

ISSUES IN THE REPRESENTATION OF SELF, OTHER, AND CONTEXT IN NARRATIVES

Alex's narrative shows the complex interplay of age, family, intimate relationships, and social conventions. You have seen how inclusive and exclusive choices are also important in constructing meaningful and plausible accounts in each of the narratives explicated. These are representational choices that the narrator makes to connect their experience to themselves and their audience as communication. Clearly, important issues of textual and representational politics need to be considered. For example, representations of self, other, and context necessarily affect the representation of the other dimensions of a story. Also, such representational choices also affect your relationship to your own experience as the narrator and the audience's relationship to the experience being narrated. Simply, your representational choices structure the reality experienced by both the narrator and the audience.

We do not advocate a prescriptive set of rules for constructing a conflict narrative. We believe narrators should be as true to their experiences as possible as they tell their stories. We do, however, believe it is important to understand the implications of the choices you make and as you listen to those of others. In this final section of this chapter, we explicate these central issues of narrative representation in recounting and interpreting conflicts.

Issues in the Representation of Life Experiences

A narrative presents a particular version of the relationship of self, other, and context. To understand conflict experiences, you need awareness of the choices you make in those representations. It is helpful to turn to ethnographic writing to determine how to write representations of life experiences. For example, conflict narratives are constructed in what Goodall (1991) calls the plural present. You live alongside others in reality, and this is always part of the narrative construction. Interpretive ethnography (e.g., Ellis & Bochner, 1996; Goodall, 1991, 1994, 1996) recognizes that the story told is always, at best, partial and incomplete. Self-reflexivity in ethnographic writing acknowledges the author's perspective, the author's filters, what Burke (1966) calls "terministic screens," and the author's representation of the experience in textual form, with all the limitations the situation implies.

Another limitation you face when writing personal narratives is the crisis of representation (Okely & Callaway, 1992; Denzin, 1997). It is not possible to represent a life as it is actually lived or experienced. As Bruner (1986) argues, there are inevitable gaps between "reality (what is really out there), experience (how reality presents itself to consciousness), and expressions (how individual experience is framed and articulated)" (p. 6). Language and expressions do not simply mirror experience but partly create experience, thereby constantly transforming and deferring what is being described (Denzin, 1997). There cannot be a final, totally accurate representation of what was stated or meant, only different textual representations or evocations of experience. Recognizing this when speaking or writing about your conflict experience opens up new ways of seeing, interpreting, and ultimately, understanding and learning from the conflict experience.

The following questions about representation may help you when presenting and/or writing your conflict story:

1. When telling your conflict story, whose story are you telling?

2. How is your story partial? What are you leaving out and why?

3. How does the way you speak or write about others influence the construction of your self in the story?

4. Is the expression of your experience a credible representation of your conflict?

5. How is your story a subjective account? What can you learn from acknowledging your subjectivity?

Some Final Reflective Questions on Alex's Narrative

1. What are some specific ways aspects of your cultural and social context influence your everyday communication, particularly your conflicts?

2. What are some ways your conflict style tends to create the context for what others are likely to do when in conflict with you?

3. What kind of climate do you create around you that others might sense when they interact with you?

4. Where do your values and principles come from and how do they influence your communication with others?

5. How might important dimensions of race, class, age, gender, and so on, affect how you would engage in Alex's conflict if you were involved?

CONCLUSION

We are rarely fully conscious of the choices we make in narrating our experience. Much of the time we simply tell what happened, and enjoy the clarification that this brings. This chapter challenges you to problematize and question your narrative practices. As you have seen in this discussion, your narratives represent the often subtle balances you place on the relationships of self, others, and context in accounting for your conflict experiences. Choices you make in balancing one of these relationships necessarily affect the other balances in your stories. These relationships of self, other, and context are thus crucial in helping you understand how and why you narrate your conflict experiences as you do. You are also challenged to examine ways you might change your assumptions about the relationships of self, other, and context as a starting point for changing your conflict practices. Your conflicts are rarely determined individually by just yourselves, or just by the actions of others, or just by the constraints of your contexts. Rather, your conflicts result from the interaction of all three dimensions, and resolving conflict involves finding the best balance among them.

4

Ways of Constructing and Interpreting Conflict Narratives

"[Stories] long to be used rather than analyzed, to be told and retold rather than theorized and settled."

(Bochner, 1997, p. 434)

"... Pay attention to the details. Ultimately, they contain the whole story."

(Goodall, 1996, p. 24)

It is important to understand how to record your conflict experiences and those of others. It is also important to learn how to reflect on and transform those field notes into conflict narratives that you can, as Bochner says, use both to represent and more deeply understand your conflicts. To achieve these goals, we need to learn the methodological principles of working with personal narratives. This chapter also draws together the theoretical framework of questions developed so far, and illustrates how these principles of narrative interpretation can be used to understand conflict narratives.

First, some fundamentals of recording notes and creating narrative accounts based on those notes are discussed. We review basic ethnographic techniques of keeping field notes in a conflict journal. This journal is used to record your personal experiences of conflict. Also, it is important to record experiences of a wide variety of cultural expressions of conflict through poetic, visual, and musical forms, as well as to record the conflicts of others around you. These conflict expressions and performances can inform the construction, performance, and interpretation of your own narratives.

Second, we describe the process of interpreting and learning from narratives. Here, we discuss how interpretive methods help in your rigorous questioning and reflective understanding of narratives in the world around you, and in making choices about changing that social reality. In short, we illustrate how personal narrative methodology offers perspective, critique, and practical insight into writing and talking about, understanding, and possibly changing conflict communication practices.

Key Concepts, Terms, and Definitions to Learn in This Chapter

- How to record, collect, and construct notes for conflict narratives as an interpretive researcher

- How to build those notes into good interpretive accounts in the form of conflict narratives

- How to learn from different forms of conflict narratives such as interviews and fictional texts

- How to apply a framework of interpretive questions to a narrative

- How to learn from conflict narratives and possibly change your social reality

Key Definitions

- *Narrative construction.* The process of transforming observations and notes into a good narrative account of a conflict experience

- *Ethnographic journal.* The often extensive notes that are taken based on observations, thoughts, and experiences of conflict in our lives

- *Personal narrative.* A personally meaningful story of our own experience developed from our journal notes about conflicts we have lived through or are living through

---

FRAMEWORK FOR UNDERSTANDING NARRATIVE CONSTRUCTION

In this chapter, you explore what makes a good personal narrative account. To prepare for this, as you read through Alexandria's narrative below, try to articulate why it is a good story from the viewpoints of the teller and the audience. Why do the details she provides, her writing style, the construction of passages, the moral of the story, and so on, make it a good personal narrative? Consider also how we can learn from her narrative construction about accounting for our own experiences. What insight does Alexandria's story give us into the dynamics of conflict communication as they are represented in narratives? These are the questions we focus on as we "think with" Alexandria's narrative (Bochner, 1997). We need to recognize that it is valuable to collect and to tell stories that are less developed as writing exercises. We may collect interview narratives of people who are unfamiliar with personal narrative methodology. We may simply decide to write about an experience as a draft flow of ideas. What follows is a discussion of how to prepare to write for an audience interested in the dialogic possibilities accompanying a carefully written narrative. Choose the writing conventions that best suit your methodological goals.

The narrative illustrates how easy it is to get caught in other people's conflicts and how they can quickly become your own. It is possible to learn lessons about truth, openness, sharing power, habits that escalate conflict, and how conflict can draw you into the strange world of others in unexpected ways. Alexandria's construction of the story makes these lessons concrete and real. We then explicate how her narrative construction leads to positive outcomes.

◄○►

Exemplar Narrative: Play Now, Pay Later

—ALEXANDRIA

BACKGROUND

Essential to understanding the following conflict, I must first put the situation in proper context by presenting a brief background. Several years ago, I had begun dating my manager at my workplace. I moved to Raleigh to attend NCSU after seeing him only a month, so we did not work together long after our relationship began. I knew him rather well prior to dating him because we were friends as well as coworkers. I also had numerous friends at that job who knew him well.

He lived at Lincoln Green apartments and had been married to an evil, cold woman for some length of time prior to our relationship. I had seen her once come into the restaurant to fight with him about something, but really knew nothing about her or the nature of their separation. He was eight years older than me and often our disputes revolved around my lack of experience with "real life." Nevertheless, I was attending NCSU—living and working in Raleigh—and he was living and working in Greensboro. We took turns traveling back and forth on weekends and, for the most part, had a relatively good relationship. We had become more serious and exclusive in the time I had been living in Raleigh, and we were spending a lot of time in metacommunication and self-disclosure.

I had begun NCSU in January so my roommate and seven other suitemates had already known each other for six months. I was still very much in a period of getting to know these people, and still forming impressions of them as they were of me. All of my suitemates, especially my roommate, had met John, and liked him a lot. I spoke highly of him as being trustworthy and responsible. Some of them had formed the impression that dating men who were slightly older was a good idea because they were tired of immature college boys. I knew some of the girls envied our relationship and this reinforced my praising him and my feelings for him.

THE EVENT

Immediately prior to this conflict he spent the weekend with me in Raleigh and had returned to Greensboro. My roommate and I as well as the six girls in the adjoining rooms were all asleep. It was approximately 3:00 am Monday morning when there was a horrendous banging at the steel door that lead to our rooms. My roommate and I assumed it was some drunk returning from a party who had the wrong door and dismissed it. The banging became louder and more pronounced. I sat up on my top bunk and listened. Jaime asked me if I had awakened due to the noise. We both sat and listened for the banging to return after a brief pause. We heard an infuriated shaky female voice through the steel door and through the thick bolted wooden door very plainly howl, "Come on, you fucking little tramp, I know you're in there. I followed him here and waited for him to go home—the lying bastard. I know what you've been doing, you little hooker!"

Jaime and I began to laugh thinking surely our suitemate, Ana, had slept with someone's boyfriend. She had a reputation for being less selective about the company she kept than most. We could hear the other girls whispering and laughing in the other rooms. We called Ana and Jenny across the hall and were speculating as to who had brought this angry woman here and how we planned to deal with it. Jaime and I were teasing Ana and asking her if she could remember everyone she had hooked up with that weekend so we could figure out whose girlfriend was at the door. The female, who had returned to kicking the door during our investigation soon cleared up the dispute, "Alexandria, I know you're in there—just like you were there with my husband all weekend. I'm going to strangle your skinny hooker ass when you get out here—and I will stay here as long as it takes. You can't just take people's husbands."

I froze. Thousands of conversations and images were swirling in my mind. Jaime could only stare at me with her hand over her mouth. I sat there in the bed for what felt like an hour, but maybe amounted to two minutes. I called campus police, but the banging and screaming had already stopped. I called John. Needless to say this was a rude awakening. I said, "Are you by any chance married?"

He said, "You know I'm divorced."

I told him what had happened and he was instantly furious—cussing, telling me not to believe her, telling me she was just mad about him being involved, and so on. I was suspicious but listened to him. I doubt I slept at all that night. Jaime and I sat up trying to build a case for or against him. There were past memories and references that seemed suspicious now, but just about anything looked suspicious if you view it in this context. I chose, against instinct, to continue seeing him until, some weeks later, his wife called me on the phone. She convinced me of her position and, unfortunately for John, I joined her side of the battle. His lie is still costing him close to $700 a month in alimony.

ALEXANDRIA REFLECTS

I have a nasty habit of playing private detective/lawyer. I gather evidence, form an ironclad argument, and argue until everyone is waving white flags. I have always been somewhat distrustful of others. It is a trained incapacity that I cannot shake. When I get involved in an issue of trust, I remind myself that I do this—snooping, questioning, arguing until I win at any cost, and I try to avoid it. If someone has wronged me I try to stick it to him or her. This allows me to reestablish control and I save face. I instinctively reestablish my fort and fire at will, sometimes shooting after the other party has died, surrendered, or fled. I do realize that it's self-supporting. If I behave in a distrustful manner, people do not feel trusted, and trust and value me less.

I am currently in a relationship with a wonderful man whom I care very deeply for. I understand that I cannot do this to him, so I try really hard to fight off my urge to question his motives. This incapacity relates to many habits I have including playing detective, lawyer, judge, fighting to the death, jumping to conclusions, winning at any cost, and assuming distrust. Winning at any cost can be synonymous with losing something valuable.

Keeping an Ethnographic Conflict Journal

Of course, you do not always have access to fully thought-through and well-written accounts of conflict that are, like Alexandria's, carefully designed to meet specific learning goals. Life is rarely, if ever, a series of completed texts with clear and obvious lessons. If you insist on this as a basic criterion for your collection of data, you are missing much of how conflict really happens in the world around you. It is more likely that you see images of conflict that move you for a moment. You may walk through a place where you catch people arguing. You walk into a room and feel that a terrible altercation has just taken place or is about to happen. You are part of conflicts that are disguised, spread out over years, or acted out through conversations that to others bear little or no relationship to the conflict. This is the reality of moving through the world sensing and making sense of fragments and moments of conflict. Your conflict journals should reflect and represent these fragmentary experiences. As naturally occurring data, they are a valuable source of learning about conflict.

Goodall (1989) has developed the detective metaphor as a useful way of thinking about and practicing ethnography as you move through your everyday lives.

Taking on the persona and practices of a detective, according to Goodall, means you naturally pay close attention to the world around you. You notice clues that point to and symbolize other, more interesting things about a conflict. You record and think about the clues to a "case" that present themselves to you. And, you develop your ability to tell compelling detective stories about your conflict experiences. Whether you take on a detective persona explicitly or just learn to pay more attention to conflicts around you, the following should also be valuable sources of images and moments—clues—as to how conflict gets done. You can use these images to create richer narrative accounts of your own conflicts. You can also collect and write about these forms of conflict expression as narratives in and of themselves.

Learning From Conversational Texts

You cannot help but hear the conversations of others. Learning to listen to others' stories and conversations can be a valuable source of learning. Certainly Alexandria's story benefited from her inclusion of the conversations and happenings around her as she goes through her conflict experience. Consider how you might ask questions about and learn from the following sample journal entry about a brief conversation witnessed by one of the authors.

We were waiting in line for tickets to the soccer game. There were probably ten or so people ahead of us, and we had plenty of time to get seated before the game started. We were looking forward to this first home game of the season. Suddenly, a family stepped out of the ticket line just ahead of us. There was a mom and dad and two children who were both in the 6 to 12 age group. Apparently, they were having problems purchasing the tickets. The woman, who was larger than the man, turned to face him just in front of us. Anger was written all over her face. "You KNEW there were four of us!" she shouted. The two children stood by and quietly watched the brief but intense conversation unfold. "You KNEW there were four of us." Again she shouted for emphasis. She had the attention of the ticket line as well as her husband.

"Why didn't you bring enough money?" she demanded.

"Well, I…err," he muttered.

He looked down at his feet like a five-year old getting scolded by his mother. As men, I think we all felt for him in his moment of humiliation. Some of us guys looked at each other as if to say, "We've been there!" Out of respect for him and fear of her we half looked away, while keeping an eye on the action in case there were any developments.

"Go and get more money now. The game is starting in a few minutes," she continued. He left without another word. Everyone seemed to look down or away as he passed by. When she had also walked away, we joked about his dilemma and relived the one-sided conversation as if we were the participants.

This was just a brief moment of conflict—a fragment of their day and a fragment of ours that occurred in a space that we happened to be sharing. We can, however, still learn from this fleeting moment by jotting down our responses to questions such as the following:

1. What questions would I have for the participants in this conflict if I could ask them anything?

2. What issues does the scene I witnessed raise about family conflicts and about male-female conflicts?

3. What questions might I raise about my own interpretive account of the conflict?

4. How is my reaction, for example, typically that of a white middle-class male?

5. How might a white middle-class woman interpret and write about this scene differently?

Such questioning can help you to recognize the layers of meaning underlying any conflict episode, as well as your own interpretations as they intersect with the episode and therefore, co-construct that situation.

Learning From Interview Narratives

Asking people about their conflicts provides insight into how others have experienced conflicts (Chase, 1995). Interviews also give the researcher insight into the ongoing dynamics of people creating narratives that a completed written narrative does not easily provide (Polkinghorne, 1988). It is particularly useful to gather stories from people who have had life experiences very different from your own. If we were building a third person account of Alexandria's narrative, for example, we should also collect Alexandria's boyfriend's story of the conflict as well as his wife's story. These additional stories would illustrate, through their different voices, the various perceptions and experiences that formed this conflict. Interviewing people from different generations, different cultures, and the opposite sex can provide rich data about the variety of contexts, assumptions, and expectations that different people have about conflict (Mason, 1993).

As a result of learning about the wide variety of conflict experiences, you can reflect on your own assumptions and expectations of conflict. Here are some questions to help you think about the variety of experiences you can explore.

- How might your grandparents' conflict experiences have been different from yours?

- How might someone from Sweden, Bosnia, or Iran think differently from you about what counts as a conflict and how it should be resolved?

- How do their stories illustrate the interpretive process you go through to create a meaningful account of conflict?

- Who would you like to interview about his or her experience of conflicts?

Learning From Poetic and Visual Conflict Texts

How conflict is expressed visually through icons, monuments, graffiti, and symbols of division in communities is an important source of learning. Similarly, it is valuable to examine poetic representations of conflict that resonate with your experience or inspire you to look at experiences differently. Songs and poems often communicate the essence of conflict between relational partners and between people and broader forces such as nature, fate, and culture (e.g., Eisenberg, 1998; Kiesinger, 1998).

1. What are the icons and monuments in your community that help you remember historical conflicts?

2. How is your town or city organized to represent the conflict, or at least the division, of racial and class groupings?

3. What graffiti and other signs exist around you that indicate particular people have a conflicted relationship with the broader or dominant community around them?

4. What song might effectively communicate Alexandria's experience with her boyfriend?

5. What poetic images are particularly effective at capturing or resonating with your experience of conflicts? How might you enrich your own conflict narratives by using or adapting such images?

Learning From Fictional and Mythic Conflict Texts

Movies, TV shows, and literature can be good sources of ideas and information about representations of conflict in your culture and in other cultures (Banks & Banks, 1998). Archetypes of good and evil, positive and negative values, and characteristics, for example, are used over and over in movies, in situation comedies, and children's cartoons. These can indicate how previous generations were presented with popular culture images of relationships and conflicts, in particular. When you examine the folk tales, sagas, legends, and children's stories of a culture, you also gain valuable insight into the deeply held values and beliefs that form part of the cultural context of how you do conflict.

1. What images and dynamics of conflict are expressed in children's literature and entertainment?

2. What are the fundamental oppositions through which drama progresses in a recent movie?

3. How do these oppositions work to create dramatic interest in those fictional and dramatic texts?

4. How do these images and oppositions become part of how you do conflict in your everyday lives?

5. How closely do the themes and elements of Alexandria's story reflect those of popular television series?

Learning to See and Think With Expressions of Conflict

As you write about the details of a conflict, it is important also to reflect on and record your own interpretations of those conflicts. These reflections form the basis of your narrative voice as you tell and retell the story. Alexandria learns about herself through her conflicts with others. Her reflective insight tells her she needs to work on particular issues and skills to improve her relational dialogues. Specifically, she realizes her overly strategic communication creates a very competitive and distrustful climate in her intimate relationships. Ask the following questions of each entry in your journal. Be as honest as possible about your responses and reactions. This honesty is where you gain valuable insight into your conflicts and those around you.

1. What does this conflict moment tell me about conflict communication in terms of why the conflict happened?

2. What does this conflict moment tell me about myself and how I view conflict communication?

3. How is the image or experience similar to or different from how I experience conflict?

4. What does this conflict moment tell me about the context of the conflict, whether in a family, neighborhood, and so on?

5. What does this conflict moment tell me about the reality of conflict in our culture and in the world more generally?

Guidelines for Keeping a Conflict Journal

The conflict journal should contain field notes of your observations, conversations, interpretations, and further questions about the your conflicts and those that you witness (Agar, 1996). Below, we outline some practices ensuring a useful conflict journal.

• *Write in it often.* Writing connects us more deeply to an experience, as well as shapes the experience through the language choices made. As you describe your experiences in writing, they become more interesting and real. Writing often, every day if possible, keeps your mind focused on your ongoing process of inquiry into conflict. If you are not in a conflict, it is useful to write about conflicts you hear about or see on the news, or even conflicts from your own past.

• *Write about a variety of conflict forms.* Just as we have outlined some of the forms that conflict takes, it is important to explore these various forms through journal writing. Write about a particular TV show. Write about a particular relationship you are in. Write about how a war or international conflict is represented on the news. Write about a song you feel captures some essence of human conflict, and so on. As your horizon of attention to conflict is broadened, you begin to see important issues and themes in a variety of forms of expression.

It is important to remember to be tolerant of others' accounts. Others' narratives represent their experiences, just as your accounts represent the truth of your experiences.

• *Write in a variety of styles and genres.* One useful exercise is to describe a particular conflict through a variety of expressive forms, including poetry, song, personal narrative ethnography, visual representation, and so on. Working in different stylistic media brings out particular facets of a conflict.

• *Write from a variety of perspectives.* Telling the story from the perspectives of the various participants in the conflict can help you understand how you create the context of choices for others and how they create contexts of choice for you. You can also gain valuable insight into the different perspectives that often create the misunderstandings and miscommunications that generate conflicts. Simply, you can gain valuable perspective from perspective-taking.

• *Be honest.* A journal is, by definition, a private account of your experiences and your thoughts about those experiences. True dialogue emerges from and connects points or moments of honesty. Write what you really think. Your thoughts as they appear on the page should surprise you. At this point, you are truly thinking with and through, rather than just about, your conflict experiences.

• *Look for, and learn from, rich points of synthesis.* There are an infinite number of possible conflict stories you can tell. There are, however, points of similarity between experiences in terms of the themes, strategies that work and do not work, tactics people use, and so on. These create points of synthesis between stories. When you periodically review your journal, it is useful to note these similarities. For example, ask yourself what the similarities are in how you deal with different types of conflict. Reflecting on the rich points of connection between the various experiences of your lives tell you a great deal about both yourselves and about your world. Learn as much as you can about conflict from these points.

• *Develop the stories that seem to ask to be developed.* Following a conflict story for a lengthy time allows you to see how a story progresses. Taking a longitudinal approach to your experiences shows you what factors help the conflict move in productive and unproductive directions and enables you to capture and represent the full story. Choose the most interesting and most personally meaningful stories to follow in detail over their duration. These make the best journal entries to build into full personal narratives.

Principles of Transforming Notes Into Narrative Accounts

This book is not about becoming ethnographers of conflict. You may choose to develop your writing into ethnography, and there are many useful sources and examples to help you (see, e.g., Agar, 1996; Emerson, Fretz, & Shaw, 1995; Fetterman, 1989; Goodall, 1989, 1991; Wolcott, 1995). However, many issues and concerns are associated with writing personal narrative accounts. These concerns also arise in ethnography, auto-ethnography, and anthropological writing, more generally, regardless of whether the narrative you create is formally an ethnography. Here, we describe these important principles and steps in moving from your conflict journal notes to writing a personal narrative ethnography based on them.

• *From meaningful parts to the meaning of wholes.* Agar (1996) uses the image of a "narrowing funnel" to illustrate how you move from notes to ethnography. In taking journal fragments and producing more meaningful narratives, the researcher needs to move from specific stories or passages of dialogue, to "more general life stories that provide self-identity and give unity to a person's whole existence" (Polkinghorne, 1988, p. 163). To do this, you need to develop research, reflection, and writing skills. Finally, you also develop a thematically clear narrative account that connects yourself and your audience to the conflict experience. For a more detailed account of this process see, Emerson, Fretz, & Shaw, 1995.

The evaluative criterion of significance or importance partly governs the way you select data and construct stories. At the end of the funneling process therefore, you should have a narrative with a broader meaning than the parts alone convey, although the meaning of the whole should be evident in each of the parts. This systemic principle should structure how you select the parts and how the end product will look.

To create a meaningful or significant story, you must construct it so the audience believes the account. Here, temporality and spatiality in narrative construction are particularly important. Bochner (1997) shows how narratives are ordered to reality based on time. You tell most stories as a series of meaningful connections that recreate the time frame in which the events took place. As such, you invite your audience to engage in the experience as events unfold in the story. Stories show you how people cope, move through, invent new ways of talking, and make sense, all as processes that take place over time. Time and space are closely interconnected in narratives. Stories promise the intimacy of detail and lived experience through time, and as a result, you feel as if you have shared the experience with the narrator. You feel, to some extent, that you have *been there* with the participants at least for some moments during their conflict. Representing the reality of space and time creates a resonance through which you might believe and identify with an account.

• *Developing the style of the text.* Personal narratives are stories you tell about your experiences. As you reflect on your notes, you choose the story's themes and broader lessons through which you connect the narrative to conflict theories and principles. These theories and principles become partial texts about your stories as you write and develop them with your commentaries and insights (Atkinson, 1990; Langellier, 1989). It is important to construct texts with a literary style that builds the account and makes the themes and lessons vivid and believable (Atkinson, 1990). Using textual conventions effectively partly determines how well you move from parts to wholes (Atkinson, 1992). Simply, the style of writing the narrative should reflect and support the meaning of the account.

Specifically, you can use juxtaposition and a variety of voices, including those of the researcher and subject, to create textual tension and realism (Miller, 1998). Also, imagery, metaphor, poetic structures, and devices all enrich the narrative text. It is important to also think carefully about the title of the narrative, as this directs the audience to read it in a particular way. You can also use hypotyposis— word pictures—to create a particularly vivid scene as an emblem of broader themes. This indicates to the audience that the storyteller was "there" (Atkinson, 1990, p. 71). Please note it takes time and effort to develop good storytelling and writing skills.

• *Reflecting on your storytelling.* Ideally, this book explicates the cultural categories or "informal logic" (Geertz, 1973) used by participants when in conflict. To some degree, you construct your texts to reflect your culture, training, and interests (Agar, 1996). It is important to recognize and document these biases. You must realize, however, that a narrative account is an interpretive representation or "picture" of a culture or experience. As such, your account reflects

1. the question about conflict,

2. the interpretation that the picture you create provides,

3. the data you select to build that picture, and

4. the way you organize these elements into a coherent "argument" (Jacobson, 1991, p. 2).

Your narratives and language generally construct a particular view of reality (Richardson, 1995). You need therefore, to be concerned with the politics and practicality of where you are in the text and how you are involved in the coconstruction of the account if it is about someone else (Brettell, 1996; Geertz, 1988; Rabinow, 1977). You need to reflect on these choices as you create your narratives. You should ask questions such as the following:

1. What parts or chapters do you "break" our account into?

2. Why do you make these choices?

3. Are they reflective of the participants' experiential categories or your theoretical concerns, for example, with race, gender, and class?

4. How are you using the data to create generalized assumptions about conflict and categories of people?

5. Do you assume all people act a particular way in conflicts?

6. How can you develop an awareness of the rhetoric of your accounts in terms of understanding the narrative strategies and language choices through which you create the truth of an experience or culture (Geertz, 1988)?

Looking at the title and research material you have selected also provides insight into the representational choices and purpose of the text.

• *Testing the text.* In the interpretive process, it is important to avoid concerns about cause, validity, justification, and so on. Remember that an interpretive approach seeks to produce "believable" results rather than be demonstrably "true" (Polkinghorne, 1988, p. 161). Atkinson talks about persuading the reader of "the authenticity, plausibility, and significance of the account" (1990, p. 57). Similarly, Hammersley (1990) points to naturalism, understanding, and discovery as the three criteria of a good account. Authenticity or naturalism concerns whether you believe the narrator has been close enough to the experience to really capture the frame of reference of the participants. Plausibility and understanding have to do with the storyteller's ability to create a believable account conveying the meaning of the event to the audience. These criteria point out the dangers of over-romanticizing experiences. Significance and discovery concern what the narrative account tells you beyond itself about conflict processes. That is, are you using stories to ask better questions and using questions to tell better conflict stories?

Bochner argues that you approach narratives not with the "illusion of transcendental observation," but rather with "the possibilities of dialogue and collaboration" (1997, p. 436). Narratives should help you talk more about your experiences. For example, Bochner tells a turning point story of the death of his father while he was at a conference. The event changed Bochner's life as a researcher and teacher. This story is a paradigm exemplar of how an event—a chance—changes you (p. 421). The turning point story carries reconceptualization, even new conflict, among the "worlds" of the narrator. For him, the event underscores the conflict between his academic and ordinary sides. The narrative pushes him to ask deeper questions about the parts of his life and their relations to the conflict. He also asks about the contexts that he inhabits and that shape him. His current approach to communication makes sense as the outcome his story documents. His story is believable because it is obvious he lived through it and learned the broader lessons of the experience, as the story documents.

Main Characteristics of a Good Personal Narrative Account

Constructing a good, versus meaningful, personal narrative account is fraught with issues of textual politics. Judging a personal account implies a position of narrative authority on your part and therefore carries a certain amount of what Geertz calls "authorial uneasiness" (1988). We do not offer rigid criteria as the prescriptive grammar of a good story. Rather, we offer some guidelines to follow so your stories effectively represent the experiences you are writing about and are accessible to a thinking audience.

Carolyn Ellis (1997) has developed a useful and concise checklist of characteristics for judging a personal narrative or auto-ethnography as "good." The following questions about narrative construction reflect Ellis's criteria. Good auto-ethnography ought to:

- Be well written, using literary devices and meeting literary standards where appropriate

    1. In what ways is Alexandria's story well written in that you believe it really happened and it is an interesting story?

    2. Are there ways that this story could have been better written in terms of style, sentence structure, and so on, to meet reasonable literary standards?

    3. What literary devices, such as special language, imagery, metaphors, phrasing, parallelism, plot structure, and so on, are effective in this story?

- Concentrate on scenes rather than on data

    4. How well does Alexandria describe the scenes and characters of the story?

    5. How well do the morals of the story emerge from the action and flow of the narrative?

    6. How well do these morals make the story into a meaningful whole?

- Concentrate on showing rather than telling

7. What does Alexandria do to show you the moral lessons of the story?

8. How well does she show you these lessons through the action, as opposed to simply stating them as abstractions from the action?

- Be processual, that is, describe the conflict as it unfolds over time

9. How does Alexandria develop the action and the subsequent explication of the story's meaning over the time frame of the conflict?

10. How well does the story move through time, or back to the past and forward to the present, to increase realism?

- Be evocative and engaging

11. How is dramatic suspense, which makes you want to find out what happens next, created?

12. How well does Alexandria pull you into her world and her personal experience of the conflict?

13. What language and imagery help create the dramatic tension and appeal of the story as it unfolds?

- Include emotions and the body

14. How does Alexandria bring to life each character's emotions?

15. How does she effectively describe her own bodily experiences in this conflict?

16. How do the emotions described and her bodily reactions to fear, anger, and so on, help to make the story effective?

- Be lifelike and believable

17. How does Alexandria's writing style make the scenes, events, and characters lifelike?

18. What details make you believe these are real events and real people?

- Use concrete experiences rather than citations as evidence

19. What evidence is presented to support the morals and lessons of the story?

20. Are these convincingly supported?

21. What broader theories and principles of conflict and communication are connected to Alexandria's story?

- Describe a particular life, but speak beyond itself and move between the personal and the social

22. How does the story balance the need to speak to the specific experiences of Alexandria's life and to represent broader or deeper issues and themes?

23. What are the broader or deeper issues and themes of relationships revealed in the story?

- Be an open text—provide no complete resolutions (open questions and ambiguities are acceptable)

24. What is left unresolved in this story?

25. What, if anything, remains ambiguous and open in this story?

26. How does this openness invite further description or audience participation?

- View readers as active participants who insert their interpretations and experience into the text

27. In what ways does Alexandria explicitly or implicitly invite you to bring your own experiences to the narrative process?

28. What questions or comments occurred to you as you read or listened to the narrative?

- Have critical and action dimensions

29. What values and practices does Alexandria problematize and question?

30. What social structures and conventions are you invited to critique?

31. What changes does, or could, the story suggest?

- Be understood as continual "works in progress"

32. How might the story be continued as another episode or phase?

33. What additional questions might move the story forward?

34. What similar or different stories about relationships can you add to continue this story into a conversation about relationships?

- Take risks and be vulnerable

35. In what ways does this narrative make Alexandria vulnerable to the interpretations and possibly the judgments of the audience?

36. What risks is she taking in telling this story?

37. Which of these risks would you also take or avoid in telling your own conflict story?

38. How might your perception of the audience for your account influence your writing?

Some Final Reflective Questions on Alexandria's Narrative

1. How might you improve the vividness and impact of your accounts of conflicts by applying the above principles?

2. Which of your experiences are as dramatic as Alexandria's or have a similar moral or plot?

3. Which specific conflicts in your journal might you develop into a valuable full-length narrative?

These categories and questions may help you sharpen your skills at writing "good" narratives. These skills also improve your abilities as observers and recorders of conflict experiences in journal form. The next section develops a framework for interpreting narratives.

A FRAMEWORK FOR UNDERSTANDING NARRATIVE INTERPRETATION

We have discussed creating narratives to achieve representational and communicative goals. The other side of the communication process concerns the main principles of listening to narratives so you can interpret and understand the conflict issues they represent. You also need to understand how narratives work as speech acts. This section briefly draws together the interpretive issues and questions we have outlined so far and develops a framework of questions that reflect on the specific communication contexts in the rest of this book.

The following relational narrative illustrates the process of interpretive representation and learning as a form of writing. As you examine Tracy's story, ask questions about the story's construction and how it can stimulate dialogue about her experience. It is possible to apply this to your own and others' personal narratives. The questions listed below are based on the topics discussed earlier in this book.

———◄○►———

Exemplar Narrative: Pick a Church, any Church

—TRACY

This conflict is between my boyfriend Todd and me. We have been dating on and off for about six years. The conflict is about our religious views. When we first began dating, it was our senior year in high school, so the conflict seemed of no real consequence. Each of us had our own views and we respected them. Six years later, this is a different story. To begin, we live together, and things are much more serious. We are discussing marriage and children, so religion is a major issue to come to terms with before making a commitment to each other, since it has such an impact over our lives. The religion issue finally came to a head about a month ago. After drinking a few beers, we got into a heated discussion of our views. We needed to come to some sort of consensus to continue our relationship.

Todd is an accountant who comes from a very close knit—very religious—family. He puts a lot of stock in what his parents want for him and expect of him. He also has trouble seeing things for himself. Tracy, a student, who comes from a divorced, then remarried family, is the other participant. Her family is very much into making your own decisions and forming your own opinions. She is very independent from her family and has formed her own views on religion. She, like Todd, is very adamant in her views and has trouble believing they are not correct.

The religion conflict finally came to a head one night when Todd and I were just sitting around and talking. We had been dating seriously for two years, and had just moved in together. We had begun discussing marriage and children and then, religion. The discussion began with Todd and I were talking about his parents.

His parents have been against us moving in together from day one; because they are so religious, they believe that premarital sex sends you right to hell. Needless to say, I cannot agree with this point of view. Todd, on the other hand, took a while, because he is so into pleasing his parents. It is not a religious issue. To begin the conflict, I said that his parents were too controlling, and used their religion as a holding device. This began the war.

Todd instantly became defensive and said that I was not religious at all. I replied that I believe in God, I think it is important to go to church, but I do not believe it should be taken to the extent that his parents take it to. They are involved in church group upon church group and are constantly inflicting their views on other people. Todd's parents take the Bible literally. They believe that anyone who does not believe in Jesus is going to hell. This does not fly with me, as I cannot see God condemning the majority of people in the world to hell. It doesn't make sense. They also believe that homosexuals are the devil's spawn, and are racist to boot. My argument to Todd was that if this was what he believed, then there is a good possibility that we should not be together. He said that he was not racist and did not have a problem with homosexuals, but he did believe that if you did not believe in Jesus, then you were going to hell. We argued that point to death. Then Todd asked what we would do if we had kids. How would we raise them, and what would we teach them? Did we love each other enough to be able to respect each other's views, or was this something that we could not get past?

Todd and I decided that when it all came down to it, we had very similar views on most of the issues that we had talked about. We decided that we loved each other, and that we could work it out. We will never be able to completely agree on all issues of religion. Between the way people are raised and the events that shape their lives, people have their own ideas or theories. Todd and I decided to compromise. Although it is a lose-lose situation, in the end it was the only option for us if we wanted to stay together. We decided that we would pick a church denomination that was neutral for both of us. We thought it was important to share the church experience, so this was the best way. We also decided that when it comes to children, we would raise them in the church, have them go to Sunday school, and from there they would make their own decisions. If they had questions, they could ask us and we would be free to give our own point of view, but not inflict our point of view. We both agreed that people are entitled to their own beliefs, and if we are at least tolerant of the other person's views, in the end, that would be enough.

Fortunately, the conflict turned out to be very beneficial because it strengthened our relationship, released some built-up tension, and also clarified our goals for the future. It helped me understand him better, and it helped him understand me better.

——————◄○►——————

Learning With Interpretive Methodology

As you interpret conflict narratives, you learn not so much to think about stories as discrete objects but, as Bochner (1997) calls it, "think with stories." That is, as researchers, you are coconstructing with the narrator rather than being merely receivers of the text from the narrator. This means you are actively pursuing particular ways of understanding conflict. This pursuit results in your version of the meaning of conflict. Simply, interpretation results in a narrative about the narrative. As such, interpretation is never a neutral activity. What you find through interpreting narratives depends on what you want to find. This is reflected in the questions you ask. What you want to find also depends on how you view the answers to those questions within a broader theoretical and research agenda (Burrell & Morgan, 1979). What you find in your stories is connected to what you want to show about conflict. If, for example, you have a critical theoretical agenda, you ask questions to explicate and deconstruct the processes of power and ideology as they affect the subjective experiences and practices of the conflict participants (Earnest, 1992; Gergen, 1992; Rosenwald, 1992). You are looking for clues to the practices of conflict as they sustain domination and express resistance. The main question for a critical interpretation is, how can the participants understand and possibly change the power structures that constrain their communication?

If you have a more descriptive agenda for your interpretation, you are interested in explicating how the participants experience their conflict from within their own perspective and world-view. You want to understand their behavior, thoughts, and communication as they participate in conflict. You are also interested in understanding how they represent that experience in narrative form. Your main synthesizing question is, how do the participants practice conflict as a meaningful form of communication? Taking such a descriptive approach means you are less concerned with the change aspects of the methodology outlined next.

Table 4.1 Main Interpretive Stages and Goals

Stages of Narrative Research Process	Main Research Questions to Guide Inquiry
Collecting/creating narrative	How can you collect and/or create conflict narratives representing peoples' experience of conflict?
Explicating narrative	What are good questions enabling you to explicate the meaning of conflict narratives?
Understanding narrative	What are the important insights and observations gained from asking good questions? How do these insights connect to illustrate or exemplify conflict principles?
Questioning practices	What further questions about conflict practices does your understanding generate?
Changing practices	How can addressing these questions generate more choices about how you might practice conflict?
Changing social reality	How might those additional choices affect your conflict practices, experiences, and relationships more generally?
Changing narrative	How might changes in conflict practices affect the richness of your narrated experience of conflicts?

As you examine the results of your interpretive questioning, your theoretically driven research questions should help you organize your observations and insights. Table 4.1 illustrates the main interpretive stages and the important research goals at each of the stages.

The Learning Cycle of Interpreting Conflict Narratives

In Chapter 2, we developed a learning-centered approach to narrative. Simply, the main purpose of interpreting conflict narratives is to better understand the conflicts you experience and witness. Here, we develop this learning process to parallel the interpretive narrative research process. The steps of the learning cycle build cumulatively to form the steps to interpretation. Table 4.2 illustrates the main research questions at each stage of the learning cycle.

To more fully articulate the stages of the interpretive learning cycle, we use Tracy's narrative to illustrate its main assumptions and details.

• Negotiated social reality with others in contexts leads to conflict narrative.

As Table 4.1 illustrates, this stage involves collecting and/or creating good conflict narratives. You are taking Tracy's written narrative as data (that which is given)/capta (that which is taken) representing how she negotiated her relational reality with Todd in the various contexts described. The conflicted dimensions of

Table 4.2   System of Interpretive Questions

Issues and Questions for Interpreting the Quality of Dialogue and Negotiation

---

How does Tracy's narrative create the sense that the conflict is both inevitable and necessary in the relationships she tells us about?

In what ways does Tracy's conflict appear to be both beneficial and damaging to her and Todd?

How are the actions and dynamics Tracy portrays similar to and different from the ideal of peacemaking and peacefulness in relationships?

What myths about conflict, relationships, and communication in general does the couple appear to either agree with or challenge through their thoughts and actions?

In what ways does this couple effectively negotiate in this relational conflict?

What clues do you have that negotiation skills and practices are absent from the conflict?

How would you describe the relational reality that these participants create through their choice of style and tactics?

In what ways are the two main participants effective and ineffective in practicing the characteristics and principles of dialogue?

How might they change their conflict communication to be more dialogic?

How does this conflicted couple exemplify the characteristics of an argumentation approach to conflict?

How might telling the story as a personal narrative have been beneficial to Tracy?

How might hearing or reading this narrative be beneficial to other participants in the conflict, such as Todd?

Issues and Questions for Interpreting Narrative and Conflict Dynamics

What is the historical, biographical, cultural, and social context in which Tracy's narrative works as communication?

What are the motives of the participants in the conflict?

How does Tracy's story work structurally to create a meaningful story?

What underlying beliefs, attitudes, actions, power structures, myths, and ideologies are supported or challenged by the narrative?

How does Tracy's narrative help you engage with and understand the meaning of her conflict?

How does Tracy's story balance the need for an appealing storytelling style and the need to be true to her experience?

How does Tracy's story combine elements of oral and written style?

How does the story provide insight into her personal experience as well as broader issues of conflict in relationships?

How might your reflection on the experience of being the audience for her narrative help you understand your social context of communication?

How does telling and listening to the story create new opportunities for Todd, Tracy, and your interpretation?

What are the lessons learned and new understandings for Tracy and you in her retelling of the story?

What changes might Tracy make as a result of narrating this conflict, and how might those changes affect the people she communicates with?

In what ways could this narrative limit, open up, or enable dialogue?

In what ways is Tracy's narrative political in the sense of creating a particular reality for the conflict?

In what ways does Tracy's narrative and your interpretations of it meet your ethical expectations?

(Continued)

Table 4.2   (*Continued*)

Issues and Questions for Interpreting Representations of Self, Other, and Context

How might this story help Tracy recognize how negative patterns in her conflict experiences tend
   to create more negative patterns?
How might the recognition of positive patterns and lessons lead to more positive patterns for Tracy?
What metaphor for conflict and life in general might underlie the thoughts and actions of the
   participants?
How does Tracy describe the bodily feel and the non-verbal aspects of being in a conflict and how
   those affect what she does and says?
How are her intrapersonal and interpersonal experiences of conflict related?
What main lessons or morals about conflict might she be communicating through the portrayal of
   others in the story?
How well do the participants show perspective-taking skills, and with what effect?
How do the participants create the context of this conflict through their actions?
How does the context also partly create the conflict?
How does Tracy represent the relationship between background and foreground, between the
   context and the events as she portrays them?
What are the important dimensions of climate, culture, history, media, race, gender, age, and so on,
   in the narrative?
What other representational issues might be important in understanding Tracy's narrative?

---

the narrative give you clues about the quality of negotiation creating their everyday reality together and their social reality more generally.

   • Inquiry into conflict narratives explicates the meaning of conflict.

Here, you ask questions of the narratives you have collected. Table 4.2 summarizes a system of questions that provide insight into how this couple practices conflict. These questions should also help explain why they practice conflict as they
do. Answering these questions produces a detailed textual analysis of Tracy's
narrative, providing insights, for example, into how the conflict progressed from
avoidance, through "war," to a compromise. Your questioning may also show how
she creates a narrative progression through the conflict when it is clearly not finished. You gain insight into how her portrayal of their conflicted religious beliefs
(free choice for her and parental domination for him) helps generate the conflict.
The questions in Table 4.2 helps achieve this interpretation.

   • Explication of meaning leads to understanding of conflict.

When looked at together, these various insights should combine to tell you a relatively coherent story of how and why this conflict happened. This story connects
your insights and helps you answer your main critical or descriptive interpretive
research question. For example, you may see connections between Tracy's portrayal
of herself as freely choosing her religious beliefs, Todd believing whatever his
unreasonable parents expect of him, and other aspects of the conflict. From this, a

picture may emerge of the relationship between this evaluative portrayal and Todd's unwillingness to address conflicts. Perhaps when conflicts arise, Todd finds it easier to give in and compromise than to hear such negative accounts of his parents and his relationship to them. Note also that Tracy portrays this specific conflict as an ultimate test of their relationship. This is another strategy to dominate the talk by raising the risks of not seeing things her way. Such an all-or-nothing approach to conflicts usually leads to avoidance, because then all conflicts appear as high stakes fights. Perhaps Todd's willingness to go along and compromise is interpreted, by Tracy, to be proof that they have "solved" their particular problem. From the relationship of these dynamics, it may be easily envisioned how they will tend to create patterns of avoidance, violent outbursts, and compromise, and how those cycles have very different meanings for Todd and for Tracy.

- Understanding conflict leads to questioning conflict practices.

Once you have a coherent account of how and why you think a conflict happens, you can ask questions about how it might have been done differently and why alternative ways of practicing conflict might be valuable. This is when you question the conflict practices your narratives represent. Here, you are concerned with a more critical, theory-based explication of how their avoidance-outburst-compromise cycle of conflict management may occur differently. You can ask why such patterns emerge, why Todd and Tracy do not handle conflict more effectively, and how they might dialogue through important relational issues such as religion more effectively.

- Questioning leads to more choices about conflict practices.

Your conflict narrative may be an account of a well-managed process, in which case you can discuss how and why it was effective. Alternatively, your questioning should lead to some specific practices to improve the dialogue of the conflict participants. Understanding these central dynamics of a conflict is an important interpretive link between questioning current practices and deciding how you might use the insights gained. You can, for example, examine how Todd and Tracy's everyday conversations might become more dialogic. As it is, they seem to accept that it is better to convince themselves and each other that everything will be fine and that they will work out the details later (presumably after marriage). Postponing dealing with their conflicts until they are married is a sure way to perpetuate those conflicts over an extended time. You can also examine how they might change the patterns and cycles of conflict they are collaborating to create.

- Changing the choices of conflict practices leads to possible changes in negotiating social reality.

When improving dialogue is realistic and desirable to those in conflict, then the participants start to change their social reality. Changes in the way you negotiate reality with others affects your relationships and, specifically, your experience of conflict. For example, if Todd and Tracy consciously tried to avoid evaluating each other's family values and practices during conflicts, their communication might be more civil. If they agreed to aim for consensus rather than compromise, they would be challenged to improve their conflict communication. If they agreed they would not portray conflicts as dangers that might end their relationship, but rather strive for a safe context in which to truly address issues, more dialogue would be fostered. Generating such realistic and tangible opportunities is important in delineating specific strategies for changing conflict communication.

* Changes in social reality may lead to enriched conflict narratives.

If you decide to change how you engage in conflicts with others, this affects how you interpret your world and therefore how you narrate your conflicts. Developing a broader range of telling the stories of your lives is a valuable form of communicative learning. This learning helps us tell better conflict stories and assist others to create better stories. It seems to be a compromise itself to tell a compromise story as if it were a major breakthrough for a relationship. It is possible for Tracy and Todd to tell a story similar to this as an example of what they used to accept as "good" communication. It is possible for them to strive to tell stories of real moments of relational depth together, rather than of avoidance, silence, anger, and compromise such as is represented here as good communication. It is hard work to change reality. Perhaps, besides a "neutral denomination" church they will both attend, they also need to decide whether it is worthwhile to create a neutral place within the relationship—their own holy ground, if you will—where they can both speak and be heard. Going to places that approximate or replace this is always an additional compromise. And compromises rarely lead to anything except more compromises.

Some Final Reflective Questions on Tracy's Narrative

1. How might you benefit from working through the stages of interpretation in relation to one of your conflict narratives?

2. How would you most want to change the social reality of one of your conflicts?

3. How did you or did you not identify with the characters and the story that Tracy shared?

CONCLUSION

Goodall's quote at the start of this chapter asks us to pay particular attention to the details of stories, as the details contain the whole. As you have seen in the narratives in this chapter, details are crucial for understanding. As you tell your conflict stories, you choose from a myriad of possible details to report. You combine these details by selecting from a broad range of possible combinations of the details. When you interpret narratives to understand and learn from them, you pay particular attention to details because you are interested in learning specific lessons. How you construct and deconstruct the details of your narratives, yourselves, and your world is what interpreting conflict is about.

This chapter has challenged you to become more self-conscious about how you represent your experiences and how you interpret those of others. Keeping a journal and learning how to develop accounts of conflict based on your considered observations improves your ability to ask questions about conflict and to have useful answers to those questions.

PART **II**

Changing Relationships
Through Conflict

Developing an insightful interpretation of a conflict narrative enables you to ask good questions about your experience. Perhaps most important, such insight provides you with coherent ideas about how you might improve the conflict skills you already have and develop new ones. Figuring what to build on and what to alter is the basis of any successful change effort, whether it is personal or organizational. The first half of this book prepared you to address issues of change in most relational contexts in which conflict is encountered. The second half of this book illustrates how you can apply the interpretive skills you have developed to the specific challenges of particular contexts.

Chapters 5 to 8 present you with narratives that illustrate the specific dynamics of conflict important for understanding some significant contexts in which you may find yourself. Besides illustrating the typical conflicts occurring in these contexts, we challenge you to consider the fundamental conflict principles important in all of them. We begin with the broadest context, communities, because we want you to consider it first as you move toward understanding conflict in your most personal and intimate friendships and romantic relationships. This way, you see how a broader context is important in understanding your selves and your personal relational conflicts.

Chapter 5 illustrates the dimensions and dynamics of conflict in our communities. This chapter challenges you to research the world around you for clues to structural and systemic conflicts where you live. You are also challenged to examine how you contribute to, and might potentially help resolve, the conflicts around you affecting the quality of your lives.

Chapter 6 illustrates typical sources of conflict in your workplaces, and challenges you to develop a systemic understanding of those conflicts. You learn how to interpret organizational conflicts as both a normal byproduct of people working together and as the expression of more serious organizational dysfunctions. Knowing how to interpret and understand organizational conflicts enables you to work through those conflicts and the issues they represent.

Chapter 7 challenges you to reflect on the conflicts that typify your families. You learn to recognize how your family conflicts affect you, and how you can choose to change dysfunctional patterns.

Finally, Chapter 8 narrows the contextual focus to examine conflicts in our interpersonal relationships. Understanding the roles that conflict plays in your relationships enables you to read conflict as clues to the health and balance of your relationships. You also are prepared to understand how to improve the dialogue in those relationships that are, after all, among our most treasured and valuable assets.

At each step along the way, you are presented with the narratives of others who have lived through conflicts and have given us their personal experiences. You are also challenged to apply the questions and the insights you generate from working through the exercises in each chapter to your own conflict experiences and practices. Interpreting your own actions is one way to create a more dialogic world around you.

Managing Conflict in Our Communities

"If we want to live a better future, we must learn to live together in the diverse fullness of our human possibilities, through a Spirit of unity that brings forth the diverse harmonies that are already there."

(Goodall, 1996, p. 224)

"Communities are living creatures, nurtured and nourished by rhetorical discourse."

(Hogan & Williams, 1996, p. 292)

It may be impossible for us to have problem-free cities, towns, and neighborhoods. However, we can, as Goodall says, move toward communities with a dynamic spirit of unity that are realistic about balancing inevitable conflicts. Conflict is a necessary part of maintaining an evolving and inclusive community and an inevitable sign of communities that ignore or repress conflicting voices. As this chapter illustrates however, you can at least learn to understand the conflicts surrounding you and change your involvement in community conflicts. From disputes with "crazy neighbors" to opposing social visions that create environmental conflicts to fundamental divisions that erupt into hate speech and even violence, conflict in communities is multifaceted, complex, and fundamental to your understanding of its contextual nature.

This chapter takes you through the meaning and functions of conflicts in your communities. You learn why conflicts occur in communities, why it is important to understand and manage such conflicts effectively, and how you can be involved in your own ways in building more cooperative communities. You learn to collect and interpret narratives from community members in conflict, as well as explore historical testimonies to conflicts in light of these framing issues.

Key Concepts, Terms, and Definitions to Learn in This Chapter

- The role of norms and normality in creating the context for conflicts

- How digital and analogue thinking and speaking create and maintain conflicts

- How to move toward more "we"-centered communities in which divisions become dialogic opportunities

- The ways communities both include and exclude, and how this leads to conflict

- How to use interpretive/narrative methodology to understand community conflicts

- The ways representations of self, other, and context interact in community conflicts

- How to learn from the community conflicts that surround and shape you

- How to ask good interpretive questions of the communities in which you live and are involved

Key Definitions

- *Communities*. The largely symbolic constructions of boundaries through which local identities are expressed and maintained

- *Digital and analogue*. The opposition between either/or and both/and thinking as it occurs in community conflicts

- *Intertextuality*. The fact that community conflicts also can have aspects of relational and family dynamics woven through them

- *Normality*. The standards or norms that a community engages to regulate membership and behavior in that community

THE DYNAMICS OF COMMUNITY CONFLICT

The following conflict is at the heart of our assumptions about communication and community. A deep and enduring conflict emerges between mother and daughter about whether the daughter should use sign or oral forms of communication. This conflict intersects with cultural assumptions and values positioned antagonistically as an either/or decision for Cindy. Either she uses sign language (visual communication) or speaks (oral communication). The conflict thus illustrates the intersection or intertextuality of community conflicts as issues about "ways of life" involving family and generation dynamics. A broader community conflict is acted out/played out in the context of a family relationship. As you read the narrative, pay particular attention to Cindy's portrayal of the deaf and speaking/hearing cultures and clues concerning opportunities to improve communication between the two.

—◀◦▶—

Exemplar Narrative: Opposing Views

—CINDY

I have a conflict with my mother; she wants me to be hearing-like, while I am proud to be deaf. We have always disagreed over which method of communicating is the best. I feel that two-way communication is the most effective, since both parties understand each other. I am trying to break away and just continue to perform my responsibilities as a deaf individual, one of which includes being *Miss Deaf Wisconsin;* she is trying to lure me into using my voice and to resist using sign language.

To understand why my mom feels strongly about the oral approach, I must assess the situation from when I was young. My stepmother and father had custody of me from six years old up until I was 15. They thought that the only way to communicate with my friends was through speaking, since there were no other deaf students at my elementary school. The idea of going to a deaf school entered their minds, but they completely objected to me being in a sheltered situation for five out of seven days a week. All they could see was that for me to be successful, I would need to learn to communicate effectively with hearing people. I do not believe they cared whether or not I was learning anything; all they cared about was my speech. In those days, deaf people refrained from speech therapy and my closed-minded parents saw them as being "retarded" or "abnormal." To prevent me from becoming one of those mutes, they never used the word "deaf," I was hearing-impaired. My mom began to pick up on the oral method and began to believe that it was for the best.

To understand our opposing views and why this conflict has emerged since I have been in college and am using sign language, one must realize that I was raised orally all of my life. My mom is a speech therapist, and decided to pursue her profession after she found out I was deaf at three years old. As my speech got refined, people commended me on the remarkable improvement, but my mom would take all of the credit.

The situation gets more complicated when we involve my grandmother, whom I call Nan. She felt strongly about good speaking skills, since she correlated speaking with intelligence. I believe this is why my mom fell for the oral approach—she wanted my Nan to approve of the way she was raising me.

After entering college and learning sign language, I realized that I had found my identity—my world. I eliminated the word "hearing-impaired" from my vocabulary, and substituted it with "deaf." I have nothing wrong with me; that is why I do not label myself "impaired." The deaf world is the world that I associate myself with. I identify myself as a deaf woman, while my mother defies it. My style of communicating is visual; people know instantly which culture I am a member of.

My self-esteem augmented after finding my support group, and I began to realize that "true communication" begins with understanding what other people are saying. Other people understand what I am saying, but I have no idea what they are saying. I no longer use my voice when in conversation with others; my voice quality confuses people. Many relate speaking abilities with how much hearing I have, and then they think I am "faking" my deafness. I, after many long years, have found what works for me, that is, using sign language because it involves two-way communication. I want to be an advocate for deaf people of all kinds. One bond that we all have is being deaf. That is what makes our community a strong and tight one.

I think that the real reason my mother is angry is because the conflict escalates and we have never solved it. I admit that I do not put enough time and effort into building our relationship, because I know we will just end up arguing. My mother wants everything to work out, but never addresses the conflict head on. My mother has tried other techniques, ranging from guilt trips to ultimatums. She says, "Either you stop hanging around with your deaf friends or I will stop talking to you." This kind of threat just sends me straight through the roof; it's one of my "buttons" that she should not push. I get angry and the conflict escalates. To avoid all of this, I just live in denial and I try to appease her.

"You never can win." This is one of my favorite sayings. I cannot be a people-pleaser and change my worldview for my mother. I have to do what I think is right for me. This ends up in a dispute about "us hearing people are attentive" versus "you deaf people are rude."

These kinds of stereotypes exaggerate the differences between the two worlds. I recognize that our regulative rules in the deaf world are different from those in the hearing world. Our stomping feet on the ground, tapping people on the shoulder, and flashing of lights to get one's attention are a nuisance to hearing people.

Now I am 21 years old and still asking the same question every day, "How shall I talk with my mom?" Our resolution is simply not to talk about it with each other—we avoid "the deaf issue" since it is taboo for us. Remembering that I am in her culture when conversing reminds me to alter my behaviors and use of language. When I adapt to her "hearing" style, then she thinks she has won because my actions have changed. I lead two separate, distinct lives. One style I embrace while at home, and the other once I walk out the door. My goals and ambitions are not shared with her; I do not want her to dispute with me over who is right and who is wrong.

My view remains the same. I am a deaf individual who is proud to be deaf, and a strong believer in advocating "true communication." How else would I learn if I did not? If my mother cannot understand my viewpoint, then she has no way of understanding; she is hearing. There will, forever, be a gap in our relationship because of a physical difference, but I hope that she will eventually accept my way of life.

———◄○►———

Community and Normality

The cultures and subcultures you belong to have a major shaping influence on you and your self-understanding, as well as how you understand and relate to others (Ochberg, 1992; Tillmann-Healy, 1996). As Ochberg illustrates, the cultural norms of your communities structure what is "permissible and admirable and what is illicit and inferior" (p. 214). Communities thus partly shape your feelings and desires, as well as what is considered right and wrong. Cindy's narrative appeals rhetorically to a number of values and practices aligning her position with the per-missible and admirable. She also aligns her mother with characteristics and prac-tices that oppose these assumptions. Specifically she is, in her mind, struggling for the cause of true communication, being authentic, accepting, and proud of who she is, and so on. Hearing/oral culture, personified by her mother, is portrayed as labeling her way of life abnormal, as being closed-minded, and forcing her to be something that she does not want to be. Appealing to cultural norms in how you characterize self and other is a powerful strategy in dividing the two individuals and the groups they represent. This propagates a divisive conflict.

Carbaugh (1996) also discusses the underlying themes of competition, divi-siveness, stratification, and strained relations reproduced in a variety of contexts and practices in your culture. So, for example, in her interest in establishing her deaf identity, Cindy is relying on these cultural habits—typifications—of doing conflict. The conflict becomes competitive, divisive, stratified, and the relations between the participants become strained, seemingly close to their limits. This habit of strongly identifying with one point of view to the exclusion of others undermines your ability to create communities. Perhaps a good place for these conflicting parties to begin is to understand how these cultural habits have informed their conflict practices so far. As Farmer (1998) argues, acknowledging that your reality is partly structured by your community involvements is the first step to valuing the differences inherent in your communities.

The Digital and Analogue Other

Community development is based on the notion that the basic elements of communities are groups and subcultures, and these contexts structure your sense of self in many ways (MacCannell, 1979). Community development concerns involving these various groups of stakeholders in finding ways to improve human interaction and the quality of life (Blakely, 1979). Morse (1998) illustrates that communities can only resolve conflicts when the participants have a stake in and contribute to the community as a shared responsibility and blessing. Ulrich (1998) reminds us that vibrant communities are built around shared values, not just prox-imity. That is, communities are not formed just because people happen to live close to each other, or even belong to the same family. Community development is grounded in the analogue relationship of both/and—us *and* them, rather than the digital relationship of either/or—us *or* them. In the conflict between the deaf/visual and hearing/oral issues in Cindy's narrative, the greatest challenge is finding ways to move Cindy and her mother closer to an analogue way of viewing their relationship in the broader community.

More than just involvement and inclusions, Austin (1996) shows that celebrating the others in your communities is key to relational development. As she says, "the celebration of others through dialogue bends back upon us reflexively, sustaining, altering, or transforming our comprehension of ourselves and our social world" (p. 206). That is, developing better dialogue with others helps you to better understand the communities you create through your habits of communication.

It is an imaginative exercise to think of these two groups celebrating one another. Perhaps a good first move might be the hearing culture taking a proactive role in celebrating the unique contribution that the deaf culture makes to understanding communication. To persuade Cindy and others who think as she does to believe they are valued rather than judged as inferior by the larger community might take significant effort, but it may be the only way to initiate dialogue between the communities.

Developing the dialogue that creates the analogue of self and other takes what Piore (1995) calls, "intersecting conversations" (p. 169). These dialogues develop shared understanding and vocabulary for the world. These intersecting conversations depend on honesty and openness as the cardinal virtues of communities (Mackin, 1997). This quality of communication reduces ambiguity about others and stimulates purposive action that, in turn, develops communities. Celebrating the other is a start toward the goal of intersecting conversations. Celebration acknowledges uniqueness and allows those who feel oppressed or marginal to start talking about ways they feel similar or different and how they have been treated. In Cindy's case, this might create points of intersection where the hearing community can listen and engage those feelings and perceptions in their responses. This is how intersecting conversations—dialogue—begins.

Despite these ideals of dialogue, inclusion, and celebration, many of you recognize that division, exclusion, and suspicion of others is far more common in your communities. Cohen (1985) shows that communities are largely symbolic constructions of boundaries and identities through which aspects of the self are expressed and maintained. This sense of self often comes at the expense of others. People instinctively defend their sense of community because they vest it with their sense of self and often feel their voices are at stake. In the divisions that are part of your conflicts, the narrative construction of a "significant other" usually exists (Cohen, 1985, p. 115), whether it is right versus left, north-side versus south-side, black versus white, progressive versus conservative, pueblo versus sierra, gay versus straight, or whatever. Differences become rhetorical resources for building an internal sense of purpose. Viewed this way, the radical deaf culture in a sense needs the conservative/repressive hearing culture for the symbolic construction of its community boundaries. What you see represented in Cindy's narrative are boundaries that create space for deaf people to be themselves, outside of the evaluative eye of the dominant community. The other—hearing culture—it seems, forces the deaf to create their own community in direct opposition to the values and practices of hearing culture.

In fact, conflict in communities has often served a valuable function in opening discourse, in bringing voices into the open, and in producing the energy to change perceived injustices and solve problems of more common interest (Kriesberg, 1998). Divisions can often create unity in those parts of the community subject to the oppressive side of those divisions, needing to find and develop their voices. For example, Gresson (1992) traces the roots of African American unity to the hostility of the "middle passage" when Africans were shipped, under terrible conditions, to the colonies. Conflict can also be a dynamic influence in communities in redistributing power and in stimulating change (Browne, 1996; Lay, Wahlstrom, & Brown, 1996). The strangeness of Cindy's "deaf power" narrative might well be replaced by questioning your hearing culture assumptions about the superiority of spoken communication and finding a more sensitive approach to the medium of communication a person uses. This positive function of conflict depends on the ability of a community to view it analogically. Conflict can be both painfully divisive *and* a creative force for change.

Etzioni (1993) traces the dangers of digital (either/or) thinking as a central dynamic in polarities, oppositions, and conflicts in communities. As he points out, communities and subcultures may become self-centered and turn against others (p. 147), thus dividing broader communities. Similarly, Davis (1991) traces the development of subcultural conflict in communities to the friction resulting from groups focusing on actively pursuing differences and self-interests. When divisions concern concepts of value, purpose, truth, freedom, and collective identity (p. 5), groups are dealing with issues much deeper than mere lifestyle choices; indeed, these issues are perceived as close to sacred. Berger (1998) calls these oppositions "cosmological" divisions in culture (p. 5).

Even a cursory glance at Cindy's narrative illustrates this is more than a conflict about the "way of life" Cindy mentions at the end. It is about her sense of self—who she is, and how this defines for her who she does not want to be. Her deaf community offers her authenticity, freedom, and "true communication." By contrast, the hearing culture she is trying so hard to avoid is portrayed as repressive, uncaring, and fake. These oppositions give meaning to the community division of deaf and hearing cultures she portrays as being in conflict. The conflict is also more than about ways of life because it is also clearly about physical characteristics that make a difference, divisions within a family concerning the best ways to "talk," and deeply held assumptions about communication. Simply, the narrative has a rich complexity that connects family, generation, and community conflicts simultaneously.

Community conflicts are often best understood as what Berger (1997) calls "normative fault lines" (p. 358). These are ruptures in everyday accord indicating that deeper questioning of cosmological differences is taking place. These fault lines are supported when the sides in a conflict are convinced they are right and this sense of rightness is supported by broader institutional connections such as organized political bodies. Cindy's narrative expresses the fault line not between being deaf and hearing, but what that means as the experience of ways of life. Furthermore, it deals with those ways of life in terms of being authentic as one-self. Such differences or fault lines can quickly become political in that they are part of the identity, belief system, ideology, or way of life of groups, particularly when these differences put one group at odds with other groups in terms of access to community resources. How oppositions between deaf and hearing communities lead to defensiveness, animosity, combativeness, and so on, and create cycles of conflict is an important concept for you to understand.

Hate is an important rhetorical dynamic in the symbolic construction of the fault lines between self and other in conflicted communities (Moritz, 1995; van Dijk, 1995; Whillock, 1995). Community tends to mean the bonds, allegiances, and fraternity that draw and keep groups together around shared values and beliefs (Campbell, 1998; Hart, 1998). Hart argues, however, that for every community, there is an "uncommunity" (p. xxv), an "other" that serves the rhetorical function of creating community by negation. To construct our community, we hate the other. Personification is used in Cindy's narrative where, for example, her mother represents and symbolizes the hearing world that must be hated. The hypothetical "they" is also used as a way of creating a consistent distinction from "we." Hate also represents the failure of dialogue between these communities.

To maintain the hate that propagates divisions and justifies even violent actions, one key rhetorical act involves defining the "enemy" or threat to the com-munity (Hogan & Williams, 1996). At the boundary with enemies, conflict and repression usually prevail. Once opposing narratives of "us" versus the enemy are developed into melodramas or highly stylized and simplified dramatic opposi-tions, then a conflict becomes polarized, personalized, and overly simple. This escalates the rhetoric of conflict and the actions of those involved in the conflict (Osborne & Bakke, 1998). Very close to this sense of fighting an enemy is war rhetoric. Rhetorical wars create the imperative that the struggle against common enemies and what they represent is essential to the existence of a community (Condit & Greer, 1998). In Cindy's narrative, the conflict appears to have taken on the stylized form of a group struggling for freedom (of communication), from the uncaring and repressive group that has the power to define normality. From here, the struggle for "deaf power" becomes one that appeals to mythic archetypes dear to American culture. A symbolic war thus evolves.

The Analogue of Community Conflict and Dialogue

Ronald C. Arnett (1997) calls the underlying systemic tendency for communities to simultaneously include and exclude people, ideas, and so on, the "oxymoronic character of community" (p. 27). He argues that "community is vital to the quality of our lives" (p. 28), but that you must recognize the dialectical tension of inclusion and exclusion. He suggests that your inclusion in a community rests on the exclusion of someone else. He also prompts you to examine the sacrifices required for a sense of "we," notably giving up some of the "I" aspect of community. Simply, you have to negotiate community with others as they negotiate with you. When you focus on your personal goals, then you undermine the possibility of community.

Cindy appears to focus on self, what her mother (hearing culture) has done to her, and what she really wants. The sense of inclusion in deaf culture is grounded on her choice to no longer be a member of speaking culture. Hence, the community divides into "us versus them," and she does not want to be included with "them." The community is two-sided—good and evil. The contrary demands of community make it elusive for all. Arnett realizes that the ideals are themselves privileged voices and that inclusion is never complete. What can be hoped for between the deaf and hearing cultures is a sense of understanding and mutual respect based on a movement from "I" to "we." Simply, the division that drives Cindy's conflict is approachable if she can think about how both hearing and deaf cultures share common communication challenges.

Barriers to community dialogue arise from a focus on self, or "I," and a reliance on monologue over real or existential listening. Monologue creates and sustains separation, while dialogue invites the community of relation. Arnett illustrates the main principles of dialogic ethics and in particular, that you need to strive for the "acceptance of disagreement and conflict with the desire to resolve them" (1986, p. 96). The important question becomes how to get these conflicting parts of the community to a sense of "we"?

Wheatley and Kellner-Rogers (1998) offer some insight into this challenge when they suggest thinking of boundaries not as "self-protective walls," but as a "place of meeting and exchange," as well as points of distinction and division (p. 12). In living systems, boundaries occur where new relationships form and information is exchanged. Cindy's conflict can be seen as the narrative representation of a boundary between deaf and hearing groups in the community. Our interest in exploring this narrative is similar to Goodall's (1996) in his insightful account of how to read the "signs" of community and lack of community in extraordinary and everyday communication. His approach enables you to use Cindy's narrative as a starting point to dialogue exploring the "everyday possibilities of expanded consciousness" (1996, p. 225). Simply, we are interested in the possibilities for expanding the conversation between these two seemingly opposing community groups through an understanding of their communication about themselves and each other. As Kofman and Senge (1995) remind us, language is the generative practice through which it is possible to understand the primacy of the community as a whole over the parts and to value the relationships between the parts. In the next section, we ask interpretive questions leading to helping these parties renegotiate their community relationship.

ASKING THE INTERPRETIVE QUESTIONS

At the end of Chapter 4, we developed a system of questions for interpreting conflict narratives (see Table 4.2). Rather than ask each question in turn, we have synthesized our observations wherever possible. In applying these questions to Cindy's narrative, you can explicate the following insights.

Interpreting the Quality of Dialogue and Negotiation

Cindy and her mother have negotiated an enduring and consistent reality for themselves. Their reality, most likely, parallels that of the deaf and oral groups they represent. If you compare and contrast their reality with the guidelines for dialogue and peacemaking, you find their reality has more in common with two opposing and ongoing monologues than one dialogue. They epitomize what we have termed polarized discourse, and do not even seem to argue effectively.

First, they actively avoid creating any sort of relational container in which collective thinking might occur. They do this by both avoiding the issues and not acknowledging that deep issues really exist. Second, they are so busy building their own individual senses of being right that they probably do very little reflective thinking about either their own or the other's perspectives. Third, they appear to be content to allow avoidance to prevent any opportunity for mutual understanding of deafness as Cindy's way of life. Fourth, as there is no reflective questioning, they do not appear to want to express the reasons they feel and act as they do. This means that new possibilities for their relationship do not readily emerge. Fifth, Cindy's portrayal of her mother indicates that both parties are devaluing each other. Cindy caricatures her mother as much as it seems her mother caricatures her. Few of us truly listen to a caricature. Sixth, rather than exploring diversity, Cindy's narrative implies that both she and her mother feel their separate communities are superior to the other one. Her mother belongs to the normal majority, and Cindy belongs to a minority of authentic communicators. In this type of communication relationship, change is viewed as something the other needs to engage in, not the self.

Cindy and her mother's lack of dialogue has implications for their conflict relationship more generally. Specifically, cast as a struggle for authentic communication against the oppressive pressures of an uncaring community, this conflict takes on a sense of inevitability and necessity. It is inevitable that her mother and the oral community have forced Cindy to act the way she has because they do not listen to the concerns of the deaf. It is necessary that the conflict occur to gain recognition for the issues and experiences of the deaf community.

Changing their relationship is not likely to be easy. If they can recognize the limitations their communication style places on dialogue, perhaps they can visualize how they might encourage each other to open their relational dialogue. Perhaps they can begin with the more neutral issues of community perspectives on communication, deafness, and the biases of oral culture. Perhaps if they both reflect closely on this narrative, and you were able to collect and reflect on Cindy's mother's narrative, they might be guided toward opening their dialogue in useful ways.

Interpreting Narrative and Conflict Dynamics

The issues and questions for interpreting narrative and conflict dynamics help you understand why Cindy and her mother's dialogue and negotiation occurs as it does. As all conflict narratives do, Cindy's narrative represents the communication of a particular experience of conflict for herself and her audience. First, her struggle for authentic communication represents a specific biographical moment within a broader historical movement in the development of the voice and power of the deaf community. As such, the experience takes on a deeper meaning beyond the struggle between herself and a seemingly controlling mother. Cindy is fighting for her version of "free speech," and the audience can identify with this as a cultural archetype in the United States.

Second, this broader cultural context gives her license to portray the motives of the participants in ways supporting the "struggle for freedom" archetype. While Cindy is trying to break away and be true to herself, her mother is constantly trying to lure and bully her into speaking. While Cindy seeks authentic communication in which she is understood, her mother is trying to keep her in the world of hearing people to please herself and the dominant community she represents. Clearly, the story sets up a simple opposition between the goodness of authenticity and freedom and the wrongness of the dominant speaking community.

Third, Cindy structures the story to bring to life this communicative intent and the apparent motives of the participants in the conflict. If we simply paraphrase the main developmental points of the story, we can see how this is achieved. The structure emerges as follows:

1. You are shown the basic opposition of the conflict. Cindy wants to live a deaf life, and her mother wants her to be part of the speaking community. As a pageant winner, Cindy represents herself as an emblem of deaf culture.

2. You go back to Cindy's childhood. Her mother's motive is placed in the historical context of a culture that does not understand or tolerate deaf communication as normal. For fear of being labeled retarded, Cindy is forced to use oral speech.

3. Until Cindy enters college, her mother crusades (that mirrors oral culture) to raise her to use oral speech, partly to comply with social convention and partly to please her own mother, that is, Cindy's grandmother.

4. In college, Cindy finds authentic communication, a caring and understanding community, and improved self-esteem as a deaf person. She eliminates oral speech from her life.

5. Cindy's relationship with her mother suffers. They lose any shared understanding of her choice. Her mother tries manipulation, threats, and stereotypes. Cindy tries avoidance and appeasement.

6. Cindy and her mother settle on a compromise and avoidance approach to their conflict. No one addresses "the issue" directly and no one gets too upset.

7. Cindy accepts that their relationship may forever be divisive on the deaf/oral issue, as she is committed to living a deaf life.

This is Cindy's historically coherent account of the personal and ideological reasons for how and why the conflict emerged, why it remains unsolved, and what the future of her relationship to her mother and the oral community is likely to be. You understand the choices she has made throughout the conflict and, probably to some extent, identify with her commitment to authenticity.

Fourth, these narrative dynamics are used to support and challenge particular beliefs and actions, as they relate to conflict and communication. Our account of these dynamics is represented in Table 5.1.

Table 5.1 Conflict Issues Supported and Challenged

Underlying Beliefs/Actions/Ideology Supported	*Underlying Beliefs/Actions/Ideology Challenged*
It is better to be deaf and authentic than oral and inauthentic	Viewing communication only through an oral competency model
It is acceptable to have varying and even opposing views of what competent communication means	Minorities should comply with the values and practices of the dominant culture
True communication is about understanding, whatever the medium	Labeling deaf people as retarded or abnormal
Being true to yourself is more important than complying with family/community pressures	Deafness is an impairment.
Addressing issues head on is the best way to resolve a conflict	Pushing someone to be oral to please themselves or others
	Using threats, manipulation, avoidance, and compromise as a way of managing conflict

This system of issues forms the basic structure and meaning of the conflict. This is clearly a conflict about fundamental assumptions concerning community norms, expectations, and beliefs about communication.

Finally, through this explication, you can engage in further questioning and dialogue about the meaning of the story in terms of conflict practices and how Cindy conveys these issues through her narrative. You can imagine what the participants might learn from the story. Perhaps Cindy might develop a deeper appreciation of the constraints that her mother is responding to. Perhaps her mother might develop a deeper appreciation for Cindy's actions in the context of how she views her experiences of oral and deaf culture. Perhaps they can both begin to explicate or unpack the politics and ideology of their own accounts of the conflict and recognize how they construct their apparently opposing versions of reality. Perhaps they can begin to talk about their specific practices that maintain the conflict. These are some of the ways that understanding narrative dynamics might enable their conversation.

Interpreting Representations of Self, Other, and Context

Neither Cindy nor her mother appears to engage in very much perspective-taking. Rather, their communication supports and maintains their opposing relationship and views on communication. In Table 5.2, we explicate the representation of

Table 5.2 Representations of Self, Other, and Context

Representations of Self	*Representations of Other*	*Representations of Context*
Is proud to be deaf	Mother tries to "lure" her into oral culture	Am successful as Miss Deaf Wisconsin
Is a deaf woman		
Advocate and ambassador for deaf culture	Views deaf culture as being too sheltered and limits possible success	No other deaf students at school (minority)
		Oral culture defines deafness as impairment, retarded, abnormal
Has real responsibilities to the deaf community	Mother took all credit for her oral competencies	Found her deaf community and her identity in college
Believes in true or authentic communication	Pushed orality to please her mother (inauthentic)	Visual versus oral culture
Life is a struggle for freedom of true communication	Defies her daughter's deaf self-definition	Relational gaps are based on physical differences
	Views deaf people as rude	
	She needs to understand her daughter	

self, other, and context in Cindy's narrative. This explication examines specifically how such representations support this divisive conflict.

How Cindy represents self, other, and context in her narrative maintains the conflict by supporting her sense of rightness, her mother's wrongness, and a context forcing her to insist on her convictions about the equality of visual communication. Explicating these representational choices might be a useful first step for Cindy in exploring how she participates in maintaining the negative patterns of conflict with her mother. She might also identify ways she could change these representations so positive conflict patterns could emerge. Perhaps, for example, there are more noble reasons her mother felt it necessary to push oral speech culture on her. Her representation of her mother supports Cindy's sense of persecution, but this comes at the cost of drawing a largely negative caricature of her mother. How Cindy represents her mother partly creates the context for the conflict, but to Cindy there are real constraints she feels she must resist. Hence, the conflict is partly created for Cindy by the other (her mother) and the context they both create.

As you can see, context plays an important role in Cindy's construction of her self, her mother, and their relative motives in life. Besides their immediate relationship, this conflict is also about creating a broader context, that is, they are also representing the conflicted relationship of deaf and hearing groups in the broader community. This conflicted relationship, in turn, creates a climate and set of cultural assumptions about deaf and hearing cultures more broadly. How many of you, for example, knew that feelings of marginality and even oppression ran so deep in the deaf community? Now, you probably know much more about how groups who perceive themselves as marginal create narratives offering them the hope of change, of power, and what we hearing people somewhat ironically call "voice" in our communities. Unless such narratives are "heard," it is very difficult for the concerns of such groups to become part of the "talk" and history of a community.

LEARNING FROM THE DYNAMICS
OF COMMUNITY CONFLICT

In a broader framework, learning from Cindy's experience of community conflict can help you think about the various conflicts around you. Specifically, you can understand the important balance between development and destruction, freedom and responsibility, individual and community, and different stakeholders in your community. In managing conflict, you can recognize the need for unifying goals, understanding and tolerance, and communication about conflict. As communicators, you can increase your sensitivity to signs of conflict in communities. Conflicts are indicated by both verbal and non-verbal signs. There are violent signs of conflict and subtle expressions of hate. There are signs of racial, class, gender, sexual, and age oppression around you. There are signs of emerging conflicts in your communities, and signs that historical conflicts are still important.

There are signs of the spirit of reconciliation. Becoming a better collector and interpreter of these signs and clues improves your understanding of your communities and the need to generate the signs you want to exist for yourselves and for others. Also important, you can improve your abilities to critique narrative accounts you hear about community conflicts and to imagine ways to narrate into existence the community in which you want to live.

Some Final Reflective Questions on Cindy's Narrative

1. How did Cindy's portrayal of hearing culture make you feel?

2. What community issues do you feel as strongly about in your community?

3. What could you do to find out more about non-speaking subcultures in your community?

4. What can you do to increase dialogue between deaf and hearing members of your community?

5. What would have to change in your community so deaf people felt valued and included in the broader community?

Exercises and Dialogue Questions About Community Conflicts

Community Conflict Exercises: Learning From the Analogue and Dialogue in Communities

A. Research a conflict that has significant impact and meaning in your community. It could be a currently unfolding conflict, or historical case that is still part of the public memory. Try to interview or collect narrative accounts of the conflict from the different sides or positions. Work through the following questions:

1. What are the main reasons for the conflict from the different positions?

2. What material or symbolic resources are at the core of the conflict?

3. How do these differences structure the dynamics and progress of the conflict?

4. What impact has the conflict had on the community?

5. What cultural clues could you collect from the community as to the meaning and intensity of the conflict? Are there common stories about each other, visual displays of division, and so on?

(continued)

(*continued*)

6. What needs to happen to break down some of the barriers and heal some of the scars that such a community conflict leaves?

7. What did your community learn from this conflict in terms of changing relationships?

8. What more could it have learned from the conflict?

9. What did you learn from constructing your third person account/report of the narratives of other peoples' conflict?

B. Research the programs, volunteerism, and learning opportunities your town or city has for developing relationships among members of your community. Contact your local Chamber of Commerce and other civic organizations for examples of their community development programs.

1. Does your community have any programs for developing skills in visioning, leadership, and change so you are prepared for the challenges of the future?

2. Does your community have any programs designed to improve communication, understanding, and cooperation between groups in the community?

3. What communication strategies are these programs based on?

4. What is the philosophical basis of how these programs develop communities better able to manage their conflicts?

5. How well do these programs work to include stakeholders, share voices, and develop more peaceful communities?

6. What programs would you like to see in your community that are currently unavailable?

Questions for Dialogue About Your Community Conflicts

1. What are some of the important current and recent conflicts in your community?

2. In what ways are you involved in these conflicts through your stake in the outcome or through your membership in particular groups in your community?

3. How do these conflicts center on disputes over material resources (which neighborhoods get new businesses, school zoning, whose property values are affected by growth, and so on)?

4. How do these conflicts center on disputes over symbolic resources (recognition of particular groups in the community, prestige associated with particular areas, display of flags and other historical emblems, and so on)?

5. What role do perceptions of marginality, unfairness, or even oppression play in the conflicts in your community?

6. What role did the news media play in representing the positions and issues in the conflict and in the dynamics and direction of the conflict?

7. What is the earliest historical conflict still playing a meaningful role in dividing or uniting members of your community?

8. How is the meaning of this historical conflict maintained culturally in your community?

9. What are some conflicts emerging in your community you would point to as opportunities for creating greater unity and self-expression?

10. How well do you think your community is prepared for the demands of the future?

11. In what ways might you help improve that preparedness through your knowledge of community dynamics, conflict, and communication?

CONCLUSION

As the quote from Goodall indicates at the beginning of this chapter, in any community there are diverse harmonies—points of connection and points of difference that can always make a difference. You can, to some extent at least, choose the connections and differences to make a difference and specifically how they make a difference in your relationships with others in communities. You have to decide whether differences divide you intractably or enrich the ideas, skills, and experiences on which communities of the future are built. Simply, to relate to Hogan's quote, also at the beginning of this chapter, you can choose to nourish your community through communication or to nourish the rhetoric of enmity. We have examined how deaf and hearing cultures have opportunities to examine their conflicts for ways to make explicit community beliefs, myths, expectations, and so on, about communication itself. They also have the opportunity to use their conflict to create and maintain deeper divisions that perpetuate opposition and all the beliefs, myths, and expectations coming with that. Of course, there is always the opportunity for some of both.

This chapter should challenge you to examine conflicts that make up the complex, textured layers of relationships between the various groups in your own communities. You should also be challenged to think of ways you can use your understanding of communication to make a difference in those communities.

6

Managing Conflict at Work

"A dialogue-based process of [organizational] change takes place through the systemic understanding and negotiation of... conflicts."

(Kellett, 1999, p. 228)

Conflicts experienced at work can be a major source of stress and other difficulties that can erode your health and permeate your nonworking lives. Conversely, workplace conflict can be a major source of creativity, performance motivation, and productive change. In either case, conflict is an inevitable part of working life. This chapter illustrates the systemic necessity of conflict in driving organizations to achieve their goals. Also described are the benefits and dangers of conflict at work and the difference between constructive and destructive conflicts. More important perhaps, you learn to better understand and interpret workplace conflicts as signs or clues to broader organizational issues. Specifically, conflicts point to underlying tensions in organizational structures, processes, and changes. This chapter develops your understanding of how improving dialogue in organizations means members can more effectively negotiate the structural and process tensions that are inevitable when people work together. Methods of achieving this proactive approach to conflict management are explored and illustrated through our interpretation of organizational conflict narratives.

Key Concepts, Terms, and Definitions to Learn in This Chapter

- How to evaluate the quality of dialogue and negotiation in your workplace

- Understanding conflict dynamics in your workplace

- Understanding how workplace conflicts can be constructive and destructive

- How to conduct a systemic analysis of a workplace conflict

- Understanding the conflicted nature of organized systems

- Understanding the structural and processual origins of conflict

- How to improve organizational dialogue

Key Definitions

- *Organizational dialogue.* The approach to communication in an organization enabling members ask serious questions about their effectiveness, such that the organization is willing to listen to, live with, and learn from the answers such talk produces

- *Systemic analysis.* Mapping the network of relationships through which a conflict occurs and is maintained or managed

- *Plausible scenarios.* The construction of narratives about conflicts that are as accurate as possible, based on all of the available clues or facts

INTERPRETING ORGANIZATIONAL CONFLICT NARRATIVES

Exemplar Narrative: Deep Ethics

—ANNE

Prior to returning to school to complete my undergraduate degree, I worked for a mortgage company. For one year, I was the branch underwriter and was then promoted to branch manager. In these positions, I developed a degree of distrust and cynicism. This is due to the behavior of a great number of the brokers I dealt with on a daily basis. There were always some deals that were simply unworkable. But, for the brokers, this factor didn't stop them. Forged pay-stubs came across my desk, as well as fabricated letters with attorney's names. After a while, I became acutely aware of which brokers followed this "policy" as well as which managers endorsed it.

I wanted to work a deal as much as the next person, and searched for legal loopholes, but was also developing the attitude that no one was going to pull the wool over my eyes. I dreaded deals from certain individuals because I knew I was being used as their last resort. They knew the deal didn't fit our guidelines, but they were going to pull any illegal move it took to slip a deal by me to get me to approve it. Soon I began killing deals.

I suppose my emotions got in the way of professionalism. I sought to protect my reputation by not allowing bad deals through or, if possible, finding a loophole to make the deal. Perhaps not at the amount requested but nonetheless a deal. At the same time, I didn't want to be "taken," either. It was that part that took over me.

I never yelled back at the brokers. I never hung up on anyone, and I never threatened our professional relationship. All of these I endured from time to time from certain brokers. It became overwhelming at times. As I look back, I see that this problem was never put on the table to overcome. We just went from deal to deal, or the broker would withdraw his/her business for a few weeks. That was fine with me. It allowed for quality time with my other deals and other brokers. At the same time, I knew these bad brokers had good deals also, and I wanted them. After all, the bottom line was numbers—high numbers at the end of the month.

I didn't work this problem out. The bank we were a subsidiary of went under and soon my position was transferred to the home office in New England. I was given the opportunity to create a new position for myself with the company, but opted to leave altogether. Soon, thereafter, I returned to school.

————◄○►————

ASKING THE INTERPRETIVE QUESTIONS

Interpreting organizational narratives provides a valuable window into the experience of members (Boje, 1991). We begin our interpretive analysis of Anne's account of her conflict by asking the interpretive questions listed in Table 4.2.

Interpreting the Quality of Dialogue and Negotiation

In Anne's narrative, a deep ethical conflict between her own convictions about what is right and wrong and those practiced at the mortgage company proved to be an important turning point in her life. As her narrative construction of the experience indicates, her conflict at work led Anne to where she is now—in college with more opportunities to choose where she works. Conflict has, for her, played a creative—even transforming—role in life. Specifically, this conflict probably pushed her to do much soul-searching during her time there. She probably spent some

Table 6.1 Work Myths Adopted and Rejected by Anne

Work Myths and Beliefs Adopted/Reinforced	*Work Myths and Beliefs Challenged/Rejected*
Rely on what is important to you, not what "makes a deal"	Success in the form of "promotions" will in and of itself make you happy
"Professional relationships" are often neither	People in organizations generally have similar ethics to you
"Good" and "bad" are often complexly intertwined, but you can make distinctions	Playing by the rules of the game, not what is right
You are not necessarily stuck where you are; there is something better ahead	You can distinguish how you feel from what you do
Sometimes leaving for the possibility of satisfaction is better than staying for the probability of success	

time thinking about who she is and where she wants to go in life. The conflict helped her to fully recognize just what her own convictions and ethical boundaries are. The conflict helped her to recognize whom she respects and, given the choice, whom she would not do business with in her community. The conflict helped bring her to a sort of crossroads whereby the choice to leave her job and go back to college became both real and desirable—perhaps even inevitable—for her. When we make sense of events retrospectively in this way, as a valuable part of a journey, then it is easier to manage those conflicts and the pain they often bring. An additional benefit of a conflict such as this one is that Anne will probably have an easier time addressing and dealing with similar conflicts in the future.

One of the underlying themes of Anne's story is that she decides which deeply held myths and beliefs about work to adopts and reinforce, and which she confronts and rejects. These myths and beliefs are summarized in Table 6.1.

The myths and beliefs she adopts, or at least reinforces as part of how she views work, enable Anne to distinguish herself from her job and the culture of the workplace. In so doing, she is able to end her relationship to that organization and build her desire to move on to the next, more promising, part of her life. The myths and beliefs she rejects are good learning experiences about the work world and why people behave as they do. Challenging these myths also enables her to view leaving the mortgage company as not just something desirable, but as necessary to her long-term wellness and sense of personal integrity.

One of the key lessons about this mortgage company is that Anne's experience was valuable and even productive despite the lack of effective dialogue and negotiation. Anne found peace with the conflict, but only after leaving the organization with the hope of better things to come. The reality she negotiated involved distrust, deception, and occasionally moral and ethical dilemmas. The cultural rules of success in the organization concerned making the numbers by the end of the month, even if this involved illegal and unethical practices. This negotiated reality proved to undermine Anne's wellness in a variety of ways. For others, it probably did not create the internal conflicts that Anne felt. The long-term result might well be that those who share Anne's convictions decide to leave and those who thrive on the "kill" of making the deal will flourish.

As the organizational value of making the deal at all costs thrives, this, in turn, will likely make dialogue about experiences like Anne's even less realistic. Dialogue was minimal when she left the company. Very little real talking occurred at the mortgage company. Active avoidance of engagement among members of the organization was more the rule. Hence, no time was taken to address, reflect on, or change the issues Anne raised. There seems to be no point at which her diverse concerns would be listened to, valued, or learned from. Deep issues are too threatening or too dangerous to address; talking about illegal activities, for example, does have legal implications. People were too busy charging ahead to the end of the month to worry about their long-term wellness or that of the organization. Because of this, conflicts were not addressed, and, therefore, they built under the surface and manifested themselves in private thoughts and feelings. Distrust and cynicism were just around the corner for Anne.

Other symptoms occurring in people who work where conflict issues are not addressed often include stress, burnout, absenteeism, sabotage, and, as it did for Anne, leaving the organization. The costs of these problems should be weighed against the apparent current success of the mortgage company.

This mortgage company may be very successful without developing internal dialogue very much. However, we believe some simple developments to improve feedback, such as exit interviews, might make the company even more competitive over the long term. At the very least, such activities might help employees, particularly new ones, understand the expectations and cultural rules that determine whether someone "fits" with the company. We also believe that the company's current lack of dialogue makes it vulnerable in some crucial ways. First, it risks losing good employees who take valuable knowledge, skill, and even clients with them, and who might continue to resent the organization. These employees may even talk badly about the company to potential clients. Second, in an organization where no one talks about business practices because unethical and illegal activities support the hard-driving competitive organizational culture, it is easy to make big mistakes. Avoiding talk about the reality of an organization's success puts that success in jeopardy. This is because those employees who take the bigger risks and make the shadier deals that often lead to big successes, make it more likely that someone will cross a line in a visible, public, and very damaging way.

Clearly, sometimes it is necessary to leave an organization to maintain one's wellness and sense of purpose and integrity in life. Because your work can become closely tied to your views of your selves, this is often not an easy thing to do. Often people cling to what they know how to do, even though inside they may feel the conflicted emotions that Anne felt regularly. As Anne discovered, it can be valuable to tell an exit story that makes moving on with one's life the right thing to do. It is a form of peacemaking.

Hearing narratives such as this one can also be a valuable learning opportunity for organizations. When exit interviews are conducted so an honest and full account of an employee's experience is solicited, then this can be valuable feedback. If they listened to Anne's narrative, the mortgage company could learn more about what motivates and demotivates its employees, how employees feel about doing business as it is done, and what changes in communication and business practices might be considered. An organization does not necessarily have to believe all that an exiting employee says about it. There is be a tendency for those leaving to valorize themselves, particularly if they leave with ill feelings toward the organization. However, such narratives can still provide valuable points from which to begin dialogue about the conflict issues employees feel strongly about.

Interpreting Narrative and Conflict Dynamics

Anne appears to have two sets of interrelated motives in recounting this narrative. First, she illustrates her own motives in explaining how she managed the conflict—why she acted as she did throughout her workplace ordeal. Second, she is interested in placing the narrative within a broader interpretive framework that the audience understands and believes. Besides the representations of self, other, and context, which we examine later, Anne achieves these goals through the choices and combinations of narrative elements and language supporting a particular interpretation of the narrative. The narrative structural elements and supporting language elements are summarized in Table 6.2.

This narrative structure works as communication because, as the audience, you recognize Anne's struggle within a broader cultural and historical moment that shapes its meaning for you. Specifically, Anne learns a valuable life lesson about going back to college and finishing her degree. The alternative she lived through was an unfulfilled life of struggling to keep her emotional health and ethical integrity without being absorbed by an apparently amoral work culture that was making her cynical. Through the experience, she learns valuable lessons about balancing professional performance with firmness and integrity. She learns to listen to her own heart and not settle for what the world does to her. To do this, she draws on the U.S. cultural archetypes of self-determination and self-reliance, choosing integrity and doing the right thing, taking her opportunities where they present themselves (the conflict was, in a sense, resolved for her), and realizing the practicality and good sense of finishing something that she started. These archetypes, when combined with her vivid language, effectively connect the audience both to her experience and to a cultural context in which the experience takes on a broader meaning. Most of her audience, including herself, probably believes

Table 6.2   The Thematic Structure of Anne's Narrative

Main Narrative Elements	Examples of Supporting Language Choices
1. Anne is completing her undergraduate degree.	1. Language shows the magnitude of the problem:
2. Prior to this, she was an underwriter/branch manager for a mortgage company	"a great number of brokers" "forged" "fabricated"
3. She became distrustful and cynical at illegal and unethical business practices	"the policy" "being use"
4. She became savvy and proactive by killing deals that she knew were shady	"they were going to pull any illegal move it took to slip a deal by me"
5. She struggles with the emotions of maintaining professional relationships while not being "taken."	"the bottom line was numbers" 2. Language that shows her reaction: "I developed a degree or distrust and
6. She left and returned to school.	cynicism" "it became overwhelming" 3. Language that showed her resolve: "no one was going to pull the wool over my eyes" "I began killing deals" "I didn't want to be taken"

that although she did not really resolve the conflict for herself, these were good lessons and good decisions. Hence, you might tend to read her motives through the conflict in this light as good ones.

The motives of the others in the conflict appear somewhat less appealing. On examining the language she uses to build her representation of the experience, we see a problem of dishonesty widespread and powerful in the culture of the organization. People are "pulling moves, fabricating," and "forging" to get a deal slipped through. Her reactions are also couched in very vivid language. You can see the overwhelming energy it must have taken to stay one step ahead of the slippery brokers. She gets tough, "killing" deals and avoiding being "taken" or having the "wool pulled over [her] eyes." You might get the impression that the mortgage company is a somewhat shady, bottom line at all costs, place that breeds an amorality that squeezes good intentions until they have to leave.

Of course, Anne is portraying things the way she is partly so her turning point story works as an endorsement of what she believes is right. You are definitely hearing a partial, position, and partisan account of her work experience. It is a story told entirely from her position, with her perspective permeating the details shared and the details not shared, with her own narrative goals in mind. Nothing is included that would dissuade you from her representation of the organization. You do not gain any insight into why the brokers believe that their actions are justified or reasonable in that context. Simply, you have only her side of the story, and there are ethical issues and questions we can raise about that. However, greed does appear to be the overpowering motive of others in the organization.

In telling her story, Anne has managed to remain true to her experience, while telling a tale many of you can relate to and learn from. That is, her narrative has social and cultural significance. This means that she has also created an opportunity for dialogue, both about her experience and the type of story she is telling. You probably all have experiences quite similar to or different from hers. You have probably all worked for an organization that seemed to go out of its way to practice poor communication. You probably have all had work experiences that were turning points for you in that they forced you to realize you need to expect more or at least different things from yourselves and from your lives. These are all points of possible dialogue for you in exploring the role of such organizational conflicts in your lives. Anne, herself, can probably articulate the main lessons she has learned and what she will never do again as a result of this experience. She will most likely search for work she believes in, and she will be a happier employee for that.

Interpreting Representations of Self, Other, and Context

Pattern recognition is an important practice in learning and changing. For Anne, understanding the patterns she is experiencing enables her to make decisions to change those patterns. There must have been a point toward the end of her time at the mortgage company when she recognized how she was feeling and how she was acting, and how these repeating patterns were related to her work world. She gives you some glimpses of her feelings as she describes her distrust and cynicism. Imagine how she felt at seeing others trying to deceive her, at being taken, at being unable to talk about what bothered her, and generally at being in a place where her sense of self clashed so resoundingly with the context and with others in that context. To create a narrative clearly illustrating this sense of clash and making breaking these patterns by leaving the organization into a logical conclusion to her narrative, Anne has developed a strategic representation of self, other, and context. The moral of the story can be presented as, "be true to yourself when you are experiencing deep ethical conflicts at work." Table 6.3 summarizes the main representational choices she makes in supporting this moral.

As you can see from the relationship among these representations, Anne is faced with the choice of staying in a context supporting the unethical and sometimes illegal actions of others or leaving it. Her workplace seems to care only about production numbers, regardless of how those numbers are kept high. Coupled with this, there is no communication about problems relating to work practices or ethics. No effort seems to be made to develop any perspective-taking on the experiences of employees. Success seems to depend on a policy that completely compromises wellness for the sake of production numbers. If Anne

Table 6.3   Anne's Strategic Representations of Self, Other, and Context

Strategic Representations of Self	Strategic Representations of Others	Strategic Representations of Context
I wanted to deal (be productive) but did not want to be deceived.	The behavior of other brokers made me distrustful and cynical	The culture supported unethical/illegal policies.
I dreaded unethical people	Some others were engaged in an illegal and unethical "policy."	Problems are "never put on the table to overcome."
I began killing deals that were unethical.		The company has a bottom line concern with production numbers, not practices.
I wanted to protect my reputation as a professional.		The bank went under and her position was moved.

stays with the company, her sense of self and deeply held convictions about what is right and wrong—regardless of the fact that it is a workplace—suffer. If she leaves, she has the opportunity to find a better fit between herself and her work. She sees herself as wanting to be a productive, ethical professional, but has found herself in a place that does not value these qualities. Because these qualities are not valued, others are practicing an illegal policy she is forced in part to endure, and this is deeply affecting her wellness.

The context shapes the conditions for the unethical behavior. In turn, the actions of the brokers partly shape a context that is highly demanding and competitive. Anne is highly principled, but young and relatively powerless in a corporate culture that does not appear to listen to anyone very much. If she leaves, she is no longer subject to the powerful hold that the context and others have over her experience and her actions.

Her narrative representations present her with an experience she learns from and that moves her forward in life, and a decision that makes perfect sense for her. Her account of her unhealthy time at the company can thus become an important part of a broader and much healthier story about her work life or career.

DIALOGUE AND ORGANIZATIONAL CONFLICT MANAGEMENT

When organizations talk about their history and learn from the successes and mistakes of that past, then they are applying dialogue to their own development. Similarly, when an organization engages in self-assessment of current practices for ways it can better achieve its mission and vision, it is also effectively doing dialogue. Finally, a great many organizations today are engaging in so-called futuring and visioning processes to learn to change now to better meet the challenges and opportunities of the future (Schwass, 1992). These are some of the important applications of dialogue in organizational change (Weisbord, 1992). When these practices are part of the ongoing conversations of the organization, many of the conflicts arising from lack of adaptability, over-constraining employees, or the high pressure of reacting to sudden changes, are minimized. In this section, you examine the importance of organizational dialogue in effectively managing conflicts such as the one at Anne's former workplace (Kellett, 1999; Schindler-Rainman & Lippitt, 1992).

Understanding Constructive and Destructive Conflicts at Work

Conflict can have a constructive impact on organizational functioning and communication. Even where a direct causal relationship cannot easily be seen between a conflict and its effects, it can have an impact on a variety of organizational functions. Conflict can be engaged, for example, by developing cross-functional focus groups that address the conflict generated by falling levels of customer satisfaction. Conflicts inevitably arising during times of organizational change can push people to work harder so their future becomes less uncertain. The conflict generated by the need to find faster or more efficient ways to meet consumer demands can stimulate creativity. Conflict in a work team generated by deadline pressure, for example, can bring people together around the common goal of meeting that deadline with high performance work. The conflict between an organization and its main competitor can stimulate commitment internally. Because conflict can stimulate creativity and commitment, it may also contribute to the sense of wellness that comes from engaging in challenging and fulfilling work.

Similarly, workplace conflicts can be avoided or can even become violent. Conflicts can lead to indifference, constraints, division, resistance, stress, and even addiction. The key issue is to understand how communication makes a difference in what direction conflict takes.

Central to why some organizational conflicts have a positive impact on productivity and experience and some do not is a systemic understanding of the following issues:

1. where the conflict comes from,

2. how it is managed,

3. how people react to it,

4. how it affects key organizational functions, and

5. how it manifests systemically in other organizational practices.

Table 6.4 connects these issues of systemic analysis to Anne's narrative so you can gain a deeper understanding of her particular conflict and of how to think systemically about organizational conflict dynamics more generally.

Using Plausible Scenarios to Understand the Systemic Nature of Conflict

Understand that the conflicts experienced in organizations are related to deeper processes in the way reality is organized. That is, conflicts often reflect deeper systemic issues in the political structure of the organization, such as power differences and access to decision making (Cheney, 1995; Mumby, 1993). Conflicts can also be connected to deeper organizational cultural processes and themes (Smith & Eisenberg, 1987). It is useful in developing a systemic understanding of a conflict and its relationship to these underlying structures and processes to put the clues together into what detectives often call a plausible scenario. That is, after reflecting on the issues and clues you have found in analyzing the narrative, it is useful to build a coherent account of the key parts of the narrative that helps to make sense of what happened. The narrative may not be completely accurate because you rarely see all the clues working together in practice. This process does, however, help you to see how things might fit together. If holes can be punched in the story—a clue does not fit—then you need to go back and rethink the scenario. This exercise also helps develop useful follow-up or dialogue questions to go from there to thinking about change. One plausible scenario we can build from our questions and narrative clues above might be as follows.

————◄○►————

Anne works for a mortgage company for a year or so. She does well, finding herself promoted after only a year to branch manager. She is good at what she does but a nagging internal conflict builds to intolerable levels for her, making her question her place in the organization. Anne cannot resolve the conflict she feels over the unethical and illegal policies of deal making. The conflict is avoided because no one wants to acknowledge that the policy exists, or that it is unethical. Plus, the policy does seem to result in high productivity numbers, although risks are taken to make this happen. Her stress level and sense of disaffection are high, but it's a "stay busy and say nothing" kind of place. People do not realize it yet, but the energy put into avoidance and denial will have effects on other aspects of the organization over time. We might assume, for example, that the culture will propagate itself, wellness will become increasingly difficult to maintain, and dissatisfaction and turnover levels of ethical employees will continue to be high. There will also be effects that we cannot predict with other consequences.

————◄○►————

Table 6.4   Systemic Analysis of Anne's Conflict

Systemic Questions for Narrative Analysis	*Examples From Anne's Narrative With Dialogue Questions*
Where does the conflict come from?	Ethical opposition between Anne and the prevailing "policy" of make deals at any cost.
How is it managed?	High levels of avoidance and low engagement of the issues generating the conflict.
	The problem is never put on the table.
	Anne avoids public clues to her internal conflict, and experiences private turmoil.
	Management avoids any discussion of marginal practices or the conflicts they generate.
How do people react to the conflict?	Say nothing and stay busy. Priority placed on rewarding those who make deals to keep productivity numbers high.
	Anne feels internal stress and tensions of lack of ethics and lack of authenticity about the problem.
	Anne thinks of her job as enduring the behavior of others. It is almost overwhelming.
	Ultimately she leaves the organization and the industry.
How does it affect key organizational functions?	Productivity is high but so is illegal risk-taking.
How does it manifest systemically in other organizational practices?	Stress levels are high for those with ethical conflicts.
	Satisfaction levels are extremely low for Anne. Satisfaction levels will be high only for the hard-driving, numbers-oriented members who are rewarded.
	Denial and blame shifting is likely to be prevalent. The organization will likely deny that it creates the conditions for unethical practices. If people are caught, they are likely to blame the organization.
	Turnover of people with ethical dilemmas will likely continue.
	Wellness of all members becomes questionable in a culture of deceit and denial
	Anne and those with the same conflict will likely feel isolated from the power bases and from each other. People with the same conflict probably do not know each other.
	A numbers-only culture propagates a numbers-only culture as it attracts like-minded recruits.

Developing a plausible scenario enables you to ask the following dialogue questions about systemic conflict. Imagine the members of the organization are asking themselves these questions. As you work through the questions, think about what might be their first reaction to the questions, and what they might learn if they genuinely address these questions.

1. Why did "the policy" first develop in our company and/or in the broader mortgage industry?

2. How has the policy affected both the productivity and experience of members?

3. What are likely to be the short-term and long-term effects of how we do business?

4. What might some of the negative effects of the policy, and our organizational culture on our employees and on our health as an organization, be?

5. Will more be gained if the mortgage company engages or avoids the conflict?

6. What are the relative benefits and risks of avoidance versus engagement of the conflict?

7. How can Anne address the conflict while allowing those who engage in the policy to save face and not become defensive?

8. What formal and informal aspects of power and position does Anne risk if she addresses her ethical conflict openly?

9. How does the culture of the mortgage company help to maintain the silence over ethical conflicts? What might people say to Anne if she starts voicing her concerns?

10. What would have to change at the company for the voicing of experiences similar to Anne's to be listened to and even valued as feedback?

11. Is it worth the effort to engage in the changes you specify? If so, why?

12. What could the organization learn from Anne's experience?

13. What is the thing you most agree with in our plausible scenario, and what do you most disagree with? Why did you pick these aspects of our interpretation?

14. How would your story of working at the mortgage company be similar to, or different from, Anne's?

Understanding the Conflicted Nature of Organized Systems

Conflict is inherent to organizational systems. Here, we are not necessarily referring to the dysfunctional conflict that is a major clue to deeper dysfunctional organization at the mortgage company. Rather, conflict is an integral part of the dynamics of how organizations manage the balances keeping them functioning effectively. First, the tensions between creativity and constraint need to be balanced. Contemporary organizations thrive and keep their employees productive when they allow them the freedom to voice experiences and the participation that stimulates creativity in employees. There is also a need for order—constraints—so creativity is directed at achieving organizational goals. Hence, performance goals people are accountable and responsible for are needed. This often generates conflicts when rules, assessment procedures, or policies are used to channel people's activities toward organizational goals. Conflicts are particularly prevalent when power is abused, when people are dominated, and when individuality is stifled.

Second, linked to this, there is a need to balance the priorities of the individual and the various collectives (teams, divisions, departments, and so on) that make up the broader organization. This may take the form of tensions between valuing diversity and demanding the unity essential for high performance. The conflict may arise from the various definitions and approaches to work people have. It may arise when individuals or divisions are accountable to each other and move only as quickly as the collective unit moves.

Third, a balance between the tensions of a desire for stability and the necessity for change is needed. All organizations have an inherent instinct for survival and development. This depends on the ability to balance the need to be open with the desire to be closed. Many contemporary organizations have adopted mission-based planning programs to develop a sense of their core or unchanging identity. On the other hand, organizations need to change to remain competitive and survive. Ideally, periods of change are balanced with periods of recovery during which sense can be made of the changes and they can be adopted.

Fourth, for learning-based organizational development to occur, an effective balance between action and reflection or questioning is also needed. Organizations that take the time to question how well they are meeting their goals, how well they are serving their clients, how well they live up to their mission and vision, and so on, are likely to learn from both their successes and their failures. Organizations that charge ahead and never reflect on where they are going usually find themselves going in a different direction from what they had planned. They also are less likely to learn as much as they could along the way. How to better balance the everyday actions associated with getting work done and the reflective questioning and self-assessment of dialogue is an important organizational tension to balance.

The following questions help you to explicate how these dynamic tensions are played out at the mortgage company.

1. How would you describe the balance at the mortgage company between the creativity allowed employees and the constraints keeping that creativity directed toward organizational goals?

2. How might this balance be improved so that conflicts are better managed?

3. How does the balance between the needs of individuals and the needs of collectives affect the employees' performance and other aspects of organizational life?

4. How might the organization improve this balance to better manage conflicts?

5. How effectively does the mortgage company appear to balance openness with a reasonable need for stability?

6. How might the company improve this balance to better manage conflicts?

7. How effectively does the mortgage company appear to balance action with reflective questioning of those actions?

8. How might the company improve this balance to better manage conflicts?

9. How effectively does the mortgage company use dialogue to negotiate the balance between these and other tensions?

Understanding Conflict in Organizational Structures and Processes

The choices you make and that are made for you in designing the structure and processes of organizations have a considerable impact on the conflicts occurring in our organizations. Organizations are structured to achieve chosen goals and choices in how you manage the everyday processes of doing work have important consequences for work communication. In particular, one's ability to handle conflict is often closely constrained in the workplace (Eisenberg & Goodall, 1997). The following questions help you explore Anne's narrative for clues as to how the structure and process of work at the mortgage company created the conditions for her unfortunate conflict experience.

- Power and Conflict in Hierarchies

  1. How might the organization and relationship of management and employees have contributed to Anne's conflict?

  2. How was power abused in the policy of how work is done?

  3. In what ways was she resisting power and domination through her behavior and thoughts in the conflict?

  4. How might the mortgage company be prone to workplace violence?

  5. How might work-hate narratives emerge and contribute to the climate of conflict?

  6. How might the mortgage company reduce the negative effects of too much hierarchy by encouraging participation, inclusion, and voicing of questions and concerns?

- Power and Conflict in Team-Based Organizations

  7. How might conflicts like Anne's be better addressed and resolved in a team-based organization?

  8. What different conflicts might arise if the mortgage company developed team-based work structures?

9. What conflicts typically occur in organizational teams?

10. How might more team-based work improve the mortgage company's performance and their employees' experiences?

- Human and Managerial Dynamics of Conflict

    11. How might personality and personal values and beliefs contribute to the dynamics of conflict?

    12. How might the everyday style of work relationships between people have contributed to this conflict?

    13. How might the leadership style of management affect Anne's conflict?

    14. How might the approach to motivation, assessment, and reward practices have contributed to the conflict?

    15. How might the predominant management style at the mortgage company have contributed to the conflict?

    16. How might gender communication styles and gender differences have played an important role in this conflict?

- Organizational Culture

    17. What broader social and ethical issues are negotiated or in conflict at the mortgage company?

    18. How might Anne's narrative capture broader organizational conflicts?

    19. What seem to be the beliefs and values about work and people embodied in the everyday practices of organizational members?

    20. How does the culture of the organization contribute to creating and maintaining conflicts such as Anne's?

- Organizational Change and Conflict

    21. What changes made prior to Anne's employment at the company might have created the conditions for her conflict?

    22. How does this conflict show that the company needs to change?

    23. What does the company need to change most about its organization?

    24. How might Anne help them recognize the signs indicating they need to change?

    25. How well prepared is the organization for proactive change?

    26. What type of crisis is it vulnerable to that might force this organization to change in the future?

27. What forms of resistance and conflict might you expect if the organization began to implement the changes you recommend?

28. What communication skills would the organization need to develop to implement change effectively?

Exploring these questions in light of Anne's narrative and your own organizational experiences may help you understand the complex organizational dynamics that both generate and react to conflict.

Improving Organizational Dialogue

Having discussed the need to address the quality of dialogue at the mortgage company, we now review specific ways that organizations may improve their dialogue to create a more open climate for addressing conflicts. This is more difficult than it sounds. Not everyone values communication, and not every organization is ready to become dialogue-based or learning-oriented. However, it is worth asking the following questions to stimulate thinking about how dialogue improves an organization's conflict management processes. Conflict is not eliminated as a result, but increasing the organization's "smarts" by building skillful communication throughout and about the organization helps (Albrecht & Hall, 1991; Morris, 1995). Specifically, becoming more learning-oriented increases an organization's ability to manage conflict and reduces negative conflicts that can divide and conquer the organization.

These concepts of dialogue—learning orientation, smartness, and so on—come from the body of research and practice often referred to as learning organizations (Chawla & Renesch, 1995; Kofman & Senge, 1995; Senge et. al., 1994; Shipka, 1995). Learning organizations recognize that smartness, or systemic intelligence, is key to long-term viability and success (Handy, 1995). Intelligence or smartness is achieved when an organization—or any system—steps out of the flow of ongoing action and reflects on reality, asks questions about that reality, and compares and contrasts its reality to that of other real or possible organizations. From this questioning process, the organization can imagine alternative or better ways of improving quality, meeting changing consumer needs, and so on. From this reflection, the organization can develop workable strategies for making those imagined realities into its organizational reality. Higher levels of intelligence are achieved when an organization does this on an ongoing basis as part of a culture of continuous improvement (James, 1996). These are signs of an intelligent system.

When an organization strives for this level of intelligence, it is becoming learning-oriented. This simply means an organization is open to learning about how it is and is not prepared to meet the challenges of an intelligent system. The ability and willingness to learn from successes and failures, to learn about ways of organizing and changing, and to develop both the people and the systems needed for constant improvement, makes an organization learning-oriented (Marshall, Mobley, & Calvert, 1995).

Clearly, learning that results in intelligence is based on an organization's ability to communicate effectively. Asking challenging questions in a supportive context is necessary for dialogue (Bennett & Brown, 1995; Bethanis, 1995). Commitment to bringing constituents together to develop collaborative answers to those questions, as well as collecting and synthesizing the knowledge and experience existing in the members of an organization, is important (Brown, 1995; Putnam, 1996). Doing the talk necessary to develop strategies to put those answers into practice, while learning to question the answers so constant learning becomes a habit, is a communication challenge (Ford & Ford, 1995). Finally, allowing the answers to drive needed change, and responding to those needs, is crucial. These communication skills take energy and even reorganization into teams, but they are essential for the learning and intelligence ensuring the organization is prepared for most conflicts. These skills also help ensure that people approach change willingly. The following questions help you examine the mortgage company and your own work experiences for signs of intelligence, learning, and dialogue.

1. How would you advise the mortgage company to change so organizational dialogue might improve?

2. What specific communication skills and structures would you advise the mortgage company to develop?

3. How would you advise the company to develop the skills and structures you think are important?

4. How might the company develop better internal communication relationships, for example, through mentoring programs and social support systems that promote cross-functional understanding?

5. How might the company build networks and connections between people at different levels and divisions to improve communication and build a culture of advocacy?

6. How might you help the company to build negotiation, balance, listening, improvement, tolerance, and ethics into core organizational values and practices?

7. How well does the company currently learn from successes and failures?

8. How well does the company currently talk about and imagine alternative work approaches?

9. How willing does the company seem to learn and develop—the basis of a learning organization?

10. How would you advise the company to improve its capacity for learning?

11. How smart is the organization about itself and about where it is going as a company?

12. What aspects of intelligence does the company need to work on initially?

13. How would you advise the company to start to become a more intelligent workplace?

14. How would you help the company create a climate of dialogue, learning, and intelligence, so conflict skills improve?

Some Final Reflective Questions on Anne's Narrative

1. What typical conflicts happen where you work?

2. Why do these conflicts tend to occur, and what effects do they have on the effectiveness of the organization?

3. How might your organization get smarter about understanding the positive and negative dimensions of conflicts?

4. How might you contribute to the organizational learning that could come from your workplace conflicts?

5. From what conflicts might your workplace benefit if they could be brought up for discussion?

6. What would you have done, and how would you have reacted to, the conflict in which Anne found herself?

Having discussed Anne's narrative in some depth, we have developed the following exercises to help you think about conflicts in your workplaces more deeply. The exercises may help you relate your experiences of workplace conflicts to the issues we have discussed in the chapter so far.

Exercises and Dialogue Questions About Workplace Conflicts

Dialogue Exercises

The following exercises are useful in developing your ability to recount workplace conflicts, question what they mean, and suggest ways an organization and its members might learn from the narrative.

The Magic Question Visioning Exercise

The magic question is an exercise developed by our friend and colleague H. L. "Bud" Goodall, Jr. The exercise is designed to stimulate imaginative

(continued)

(continued)

dialogue about what members of an organization would most want their work and workplace to be like. From the visioning part of the exercise, members spend time developing strategies that might move them closer to that ideal, while considering what is realistic and unrealistic.

The magic question is as follows:

- If you could wake up tomorrow and your workplace were everything you could dream of, what would your workplace be like?

The follow-up questions are as follows:

1. How would you describe your first working day in that ideal organization?

2. What would communication between people be like?

3. How would you effectively meet your corporate goals?

4. What are some changes you could implement leading you closer to that vision?

5. What is currently preventing your organization from becoming closer to your imagined ideal?

Narrative Application of the Magic Question

The first half of Alison's poem, below, gives us an interesting vision of what she would like her work to be similar to. Unfortunately, her vision is a fleeting moment of a daydream between glances at the clock. Her work conflict is between what she would like her work to be and the reality of a mundane restaurant job. It seems she would like to have work that heightens rather than dulls her senses. She would like to be relaxed, yet have her mind focused on what she is doing. She would like to put her soul into something challenging that has beauty and goodness and gives her a sense of achievement. Ironically, her work does not seem to be anything similar to this vision.

Work Time

—ALISON

Heightened senses;
Relaxed yet brilliant with perception.
A nirvana of challenge, beauty, light, and achievement.
Synchronicity of the soul...
(watching myself stack)

(continued)

(*continued*)
        fork-fork-spoon-knife
        fold the napkin nice and tight
        place it swiftly on top and...
        look at the clock.

——◄○►——

Go back and ask yourself the follow-up questions to the magic question, imagining you had Alison's mundane job. This exercise creates a dialogue about the experience of meaningful versus meaningless work.

1. What does your dialogue tell you about what you desire from work?

2. What does it tell you about the conflicts that many people experience between the desire for meaning and the lived reality of work?

3. What are some ways such organizations can change work practices to improve the meaningfulness of work?

4. What are some of the typical barriers that prevent such changes from being implemented?

The Conflict Empathy Exercise

——◄○►——

May I Help you, Mr. Smith?

—BROOKE

As I work and talk and type
Someone's listening to all the hype
"May I help you, Mr. Smith?"

She scribbles, jots, critiques, and preys
On all the things that I don't say
"May I help you, Mr. Smith?"

Lying on my desk I see a sheet
Where my faults are tallied nice and neat
"May I help you, Mr. Smith?"

(*continued*)

(*continued*)

I don't agree with one thing marked
I'll have to ask her about that remark
"May I help you, Mr. Smith?"

She says I rarely say the name
This is not true I proclaim
"May I help you, Mr. Smith?"

When I'm helping each person on the phone
I say their name and not just once, alone
"May I help you, Mr. Smith?"

I ask my boss about the names
She's made a mistake, she takes the blame
"May I help you, Mr. Smith?"

I did not doubt not for a bit
'Cause I do not go for petty bull@#$!
"May I help you, Mr. Smith?"

———◄○►———

Brooke's poem illustrates the tensions between her internal feelings of resentment and injustice and her public performance of being customer-oriented. Her way of resisting the perceived injustices at the hands of her apparently unfair but powerful boss comes out in an ironic performance of the required script and her true thoughts. The following questions help you use Brooke's narrative to explore your own conflicted work experiences.

1. What conflicted feelings and experiences is Brooke communicating to you through her poem?

2. What is it about the communication processes and structures in her workplace that help to generate the conditions for these feelings and experiences to emerge?

3. How do you think she relates to her boss on an everyday basis?

4. How would you describe their communication with and about each other?

5. How would you manage the conflict similarly or differently from Brooke?

6. How much do you think the employees and management at Brooke's workplace talk about this type of employee experience?

(*continued*)

(continued)

7. Have you been in a work situation where you had a similar experience of unjust and unfair use of power?

8. How would you describe that experience in narrative form, perhaps using a poem?

9. As you recount your experiences of workplace conflict, what insights do they give you about that organization?

10. What insights do they give you about yourself, how you resist abuses of power that affect you, and how you deal with workplace conflicts?

11. What might Brooke and your workplaces learn from your experiences?

12. In what ways is your experience of workplace conflict similar to or different from Brooke's?

CONCLUSION

How people create the collectives that enable them to accomplish more work together than they could individually—how people organize—brings with it the challenge and opportunity of conflict. Conflict in organizations can unite and motivate people, or it can divide and dampen the spirit of their collective and/or individual purpose. These effects and manifestations of conflict can be serious business. Organizational conflicts are further complicated by the fact that constructive or destructive conflicts can be propagated by the choices you make in organizing work.

As well as being serious business, managing organizational conflict is a difficult business. If you learn to think systemically about the relationships among how you organize, how you behave and think in those organizations, and the workplace conflicts you experience, this can make an important difference. You can learn to better interpret the meaning of your workplace conflicts. You can learn to see the connections between your conflict practices and your experience and productivity at work. From there, you can learn to make better choices about how you engage in your conflict and how you participate in and react to those of others who work with you. Such overall changes can often make a significant difference to your workplace culture and your own experience of work.

7

Managing Conflict
in Family Relationships

*"For storytelling is a primary way that families are produced, main-
tained, and perhaps transformed."*

(Langellier & Peterson, 1993, p. 50)

Our families are, for most of us, the communicative context in which we learn how
conflict should and should not be done. The assumptions and values that permeate
everyday communication in our early family experiences become powerful guideposts for how we approach conflict through our adult lives. As the quotation
illustrates, it is through communicating stories that our families are created and
changed; the familial reality thus created affects our thoughts and actions. Our early
experiences can also become powerful guideposts if our decision is to change our
conflict communication, that is, to avoid repeating the past in the families that we
create. Learning to locate your effective and ineffective conflict practices in your
early family experiences is a valuable exercise. Doing this can lead to greater
understanding of why you handle conflict in particular ways, and what opportunities for change exist enabling you to break from practices inconsistent with what
you desire.

Besides helping you to connect the past to the present, this chapter explores
some of the typical conflicts that pervade families. You learn to connect family
conflict issues to the narratives you collect or create from family experiences.
The typical sources of conflict in managing relationships to achieve family goals

are explored. How conflicts arise in the complexity of family dynamics is also discussed. Conflicts are connected to the broader culture surrounding the family. Finally, you can learn to understand opportunities for changing family communication implied by your narratives. You can do this by applying the dialogue skills and narrative understanding from Part I of this book to your family experiences.

Key Concepts, Terms, and Definitions to Learn in This Chapter

- The importance of shared stories or narratives in building family culture

- How to analyze and interpret family conflict narratives

- How having multiple family goals can lead to conflict

- How the typical but complex dynamics of contemporary families often results in conflict

- How particular types of conflict tend to occur at different stages of a family conflict

- How to improve the dialogue in your family

- How to learn from conflicts as a family

- How your cultural context partly shapes your family's conflicts

Key Definitions

- *Family.* A network of people who have strong commitment, including living together and expecting to share a future together

- *Dysfunctional and functional families.* Functional or healthy families are able to negotiate the goals and identities of members such that positive patterns exist in members' conflict practices; dysfunctional families tend to promote negative conflict patterns

---

FAMILY CONFLICT NARRATIVES

As the opening quotation indicates, Langellier and Peterson (1993) explain that telling family stories is a discursive practice producing familial culture. They continue by saying that the term *family* is not always a natural, biological phenomenon, but a form of small group culture produced strategically in family stories.

Family stories both generate and reproduce the family by validating meanings and power relations. This definition is somewhat in contrast to Bochner's (1976) definition of family as "an organized, naturally occurring relational interaction system, usually occupying a common living space over an extended period of time and possessing a confluence of interpersonal images which evolve through the exchange of messages over time" (p. 382).

It is necessary to be careful when defining family, as Langellier and Peterson (1993) caution, not to focus solely on the relationships within the family and ignore the family as a social and cultural product whose dynamics are historical, gendered, and generational. Perhaps we are best served by using Galvin and Brommel's (1982) more inclusive definition, while at the same time recognizing the family is also a product of the context within which it is created. These authors define families as "networks of people who live together over long periods of time bound by ties of marriage, blood, or commitment, legal or otherwise, who share future expectations of connected relationship" (p. 4). The notions of "living together over long periods of time" and "ties" of commitment are what make the family different from other groups to which you may belong.

Stories are the "cornerstones of family culture" (Stone, 1988, p. 17). Family stories are how lived experiences of family are both organized and legitimized (Langellier & Peterson, 1993; McLain & Weigert, 1979). Three goals should be remembered as you collect, examine, and interpret family conflict narratives. First, you can be more effective at learning from your narratives of family conflict. Second, from this learning emerges the goal of negotiating family conflict. Third, ultimately, through this negotiation process, you should strive to build family dialogue. We know the way we approach and manage our conflicts affects the health of our relationships. You can challenge yourselves through your interpretations of your family conflict narratives to rethink and reshape your actions and change unhealthy conflict patterns. You can reflect on your family stories and see them as an inevitable expression of the conditions of which others are a part and how these others create, or how together with them you negotiate a family reality. Some of your experience is your responsibility, but you also must recognize you do not create your family reality alone. Family culture or familial reality is multifaceted, the construction of which is affected by your childhood, the members of your family, family history, your culture, and so on.

Family stories are a product of "the process and structure of interpersonal and small group communication, the information exchange and network of organizational communication, the generation and evolution of intercultural communication, the creativity and force of poetic of rhetorical communication, and so on" (Langellier & Peterson, 1993, p. 50). They are rich sources of learning and opportunity that challenge you to examine myths limiting your willingness to do conflict and your understanding of conflict as a potentially positive experience.

———◄◦►———

Exemplar Narrative: To Father, or Not to Father

—NATALIA

Before I begin my dialogue, I want to make it known that I do accept my father for who he is, and I do respect him for a few of the sincere efforts he has made. But I am admittedly bitter, and I tend to speak passionately in reference to this subject. I do care for him, but I don't love him.

My parents divorced when I was five. My father threw away a brilliant architectural career and went on to practice alcoholism professionally. My mother dedicated her life to making sure my sister and I never followed in his footsteps. My father never could seem to accept responsibility for anything he did in life, and we were no exception. Now, I suppose I'm making him out to be the "boogyman," but it's really not all his fault. Your value system develops according to your family and surroundings. Considering that my dad was brought up the second youngest of eight, with a silver spoon in his mouth, and parents too social for values, his behavior is not all that unusual. Which is not to say it doesn't hurt. In the 20 years I have been on this earth, my dad has assumed minimal responsibility. He has also given little credit to the tremendous feats of my mother or the successes of his children.

My dad has now been sober for seven years, is living in Ohio, and has been remarried to a woman a few years younger than he, who is also recovering, and of whom I sincerely approve. They have been together for two years and she has no children of her own. My father still owes my mother over $50,000 in child support and has only made fleeting attempts to aid in our education as once was promised. But, until last month I was content with my father's immaturity and responsibility. Then I received a phone call that would sour my feelings indefinitely.

My 49-year-old father had had a reverse vasectomy and his wife, Ellen, was pregnant. This is where it started. It progressed when he assumed with joy that the child would be a boy—kick in the face number two—and it escalated when I could no longer bear to pretend that I was happy for him. I began to verbalize things that had been building for years that I had just let slide to save face and the little financial support he gives my mom every once in a while. My first reaction was, "How dare you." It seemed that he had wiped the slate to start over. Even though he couldn't take care of the two children he already had, he thought it would be, and I quote, "neat" to have another one. It all seemed so selfish and impractical, but that was the way I knew my dad. My tone became increasingly sarcastic, and he began to withdraw and avoid. I said things such as, "They're real fun until they need braces or they need to go to college." He skirted these issues, maybe out of guilt or maybe out of blindness, but I felt so denied. I also feared the prospect of another child and/or another mother having to suffer his impracticalities and inconsistencies. I realized by his avoidance that, once again, I would be unable to make him understand my reality. So, once again I reverted back to playing the grownup, swallowing my anger, and shallowly acting as if I accept the whole thing. I figured that some fights can't be won, and I exited the conversation very coldly.

I believed that a resolution had presented itself to me a few months later when my dad called with the news that Ellen had miscarried. As awful an experience as that is, I trust that fate is a very strong force, and I thought they too might see this as being better for everyone in the long run. I was sympathetic to my father on the phone, and I set aside all my negative feelings in the presence of their heartbreak. Deep inside I was relieved.

A month later my mother and sister informed me that Ellen was pregnant again, and I instantly returned to my previous state of mind. I've been avoiding my father's calls, which are few and far between anyway, as I am unable to figure out how to communicate with him. My only hope is that there can be some sort of civil resolution, even though I fear that it will take a very long time to occur, as I will have to monitor his behavior with his new child.

Conflict and Negotiating Family Goals

The need to coordinate activities and maintain relationships requires shared expectations, defined roles, and shared goals. When you think of expectations, you realize that you have developed ideas about who the other people in your families are and how they should behave, not just as family members, but as people in relationships with you. Often, the gaps between what each family member expects are sources for conflict in families. You also have to understand and accept your role and the roles of others in your families. Differing ideas about role definitions are also a source of conflict. Yet another challenge for families is negotiating individual, shared, and incompatible goals simultaneously.

You have to ask yourselves the following questions:

1. Are the definitions of these roles shared?

2. Do I have a sense of my role?

3. How do I perceive my role?

4. How have others defined my role?

5. What is gained in my playing this role?

6. What does it cost me to play this role?

7. Who has the power to define my role?

8. Given my role, what are the expectations for my behavior?

9. Have I ever experienced any guilt in not having lived up to my role?

You can gain much insight by examining family systems using the dialectical perspective outlined by Bochner and his colleagues (Bochner, 1984; Bochner &

Eisenberg, 1987; Cissna, Cox, & Bochner, 1990; Yerby, Buerkel-Rothfuss, & Bochner, 1990). They emphasize three key dialectics that help you understand the dynamics of families. First, family members have to balance the contradiction of being both open and closed with each other. Family members are expressive, revealing, and open and simultaneously concealing, protective, and closed.

Second, family members have to balance their individual identities with their shared family identity, which is the dialectic of differentiation and integration. Baxter and Montgomery (1996) explain the need for families to build interdependence among their members at the same time that individual family members need to establish independence and autonomy from the family unit. Balancing this dialectic characterizes healthy and functional families. A fundamental premise of a systemic view of families is that parents, children, the relationship between parents, the relationships among children, and the relationships among parents and children affect each other (Broderick, 1993; Stafford & Dainton, 1995). Family processes and patterns influence and are influenced by every relationship in the family.

Third, a family system has to manage to be both stable and adaptive. A family with complete stability is not likely to grow or adapt to new circumstances. However, a family that is always unstable and changing with no predictability is also not likely to survive. Both stability and change have to be ever-present qualities of the family.

It is in negotiating a balance between these contradictions that many family conflicts occur. Think of Natalia and her father. Are they interdependent? Do they share a family identity? Perhaps part of their conflict stems from this dialectical tension between individual (autonomy) and family (connected) identity. Her father's life is also changing, thereby changing his personal definition of family to include his new wife and the children they expect to have. Natalia and her father may also need to balance the dialectical tension of stability and change. This possibility of change can be viewed as a positive opportunity for healthy changes in their relationship.

Other potential sources of family conflict include authority, power and membership in families, role and gender identity construction tensions, and the patterns you use to approach conflicts. While conflicts between parents and their children share many features of conflicts found in other close relationships, the power imbalance makes parent-child relationships unique (Osborne & Fincham, 1994). Socialization requires parents to guide their children's behavior to be appropriate and conform to social values. As a result, the goals of children and parents are often at odds, resulting in potential conflicts (Osborne & Fincham, 1994). When we look at parent-child relationships from this perspective, conflict is an ever-present possibility.

As Ting-Toomey (1994) explains, gender refers to "the gender-based belief system developed from the primary sex role socialization process of individuals in a particular society" (p. 54). This belief system influences how individuals hold expectations for "femaleness" and "maleness." Tensions arise when expectations differ. Conflict over the division of labor in marriage, for example, illustrates specific gender roles or identities for individuals and certain forms of the ideal family (Langellier & Peterson, 1993). As Mead (1934) explained, children learn social values through communication with others, who introduce them to meanings, rules, and values of the culture. Having learned these values, most men and women embody them in their own communication, perpetuating, among other things, existing social views of gender (Wood, 1997). Also, conflict experiences you have as a part of the socialization process are likely to influence your later conflict behavior (Osborne & Fincham, 1994). Parents who manage conflict constructively are less likely to neglect or abuse their children and become less apt to teach them these behaviors (Minuchin, 1992).

You may have learned effective conflict patterns growing up that work for you as adults. Or, you may have learned ineffective conflict patterns that you want to change. You can think of how you will and will not act when you create your own families. Understanding where these patterns come from provides insight into how you can change the patterns that do not work for you.

It is no wonder that you have patterns for dealing with conflict within your families. You learn them as children; they are a part of your family history and the context in which you grow up; and these patterns are modeled and reinforced in your interaction with family members. The patterns you learned are also often reinforced by the media. For example, the media conveys mythical fantasy images of married life (Bedard, 1992). Television families such as the Cleavers and the Bradys are presumed to offer implicit lessons about appropriate family life that may affect the way people think about the family (Brown, Childers, Bauman, & Koch, 1990; Cantor & Cantor, 1992; Douglas & Olson, 1995; Greenberg, Hines, Buerkel-Rothfuss, & Akin, 1980; Meadowcroft & Fitzpatrick, 1988). As a result, television families function as social role models. Furthermore, most family interactions on television reflect stereotypical family roles. Specifically, this means in television portrayals, husbands direct wives; wives seek support from husbands; mothers do not oppose or attack; wives and children do not give directions; children seek support; and mothers give directions to children (Greenberg et al., 1980). Television portrayals are both a reflection of and a role model for family relationships (Anderson, 1993). With such unrealistic models reinforcing stereotypical roles and myths about conflict, it is easy to see why you have not all learned effective patterns for dealing with conflict. As you know, your family conflicts cannot be happily resolved within half an hour. The gap between reality and the images you see in the media help to perpetuate conflicts. As you see in Natalia's narrative, the gap between her expectations of her father's role and reality is a major issue that divides them.

Conflict and Family Dynamics

Natalia's narrative illustrates the cyclical nature of conflict. Unresolved conflicts, particularly those associated with post-divorce parent-child relationships, often return to structure relationships. Forgiveness seems to be the hardest part of resolving conflict. Communicating through dialogue is not just about talking something through; it is about approaching a situation, relationship, or experience in a spirit of forgiveness and reconciliation. The talk is often how you strategically reach these goals, but deep family conflicts cannot be resolved if the spirit—ethos—of dialogue is absent. Or, at least it should build through the talk. Sometimes the best that can be achieved is that the participants walk away feeling they did what they could, and that it makes sense within a grander scheme. This is not dialogue per se, but may be a valuable communication experience. Recognizing that others are as imperfect as oneself, and they have their own ways of interpreting and narrating conflicts, is an important learning moment for many in conflict.

It is also important to recognize the mythology that you bring to your early conceptions of families and what people in your families are supposed to do for you. What are your expectations? What is a dad supposed to be like? How is the story of a family such as Natalia's supposed to play out? It is often the gap between myth and lived reality that is so central to the experience and generation of conflicts. What are the underlying assumptions about families and the roles of parents in that system? The narrative also illustrates gaps in communication—the conversations we never have with people until we find ourselves by their deathbeds or gravesides, finally having those conversations—that generate conflicts. What conversations have Natalia and her father never had? Carefully try to construct these conversations. For example, how might those conversations have affected their relationship? How is money symbolic in this story? What does Natalia need to realize about her father? True also is that the strangest conflicts happen in families, and the patterns of the past permeate, structure, and often direct the present and future. Although sometimes it is possible to see these patterns and problematize them, it is hard to change them, at least alone.

There are several family dynamics that can play into your conflict experiences. For example, generational conflicts can take place between people because of differences in attitudes, values, beliefs, and actions. The family hierarchy can be an element or issue affecting family conflicts, as can birth order. Changing cultural values also affect family conflict experiences. For example, Bedard (1992) explains that the women's movement in the United States has been a major force in bringing family conflict out into the open and making it a public issue. This new realism shattered the myth of the typical couple living "happily ever after." Conflicts over the division of household labor are now a major source of friction between family members. Families have to negotiate communication norms and rules, family culture, and conflict styles. It is not surprising that you very often find yourselves in conflicts with your families.

Negotiating Family Stages and Conflict

A predictable series of issues, concerns, and conflicts exist that individuals experience as a result of their place in the family cycle (Carter & McGoldrick, 1988). Each stage of family development requires redefinition of family roles and responsibilities, and this presents new challenges. Typical stages of family development where members are challenged and conflict can develop include establishing a new family, having children, dealing with adolescents, and negotiating adulthood. For example, in families with adults in midlife, these individuals must focus on their own marital and career issues, their changing relationship as their children grow up, and their own parents as they grow old (Halpern, 1994). Conflict in families becomes less manageable if the combination of current and historical stresses overwhelms the family's coping abilities and strength (Bowen, 1978; Carter & McGoldrick, 1988; Minuchin, 1974). The potential for conflict increases when the stress of marriage, career, and care of children and elderly parents falls on the middle-aged adult family members who have been labeled the "sandwich generation"—a role often shouldered by adult women (Dobson & Dobson, 1985; Halpern, 1994; Lang & Brody, 1983).

One way to deal with conflicts brought about by the stress of providing care to elderly parents is avoidance (Halpern, 1994). While Cahn (1992) points out that nonconfrontation can include a variety of behaviors, one of the most powerful is avoidance. Families may have little direct conflict because of this avoidance, or what Shanas (1979) calls the "alienation hypothesis," in which adult children live far away from their parents and rarely see them.

There is no doubt that families in the United States are changing. Economic problems, rising unemployment, and high divorce rates have contributed to the need for many adult children to return to their parents' "empty nest" (Shehan, Berado, & Berado, 1984). There are benefits to multigenerational households, but the potential for conflict is great (Clemens & Axelson, 1985). With more people under one roof, privacy, overcrowding, differences in lifestyles, and disruptions all create the potential for conflict. Family conflict often leads to divorce, but the conflict does not always end there. Emotionally charged conflicts often occur between divorcing spouses over child custody and property settlements.

Cahn (1990b) explains that because Americans are living longer, life cycles, marital stages, and social changes play a large role in intergenerational conflict. Conflict between adult children and their parents occurs because of generational differences, role definition tensions, and the fact that the closer people are, the greater their potential for conflict (Halpern, 1994). Conflicts very often are related to the role reversal that happens when an elderly parent loses independence. Despite the fact that clearly defined roles exist when a parent cares for a child, there are not clearly defined roles when a child cares for a parent.

Cultural Context and Family Conflict

To most people "family" is represented by their own real family or by the stereotypical ideal portrayed everywhere in the media, politics, law, religion, medicine, therapy, and the social sciences (Langellier & Peterson, 1993). It is important to examine how culture is a part of family conflict experiences and family conflict narratives. Culture functions as a context within which family communication takes place. Culture also permeates and partly structures family dynamics. To understand your narrative representations of conflict, you must examine the communicative context that frames your experiences. Doing family conflict is far more complex than following a basic problem-solving procedure. We engage in conflict as people shaped by our family experiences, and our family conflict narratives tell us about the social, cultural, and communicative context creating the conditions for generating, escalating, and resolving conflict.

Feminists and critical theorists have repeatedly illustrated the strategic use of "family" to promote political positions (Barrett & McIntosh, 1982; Osmond, 1987; Thorne & Yalom, 1981). It is unrealistic ideals of family, such as the ones used in political rhetoric, that create dissonance or gaps between your true family experiences and what you feel you "should" be experiencing. In this example, you can see how your cultural values help create a context where conflicts of failed expectations can take place. This is true in Natalia's narrative. Her conflict with her father is situated within a context where a father is defined as someone who is a responsible, practical breadwinner who takes care of his family's emotional and financial needs. The conflict stems, in part, from her inability to resolve the difference between her actual relationship with her father and the relationship she feels she ought to have. Also, notice Natalia's emphasis on her father's age when describing his desire to start another family. Again, you see how the cultural context informs your evaluations of experience. There is a gap between the culturally appropriate age to start a family that informs Natalia's evaluation of her father and her actual experience. You can see from these examples how your communication about your conflict experiences both creates context and how the context structures your communication.

Conflict, Dialogue, and Learning in Families

One valuable goal for families in conflict is to strive to learn from their experiences by exploring their patterns of communication and deciding to adopt or change family conflict models. While some families may repeat "healthy," functional patterns, it is important to recognize when your family repeats patterns of dysfunction or "disease." By using effective negotiation skills, families can build dialogue into their family communication. It is important to keep in mind that "the purpose of dialogue is not to merge voices but to allow for the possibility of differences" (Baxter & Montgomery, 1996, p. 223). It is through these differences that families can reach a solution together. For this to be possible, families have to be open to change. Openness to change is essential to effective family communication (Wilson, Hantz, & Hanna, 1995). People and relationships change, and as family members, you have to notice and adapt to these changes. This is not to say that you should change everything or accept change uncritically. Once you recognize the patterns of your family's communication, you can use dialogue and negotiate to change only the patterns that do not work for you.

ASKING THE INTERPRETIVE QUESTIONS

In the next section, we apply our interpretive questions (Table 4.2) to Natalia's family conflict narrative to explicate some useful insights and gain a deeper understanding of her conflict experience. Rather than asking each question in turn, we have synthesized our observations into the following discussion sections.

Interpreting the Quality of Dialogue and Negotiation

It is quite clear that Natalia's conflict with her father is not an isolated episode of disagreement, but a serious matter that stems from conversations they have and have not had, their past experiences, and differing family relationship and role expectations. You can ask yourselves, What does Natalia need to resolve about her image and myths of families before this conflict progresses? Why cannot she accept that her father has a new life, and that she is not necessarily an important part of it? Why would he continue to call when he gets only her evaluation, is constantly reminded of his mistakes, and hears nothing of her background experiences leading to her anger and judgmental behavior? Would you? Where does her sarcasm come from, and how does it contribute to their conflict?

Although complete peace in this family is an unrealistic goal, striving for more peace—peacemaking—is a valuable pursuit. Natalia's monologue does a good job of justifying her perspective and proving herself right; however, it does little to resolve her conflict with her father. Instead of identifying a common goal to work toward, her narrative expresses only her side of the story. Without a common relational goal, it is difficult to begin to take steps toward dialogue and resolution. Natalia and her father can strive to engage in the creative, productive dialogue that helps produce conditions for more peaceful relationships and discover a common relational goal. Although this is difficult, it is a valuable pursuit if it is important to her.

It also emerges from her narrative that Natalia subscribes to the myth that a conflict always has an answer or solution. Because negotiation involves a collaborative exchange of ideas with the intent of creating agreements, it is clear that Natalia and her father are not negotiating. There are several clues that negotiation skills and practices are absent from this conflict. The relational reality that Natalia and her father create through their choice of avoidance tactics is characterized by separate monologues. They each have a story to tell, but they are not listening or engaging each other and telling a story together. Natalia and her father are not negotiating, but rather navigating the conflict through avoidance. They are ineffective in practicing the characteristics of dialogue.

For example, they have not created a context in which they can address and negotiate their relationship. They are not directly discussing the issue together, nor do their exchanges create mutual understanding. Natalia and her father have yet to engage in collaborative sense-making to reach a shared understanding that can help transform them and their relationship. It appears as though Natalia and her father have yet to talk openly about their relationship at all.

In some ways, Natalia and her father exemplify the characteristics of an argumentation approach to conflict. Their "polarized discourse" prevents them from negotiating the complex middle. This conflict is not made up of two opposing sides; it is comprised of a multifaceted crystal. Arguing to prove and justify your side clearly works against collaboratively developing a shared understanding. You can only imagine how this narrative could act as a catalyst for talk between Natalia and her father if he were to read it. Natalia would also benefit from reading her father's perspective on this conflict and their relationship. Perhaps they cannot hope for complete peace, but the possibility of resolution exists in dialogue. Through communication, Natalia and her father have the potential to improve their relationship, if they strive to have dialogue together.

This may seem unrealistic. Perhaps they just need to have some of the conversations that are currently absent from their relationship. When you realize conflict can be a potentially positive experience, this makes a huge difference in your lives. If Natalia and her father were able to change their communication, even in small ways, imagine how differently they could negotiate the reality of their conflict.

Interpreting Narrative and Conflict Dynamics

Natalia structures her story in a way that brings to life the motives of the participants and makes the story meaningful. By paraphrasing the development of her story, we can see how she achieves this in narrative. The structure of the story emerges as follows:

1. Natalia begins her story with a disclaimer. She juxtaposes the story of her conflict with her feelings for her father. In this way she gives herself "permission" to tell the story she wants.

2. Next, Natalia shares background information that places the conflict in context and introduces the key players: herself, her father, her mother, and her sister. Relevant facts, such as her father's alcohol problem and what a wonderful job her mother has done, are introduced.

3. Natalia then shares her version of her father's biography so the audience gains an understanding of how she sees the events in his life that play into the conflict experience. Notice how negatively she constructs him.

4. The story moves to the present where her father's current situation is explained. Another key player, her stepmother Ellen, is introduced. The scene is now set for Natalia to share her conflict.

5. Natalia explains in monologue form that the news her father is going to have another child starts the conflict. She describes the strategies she uses as she moves through the conflict. At first, she states she can no longer be happy for him and becomes increasingly sarcastic. It is his avoidance of the issue that forces her to revert to "playing the grownup"; she changes her strategy from passive-aggressive and withdraws.

6. Events change and Natalia presents Ellen's miscarriage, which she constructs as the divine intervention of fate, as a possible "resolution" to the conflict. She expresses her sympathy, but is secretly relieved, as she thinks this is for the best.

7. The conflict is rekindled when Natalia learns her stepmother is pregnant again. She returns to her previous conflict strategies and expresses a wish for "some sort of civil resolution."

You can see from the structure of her narrative that Natalia's motives in this narrative are to justify her position and persuade her audience she is right. From the very first paragraph, you can see how the construction of her father, for example, limits the possible ways she can approach the conflict. Their familial reality is not all her responsibility, and it is through a narrative such as this one that she and you can reflect on her actions and learn. It is clear that her pent-up resentment and frustration toward her father affect her conflict, thereby affecting her narrative as well. Her father's motives in this story seem to be to live his life the way he wants. For Natalia, this means acting as a barrier to her goals, continuing with his impractical and irresponsible behavior, and potentially ruining more lives.

Natalia's narrative certainly provides insight into her personal experience. There is no doubt that her relationship with her father has been a disappointment to her. However, it is important to remember that he is a disappointing father primarily when compared to the cultural myth of how a father and a family are supposed to be. He is not a disappointment occurring in a vacuum; her expectations also create her feelings of disappointment. Perhaps by telling and listening to this narrative, Natalia can come to the realizations that will help her accept that an ideal father is never guaranteed. Perhaps she can accept that her father has chosen to move on and build a new life, and that she is not that important to him. Or, she can at least begin to reflect, rethink, and reshape her actions in light of what she may have learned by examining her narrative.

This narrative limits the possibility for dialogue with her father because of its argumentative nature. However, it may still be possible for Natalia to come to new understandings about the conflict by reading her narrative. Perhaps she will decide to have some of the conversations with her father that are absent from their relationship. This would certainly change their communication and, at the very least, engage them in conversation about their relationship, this conflict, and the issues underlying it. However, her narrative creates a particular reality for the conflict and her relationship with her father that makes it unlikely that they will strive to negotiate these issues. It is possible, but her monologic story continues to silence her father, just as her sarcasm does.

Interpreting Representations of Self, Other, and Context

In her narrative, Natalia constructs herself as a mature adult who can accept her father, regardless of his irresponsible ways and the disappointment he has caused. She is bitter and passionate about the subject of her father. Her experiences of anxiety, dread, anger, and disappointment play into this conflict in important ways. She is a child of divorced parents, who feels rejected and denied. Although she is angry and hurt, she is still able, in her eyes, to be "grown up," swallow her anger, and be the bigger person. Although she resigns herself to the fact that she is unable to make her father understand her reality, she claims to understand his, in a sense. She hopes to find a "civil resolution"; however, the reality this creates is that the only suitable option would be for things to go her way. She also constructs herself as the guardian and protector of any future children of her father, as they will undoubtedly be as disappointed by him as she has been.

The metaphor in this narrative appears to be "conflict is war." She attacks her father with arguments; she views his behavior as "kicks in the face"; and she talks about conflict as fights won or lost. This metaphor guides her thoughts and actions in this conflict. The way she describes her bodily feelings affects what she does and says. For example, she "swallows her anger," which leads to more suppression of her feelings and avoidance tactics. It also frames conflict as something you do alone. Her portrayal of conflict does not include sharing, collaboration, or doing conflict together. How does this construction limit her ability to handle conflict with her father?

It appears as if Natalia and her father have not had the meaningful conversations necessary for a clear definition of their relationship and their expectations of each other. As a result, her father's voice and perspective are missing from the story. She constructs him as a brilliant architect turned alcoholic who shirked the responsibility of his first marriage, his children, and his financial obligations. He does not live up to her expectations of what a father should be. He cannot accept responsibility. He is a product of his family, growing up with absent parents and absent values. He is immature, irresponsible, selfish, and impractical. He withdraws and avoids the conflict issue out of guilt or blindness. Now he is starting a new life with a new wife and a new child. Although he is now sober, Natalia is convinced that he will disappoint his new family by repeating his pattern of impracticality and irresponsibility.

Natalia constructs her father as a barrier to her goal of reaching a resolution. Her portrayal of him influences this conflict in important ways. Her negative portrayal severely limits her ability to understand this conflict in another way, thereby limiting her possible strategies and actions.

The context of this conflict is represented as a struggle between an irresponsible, absent father and a rejected child. It is a struggle between the "old" family and the "new" family Natalia's father desires. What is important to recognize are Natalia's assumptions about how fathers are supposed to act and families are supposed to function. It is the gap between the reality of the situation and her myth that, in part, creates the context for this conflict.

Reinforcing this myth is Natalia's construction of her mother as an ideal parent. Her mother supports her assumptions of family life; therefore, her father is the problem, and not her perception of how her life should be. Another important part of the construction of the context is fate. Natalia constructs Ellen's miscarriage not only as a resolution to the conflict, but it validates her assumption that her father's plans are wrong. How can his new family be a good idea if fate has worked so strongly against it? She also constructs a context where acting "civil" in a conflict is the ideal. She presents confrontation as negative and withdrawing, suppressing anger, and "playing along" as positive conflict strategies. However, when her father does the avoiding and withdrawing, it is portrayed as negative and impractical. Direct confrontation of the issues and dialogue are missing from the context of this conflict. Think about the conversations needed between Natalia and her father. What kind of context would they need to resolve this conflict, or at least communicate about it?

The climate of Natalia's relationship with her father and its history has a very definite impact on her experience of conflict. Their lack of dialogue in the past has, in a sense, set the scene for this conflict. The pattern of avoidance and suppressed resentment repeats itself. You can guess that this conflict will end as previous ones have. They will probably fail to confront the issues directly and this will keep their relationship from changing. Natalia's father will probably continue to avoid her sarcasm and judgement, and Natalia will continue to be angry and resentful. Another important element of the context of this conflict is that it takes place in a family transformed by divorce. You can wonder how the conflicts that broke up Natalia's parents' marriage influences this conflict. Growing up as a child of divorced parents certainly affects this conflict and the lives of those involved.

Some Final Reflective Questions on Natalia's Narrative

1. What questions could you ask Natalia about how she grew up that would help you understand the context better?

2. In what ways do you think the past is repeating or affecting the present?

3. How are your family conflict experiences similar to and/or different from Natalia's?

4. What family experiences of yours would you most like to share with Natalia?

5. What valuable lessons could Natalia teach to a couple contemplating having children?

Exercises and Dialogue About Family Conflicts

Family Conflict Exercise: Learning From Others

• Contact your city's or county's mediation center and ask permission to sit in on a family mediation session.

• Take notes on the conflict the family is experiencing, paying close attention to each family member's account of the conflict.

• Write a narrative of the family's conflict experience that brings together each member's story.

• Using the narrative you have constructed for the family, work through the following questions:

   1. In what ways was the mediation session beneficial or damaging to the family?

   2. In what ways did they practice good dialogue skills? Were all the voices in the family included?

   3. Did you find yourself siding with one or more family members over others? What clues did this provide you about your own approach to family conflict?

   4. Was the outcome satisfying to all members? Why or why not?

   5. In what ways was this conflict connected to the family's past conflict experiences?

   6. If you could, what questions would you ask members of the family to gain a deeper understanding of the family conflict dynamics at work?

Family Conflict Exercise: Family Poem

- Write a poem recounting a conflict your family has experienced.

- Share your poem with your classmates and work through the following questions:

   1. What insights did you gain regarding your family and your conflict patterns by writing your poem?

   2. Whose voices are included or excluded in the poem? Why is this meaningful?

   3. What are the elements of dialogue in the poem?

   4. What conflict metaphor does the poem express? Is this metaphor true for the whole family? Does this metaphor work for the family?

   5. What changes would you like to make to your family communication and your own communication that would change the poem?

- Read the following poem and work through the above questions. This family poem recounts the internal tensions and conflict that challenge family ties and communication. Fortunately, taking the time to communicate the reasons for actions, and developing a collaborative narrative account of challenges such as change, work for these members.

————◄○►————

Exemplar Narrative: The Ties That Bind

—KELLY

I belong to a loving family of five, all bonded
together by unbreakable ties.
Although there's something that makes us unique,
moving ten times is the truth I speak.
Indiana, Texas, California, to name a few, Nevada
was the hardest, if you guys only knew.
My father was transferred when I was a teen, was a
senior in school at the age of 17.
I thought these moves had finally come to an end;
little did I know we had to leave once again.

(continued)

(*continued*)

My dad knew a conflict would arise from this, he knew Nevada was a place our family loved and would miss.
Throughout all the pain, the tears and grief, my family needed a compromise and one that could be reached.
Finally, it happened; my father, a remarkable man, sat us all down and explained to us his plan.
I know this is not the best time for us now, so I will go solo and no more crying is allowed.
My father moved to Carolina for a year all alone, making this sacrifice was his love that was shown.
We knew we were strong even through this year, for one thing was certain—that was the bond we hold dear.

The above exercises enable you to examine and express your family conflict experiences more fully. You should also have a good sense of how your experiences compare and contrast with those of others. This process of comparing and contrasting enables you to understand your self and others more deeply.

CONCLUSION

As Langellier and Peterson (1993) explain in the quotation at the beginning of the chapter, you have the opportunity to truly learn about yourselves, your family members, and conflict by examining your family stories. Your family experiences of conflict are powerful guideposts for how you approach conflict throughout your lives. Reflecting on your family conflict patterns is a valuable exercise leading to greater understanding of why you do conflict in a particular way and what opportunities exist for change.

Whether you are improving the dialogue in your current families or contemplating starting your own family, exploring your conflict experiences is a good starting point. In terms of improving an existing family, your conflict experiences identify opportunities for more dialogue. Begin with specific goals for improving dialogue and do not be discouraged when you meet with resistance. Change is difficult, especially in the complex relationships of families.

If you are starting your own family, you can examine the patterns you have inherited from your family and work at building your own family on the patterns you want to see in your children. Work hard and you may eliminate patterns that have been dysfunctional or difficult in your life. The results can be a family prepared to meet the inevitable conflict challenges that are both typical to families and unique to yours.

8

Managing Conflict
in Interpersonal Relationships

"Partners must be sensitive to each other's needs to integrate and to differentiate. They must skillfully balance involvement and privacy, revelation and restraint, disclosure and discretion, predictability and mystery."

(Bochner, 1984, p. 611)

There are probably no communication activities that present us with more challenges and more joys than creating and maintaining close or intimate relationships. However, as the quotation above illustrates, this is an extremely complicated process, filled with contradictions and challenges. This chapter explores how conflict is a productive and sometimes destructive part of romantic relationships and friendships. You learn how to interpret and understand the sources of conflict in close romantic relationships and friendships, the dangers of not addressing conflict, and the benefits of engaging in well-managed conflict. From the narrative account of conflict in an interpersonal relationship, you learn how to interpret clues that indicate whether conflict is being managed effectively. You also learn how to ask deeper questions about why conflict is being handled in particular ways, and how to explore narrative accounts of conflict for opportunities for improving dialogue in relationships. This leads to a more proactive and negotiation-based approach to managing conflict in close relationships.

Key Concepts, Terms, and Definitions to Learn in This Chapter

- How to manage the typical conflicts in romantic relationships

- How to manage the typical conflicts in friendships

- How to manage difficult and complex conflicts in friendships and romances

- How relationships can become abusive and manipulative, and how to manage conflicts in such relationships

- Why mismanaging or avoiding conflicts in relationships usually leads to unwanted results

- How conflict can be beneficial to relationships

- How contextual factors such as culture and gender can be important in a relational conflict

- How to interpret and learn from a relational conflict narrative

Key Definitions

- *Abusive relationship.* When one or more people are emotionally, physically, or even sexually hurt by a relational partner; when this is violent, this is an abusive relationship

- *Manipulative relationship.* When one or more people are the victims of coercive tactics, such as lying, dominating, forcing, or using guilt, to influence their behavior

RELATIONSHIP CONFLICT NARRATIVES

More than any other type of communication, conflict has been said to test the integrity and character of a relationship (Canary & Cupach, 1988; Canary, Cupach & Messman, 1995). People in quality relationships can manage conflict through positive interaction and avoid allowing their anger to escalate to aggression, withdrawal, and destructive patterns. People involved in close relationships, friends and romantic partners, need to learn to negotiate conflict constructively because the risk of hurting each other in interpersonal disputes is very real. Also, conflict can play an important creative and energizing role in the development of effective and satisfying personal relationships, as it often opens up the lines of communication and leads to deeper mutual understanding. Learning from your conflict narratives provides you with opportunities to grow and to develop skills to manage your conflicts constructively. Healthy conflict can open doors to deeper, more fulfilling experiences in your relationships.

Conflict in intimate relationships reflects difficulties under the surface that exist when two interdependent people negotiate being together in a relationship. How people manage their conflicts provides a great deal of information about the nature of their relationship. It provides clues to the definition, relational rules and norms, and what is acceptable and unacceptable. You can use these clues to gain a greater understanding of conflict experiences and learning opportunities for each participant.

◄○►

Exemplar Narrative: Games People Play

—PAM

My boyfriend Jon and I have a very close relationship. We have only had one major conflict during the time we have been dating, but it almost ended our relationship.

I met Jon in July when I began working at Rock-ola Café, where he works as a cook. We played cards together after work a few times, and I felt myself becoming attracted to him toward the end of the year. I noticed that he was very nice, very funny, and loved animals just as I do.

Our manager had a party at his home for the Super Bowl in January, and I went, anticipating that Jon would be there. We finally got together that night. Since that night, we have spent almost every day together. I think that our relationship has developed from spending so much time together. We see each other every day, and spend the night together almost every night. During this time, we have learned about each other mostly by interacting together. We have also had many profound conversations about our own past experiences, things that are important to us now, and what we expect from our futures. However, there are topics that I think we declined to discuss for a reason—because we didn't think they were relevant issues to our relationship. For example, we never talked much about past love relationships. More important, we never discussed past sexual experiences. It is my feeling that discussions like this can hurt both parties much more than they could ever help. This is a very important detail to remember in considering the conflict.

The actual conflict took place one night when we decided to play an old game, "truth or dare," with my roommate Val. In retrospect, I can see that the decision to play this game was unwise. Before the game began, Jon and I promised that we wouldn't get mad at each other about any of our responses when we had to tell the truth. I told Jon to be sure not to ask me anything he didn't really want to know. He agreed that this was very important. However, the three of us drank beer and took shots as we played the game, and the words began to flow more and more freely. We all started out with some silly dares, but realized after a while that once you get to be a certain age, the dares just aren't as exciting. So we continued just to play truth. After we had asked each other a lot of very basic and silly questions, Jon turned to me and said, "How many people have you slept with?" To this I replied, "Remember that we agreed not to ask each other anything we don't really want to know."

For a while, Jon left this subject alone. It really bothered me that he even asked me that, but I tried to overlook it. After it seemed that, once again, we were running out of interesting questions, Jon asked me the same question. Again, I tried to stop him from asking this. However, he would not leave it alone. Finally, with the aid of several beers, I blurted out a very honest answer to his question. He got very upset when he found out the truth. He started running around the house, yelling about how he couldn't believe I had just told him that. He was shocked that I had actually told him the number of people I had slept with in the past. I was angry that he had pressured me so much, and even more angry that I had revealed something that I never intended to reveal to him or anyone else. It was really none of his business, and it wasn't what he wanted to hear. I told him to "get the hell out of my house." Jon left my house with all of his clothes, his Nintendo, and his dog. He walked six miles home. At that point, I felt that our relationship was over. The trust and respect that we had for each other was gone.

When I went to bed that night, I told myself that I didn't want to be with Jon anymore. I was sure that he felt the same. I did not see any way that we could repair the damaged feelings that we both had after this happened. When I woke up the next day, I got together the rest of Jon's belongings that he had left behind. I discussed the situation with my roommate and two of my closest friends. Everyone was surprised by what had happened. They all agreed with me that there was no way to fix this problem.

Later in the day, Jon called me and asked me if he could come over and talk. His tone over the phone revealed little. I could not tell if he was disgusted with me, upset with himself, or a little of both. I planned everything I would say. I felt that Jon was wrong for pushing me to tell him the truth about something and blowing up when I told him the truth. I could not allow myself to feel guilty for things that had been done in the past.

When Jon arrived at my house, he had roses and a card for me. He apologized for asking me the question when I had repeatedly warned him not to do so, and for the things he said to me afterward. He confessed that the truth had disappointed him because, as he said, "No guy wants to hear that he wasn't the first." He said that the actual number wasn't important, it was the fact that I was so willing to tell him. I reminded him that I was not at all willing until provoked by his nagging. I also told him that I felt bad for revealing something that might make him feel somewhat "inadequate." We stayed calm and worked our way through the problem. We finally both agreed that this problem wasn't big enough to ruin our relationship. We agreed to accept each other's disappointment and put the past behind us. Now we laugh at what happened. I honestly feel that we have both forgiven each other for it.

◀○▶

Conflict in Romantic Relationships

When we are in a romantic relationship, whether dating or married, this situation involves some of the most intimate and powerful of emotions. Obviously, we care much more about conflicts with people with whom we are intimate than we do about conflicts with acquaintances. Cahn (1990a) explains that because of the emotional nature of intimate relationships, it is important to manage and resolve interpersonal conflicts to preserve the relationship and promote

- love;

- commitment;

- expressions of affection, esteem and recognition;

- caring, concern, interest with the partner;

- desire to help the partner;

- enjoyment in being together; and

- truth and disclosure.

Interpersonal conflict can be defined as interaction between people expressing opposing interests, views, or opinions (Bell & Blakeney, 1977). People often have differing expectations in a relationship and differing definitions of conflict, intimacy, power, norms, and communication ethics. The very definition of the relationship may vary from one person to the other.

Intimacy is described as a close personal relationship in which two distinct and interdependent people are engaged in joint actions (Braiker & Kelley, 1979). The degree of dependency and the amount of joint action may differ. By definition, intimacy functions as both a source of conflict and a component that complicates or intensifies it. In Pam's narrative, it is the very fact that she and Jon are intimate, both emotionally and physically, that makes the conflict possible; the issue would be null and void if they were not.

Relationship conflict typically occurs because at least one party perceives a violation or threat to relationship rules, themes, beliefs, or boundaries (Galvin & Brommel, 1986). For Jon and Pam, the conflict stemmed partly from the fact that they were negotiating the rules of the relationship and how much disclosure was appropriate. Her disclosure was threatening to him. His continued nagging for an answer to his question was inappropriate to her. Conflict becomes a persuasive process as partners attempt to negotiate these violations or threats. Conflict necessarily involves interpersonal influence and the use of strategies to establish, reinforce, or alter others' thoughts, emotions, and behaviors (Seibold, Cantrill, & Meyers, 1985). Expectation violations and, therefore, conflicts are likely to occur when relational partners hold fundamentally different attitudes and expectations of how to approach romantic love and how to communicate in romantic love relationships. It is a matter of partners negotiating what should be said versus what should remain unsaid.

Conflict is not at all uncommon in romantic relationships; on the contrary, it has even been described as, "a fact of marital life...frequently used to index the level of relational commitment or lack thereof" (Burrell & Fitzpatrick, 1990, p. 167). Relational conflict can take many forms. Couples can fight about a particular content issue, but they may really be fighting about a deeper relational issue. Burrell and Fitzpatrick explain that in general, relational issues fall into one of three categories: distribution of privileges or power issues, affection or love issues, and inclusion or commitment issues. How do these issues play into Pam's conflict with Jon? Potential topics for conflict in romantic relationships are virtually infinite. Couples can fight about money, sex, jealousy, sharing domestic responsibilities, the violation of a confidence, forgetting a special occasion, failing to reciprocate emotions, breaking a promise, not being there in time of need, changing important plans, or differences in attitude, lifestyle, or beliefs. Conflicts can be about specific behaviors, relational rules and norms, or personality traits (Braiker & Kelley, 1979).

Managing Romantic Conflict

While there appears to be much to disagree about, romantic conflicts can also be viewed as opportunities to learn and grow together as a couple. Not only is conflict common in romantic relationships, it is necessary for relational development. According to Ting-Toomey (1994), four specific interaction skills can help you to negotiate and manage intimate conflict effectively:

- Responsive listening
- Perception checking
- Value clarification sharing skills
- Face-management interaction skills

Responsive listening means making a commitment to listen despite the conflict. Jon and Pam were able to work through their conflict in part because they made a commitment to listen to each other. Perception checking means actively using paraphrases to gauge whether you are interpreting the thoughts and feelings of your partner accurately. Value clarification sharing skills means that both partners constantly underestimate the degree to which they understand where their partner is coming from, regardless of how well they know each other. Jon and Pam's conflict was partially the result of the fact that his perceptions of what her answer should be differed greatly from the real answer. The ideal and the real clashed.

Underestimating the degree to which you understand the other person can prevent relational partners from making false assumptions about each other. If Jon hadn't relied so much on his preconceptions of the "right" answer, he might not have been so shocked and upset.

Face-management skills address the issue of human self-respect. Everyone wants and needs to be respected. Don't say things you will regret or can't take back. However, as Pam's narrative illustrates, sometimes this can bring a couple closer. By working through conflict issues and differences, partners in a relationship may come to regard their relationship as unique and more valuable (Braiker & Kelley, 1979; Hays, 1985). When confronting and negotiating differences together, partners may increase their level of intimacy. You can certainly see this in Pam's narrative. Pam and Jon decided to accept the disappointment and move on together.

Conflict in Friendships

Relationships vary in their nature, functions, and characteristics and these differences affect how and why conflict emerges and how it progresses and is managed. Important differences exist between romantic and friendship bonds, such as the absence of an expectation of exclusivity in friendships (Healy & Bell, 1990). Friendships are fragile. Rawlins (1994) calls friendships "mortal" in that they are not constrained by the same legal or religious sanctions as marriage, the same economic contracts as business associations, or by the same blood ties as family. In other words, the possibility of just walking away to resolving conflict in friendships is very real.

Canary, Cupach, and Messman (1995) explain four central themes in the definition of friendship, and these can help you understand the nature of the relationship and what is at stake for friends. Friendship is a voluntary association with few social rules for how to enact the relationship. Equality and reciprocity are extremely important in friendship, and it is characterized by mutuality. Successful conflict management is a must for a lasting friendship, or any type of interpersonal relationship. Without a commitment to the common goal of being together, managing a conflict becomes pointless.

The problems that arise between friends stem in part from the dialectical nature of human relationships (Stueve & Gerson, 1977). There are three contradictions in close relationships, the existence of which virtually guarantee occasional disruptions (Baxter, 1988; Baxter & Montgomery, 1996):

- Autonomy-connection

- Novelty-predictability

- Openness-closedness

The autonomy-connection dialectic is central to friendship as well as romantic relationships because the development of a relationship requires the sacrifice of some independence (Healey & Bell, 1990). The contradiction exists because too much autonomy dissolves the bond that connects friends, and too little disrupts the friendship by destroying individual identities. The novelty-predictability dialectic also creates a source of potential conflict in close relationships. While the establishment of predictability is a central goal in relationship development (Berger, 1987), too much predictability can result in dissatisfaction because of boredom and repetition. Perhaps it was a negotiation of this contradiction that prompted Pam and Jon to risk playing the game of truth or dare in the first place. The openness-closedness dialectic is the struggle between the need for the open self-disclosure that creates an intimate bond and the need for privacy. This dialectic was a central issue in Pam and Jon's conflict. The conflict occurred in the negotiation of the contradiction. While self-disclosure is important, too much is not always a good thing. There is a boundary or balance to be negotiated in every relationship.

Conflicts also occur in friendships for reasons that have nothing to do with negotiating these contradictory elements. Different goals, expectations, and rules are negotiated constantly. Sometimes friends do things you cannot tolerate. Sometimes you meet someone who better satisfies your friendship needs. Dissatisfying events are an inherent part of navigating friendships. Friends' conflicts can be about issues such as competition over jobs and promotions, competition for the affection of others, having different beliefs and values, discussing personal problems, or understanding each other. Adults' friends are very often also their coworkers, roommates, or relatives (Canary, Cupach, & Messman, 1995). This blurring of relationship types can complicate friendship conflicts further. There are a variety of issues that friends must negotiate together, such as support versus competition, personal versus relational goals, relational expectations, relational boundaries and norms, and relational stages.

Difficult Conflicts in Romantic Relationships and Friendships

Conflict can be beneficial or damaging to a relationship (e.g., Hocker & Wilmot, 1995; Roloff, 1976; Rusbult, 1987). You can learn to rescue a conflict from destructive practices, making the overall effect more positive and productive, by learning to recognize destructive conflict characteristics. Conflict can be constructive, helping to resolve differences and bring partners closer together, or it can be destructive, ending in emotional abuse and/or physical violence (Cahn, 1990b; Lloyd & Emery, 1994; Retzinger, 1991).

Escalatory spirals pervade destructive conflicts. Conflicts can get out of hand. What begins as a rational discussion deteriorates into an emotional, heated exchange where strong feelings such as fear and anger change the goals of those involved from useful discussion to destroying the other person's argument. Escalatory spirals can be thought of as the "fight" pattern, and avoidance can be thought of as the "flight" pattern (Hocker & Wilmot, 1995). Avoidance patterns also reduce the chance for productive conflict. When relational partners avoid conflict, they often lose some of their interdependence, begin to harbor resentment or disappointment, and complain to a third party. Avoidance means missed opportunities. Retaliation pervades destructive conflicts. People involved in a conflict ruin chances for change when they hold grudges and wait for opportunities to retaliate. For example, think of the saying, "Don't get mad, get even!" Would Jon and Pam's relationship have continued or grown had they focused on retaliation? Probably not. Inflexibility and rigidity characterize destructive conflicts. Productive conflict management helps prevent physical and psychological aggression in intimate relationships (Lloyd & Emery, 1994).

Abusive and Manipulative Relationships

Although there are numerous occasions for differences to arise in relationships, sometimes they are suppressed rather than expressed (Roloff & Cloven, 1990). As a result, when conflict does occur, it often encompasses accumulated complaints as well as the problem at hand (Zillmann, 1990). As these differences mount, so do negative emotions that may contribute to intense and escalated conflict, a context ripe for the eruption of physical aggression. Demeaning and degrading verbal and nonverbal communication results in and reflects destructive conflict practices. Violence among intimate couples takes many forms. It entails verbal abuse (e.g. Shupe, Stacy, & Hazelwood, 1987), which can escalate to physical abuse, including slapping, shoving, punching, and kicking. In physically abusive relationships, almost anything can trigger an argument that results in an episode of aggression. A significant theme of aggression in romantic relationships is the unpredictability of the aggressive behavior (Lloyd & Emery, 1994).

The Dangers of Absent or Mismanaged Conflict in Relationships

Poorly managed conflicts can be detrimental for several reasons (Barry, 1970). For example, they can create stress and make matters worse. Unresolved conflicts often leave couples unhappy, doubting, and irritated (Cate, Lloyd, & Henton, 1988; Duck, 1988). It is also more common for negative acts from one partner to be reciprocated by negative acts from the other (Gottmann, Markman, & Notarius, 1977; Margolin & Wampold, 1981; Wills, Weiss, & Patterson, 1974).

Several dangers exist when dealing with conflict in interpersonal relationships. There is a danger of monologue. Partners must realize there is not only more than one side to every story, there are multiple ways to tell and interpret each side. Although they may be absolutely certain in their beliefs, it is crucial to recognize that monologue prevents dialogue and reaching solutions together. There is also the danger of repressing conflict. As we mentioned earlier, this can lead to explosive conflicts and in some cases, verbal and physical violence.

There is also the danger of acting powerlessly. By acting powerlessly, you close the door to a multitude of opportunities for reaping the benefits of a conflict experience. When you blame others or the situation, you close off the possibility of learning, changing, and growing from the experience. Assigning blame elsewhere means you have no responsibility for your own experience. "What can I do? It's the other persons fault." This leaves you powerless to manage the conflict constructively and gain from the situation.

The dangers of noncooperative styles, such as competitiveness (win/lose), avoidance, and compromise, (lose/lose), means missed opportunities. Missed opportunities occur, in part, because of negative conceptualizations of conflict. When you view conflict as a negative thing, one in which you compete, avoid, or lose, you miss all the opportunities to benefit from the experience and grow, both individually and relationally. Competitive conflict behavior includes directly attacking or criticizing the other person, doing whatever it takes to "win." Avoidance and withholding grievances or irritations also does not seem to be an effective way to manage conflict in interpersonal relationships (Roloff & Cloven, 1990). If the grievance or irritation is not brought to the attention of the relational partner, he or she has no reason to assume a problem even exists. In fact, relational partners who avoid conflicts have more difficulty resolving their disputes (Sillars, 1980). Although avoiding certain conflicts can be constructive in relationships, failing to directly confront important disagreements or conflicts over the course of time can be dysfunctional. Very often you avoid communicating your grievances or complaints because you fear negative reactions from your relational partner. It is not surprising, considering this may lead to an argument, which could include raised voices, criticism, disagreement, and sarcasm (Resick et al., 1981). Verbal attacks and criticisms aimed at intimates are frequently things people wish they had not said. You may avoid conflict simply because you fear that raising certain issues might be the end of the relationship. However, verbal disagreements produce increased agreement and greater understanding of others' perspectives than does avoidance (Knudson, Sommers, & Golding, 1980).

The Benefits of Conflict in Relationships

Many scholars recognize that interpersonal relationships inherently require conflict. A fundamental feature of conflict management is the dimension of engagement versus avoidance (e.g., Hocker & Wilmot, 1995). Conflict engagement implies overt confrontation of conflict issues instead of withdrawing and not dealing directly with the issue at hand. We should ask ourselves, What is the degree of directness/indirectness, activity/passivity, and unequivocality/equivocality in the relationship? Another fundamental feature of interpersonal conflict mentioned earlier is whether the conflict is constructive or destructive.

Approaching conflict positively or constructively can generate energy, both romantic and creative. It has the capability to move a relationship forward. By opening relational dialogue, partners or friends can constructively confront each other so the answer to the conflict emerges between them (Arnett, 1980). In this dialogical approach to conflict, neither person alone possesses the truth, but the truth emerges during their struggle with each other (Buber, 1972; Hocker & Wilmot, 1992; Stewart, 1978). Dialogue is by no means easy; it requires a serious commitment to the relationship and to one's own principles at the same time. However, the benefit is that dialogue leads to collaboration. As Baxter and Montgomery (1996) explain, good dialogic exchanges are not built on stubborn monologues and pronouncements, but on the ability to not only express one's ideas but also to understand the other person's point of view and work with that person to change the rules and come up with new and creative ways to work through a conflict together. This creates opportunities for change, generates mutual understanding, and creates a context where interpersonal partners can learn from their relational conflicts. Partners can learn what their relational expectations are and how to share them and revise them, if necessary. They can begin to decide together how they want to experience communication in their relationship. They can decide the conversations they want to have, and ultimately create together a relational reality they find satisfying, enjoyable, and fulfilling. Friends and couples can achieve these benefits by using conflict narratives as a starting point to learn and grow from their conflict experiences together.

Hocker and Wilmot (1995) present some basic communication skills that can help interpersonal partners manage their conflicts constructively and create an atmosphere of trust and respect that facilitates relational dialogue.

- Speak your mind and your heart

- Listen well

- Express strong feelings appropriately

- Remain rational as long as possible

- Summarize and ask questions

- Give and take

- Avoid harmful statements

Aside from specific skills you can practice when communicating with your interpersonal partner in a conflict, there are a variety of strategies you can use to stimulate relational dialogue in your interpersonal relationships. You can begin by listening for conflict clues. You can use statements and questions to express conflict experiences. Friends and romantic partners can use conflict narratives for interpreting relational meaning and learn from sharing their narrative interpretations. From this, you can develop shared narratives about conflict that demonstrate a deeper relational understanding.

Understanding the Context of Relationships

The Cultural Context of Relationships

The relational culture friends and couples develop over time represents their shared symbolic world reflecting the nature or identity of both the relationship and its partners (Canary, Cupach & Messman, 1995). However, humans are cultural beings before they are beings in interpersonal relationships. "Individuals first learn the implicit scripts of interpersonal relationship development within the webs of their culture...people learn the values, norms, and rules of appropriate or inappropriate conflict conduct, and effective or ineffective conflict behavior within the primary socialization process of their culture" (Ting-Toomey, 1994, p. 47). Your cultural perspectives or lenses influence how you view conflict itself and its management and resolution. For example, in U.S. culture, we tend to view the other in a conflict as a competitive opponent. Your cultural perspective provides clues you can use to gain a greater understanding of your conflict experiences and why you approach conflicts the way you do.

Gender Dimensions of Relationships

The incorporation of gender is critical to any serious attempt to understand intimate relational conflict between men and women (Ting-Toomey, 1994). Sex differences in perception and interpretation may function as a source of conflict in intimate relationships (Cahn, 1990a). There are different cultural expectations, demands, and stereotypes for men and women in intimate relationships. How do these cultural expectations play into Pam's narrative? What cultural assumptions about women and sex play into the conflict? Why is Jon's past sexual history not a part of this conflict narrative? What does that say about your culture's expectations about appropriate sexual activity for men versus women? Examining the gender dimensions of a relationship, as well as the gendered stereotypes, can help you understand the underlying issues of a particular conflict experience.

Women and men also differ in conflict communication behavior. These different behaviors are demonstrated in the common cycle that occurs in intimate relationships known as the demand-withdrawal cycle. In this cycle of behavior, the female makes demands or "nags" and the man withdraws, and because he withdraws, she continues to nag. It is a never-ending and unproductive cycle where both parties are to blame, although they each see the other as the one at fault. Women view their more confrontational behaviors as legitimate attempts to get closer to their partners and as a means of resolving issues. Men, unfortunately, experience these attempts as threatening ("nagging") and unproductive. Clearly, these behavior patterns indicate opposing, strongly held meaning, which provides fertile ground for demand-withdrawal escalation sequences (Weiss & Dehle, 1994). Although both men and women may be inclined to demand when they seek a change in their partner, men may be more inclined than women to withdraw (e.g., Gottman, 1990). This is just one example of how gender differences affect how you both approach and behave during a conflict. Understanding the influence of your own and your partner's gender on your conflict experiences can help you understand the dynamics of the conflict and why you approach it the way you do. The style you use when approaching interpersonal conflict has a huge impact on the outcome. What is important to recognize is that your gender affects that style.

You can learn much about how to manage conflict from Ting-Toomey's (1994) approach to managing intercultural conflict. She explains that of all the elements involved in managing intercultural conflict, knowledge is the most critical. Without cultural-sensitive knowledge, couples cannot learn to uncover the implicit ethnocentric lenses or assumptions they use to interpret and evaluate events in their intimate conflict situations. If you broaden this idea and use it to approach a variety of personal differences in interpersonal conflict, whether these differences are gender, race, culture, or age related, you can begin to engage in dialogue together. Knowledge of your interpersonal partner's background provides valuable clues that aid in understanding where your partner is coming from and how you can work together in a conflict situation.

ASKING THE INTERPRETIVE QUESTIONS

The system of interpretive questions developed at the end of Chapter 4 to help you interpret conflict narratives (see Table 4.2) guides the following analysis of Pam's narrative. Instead of asking questions one by one, we have synthesized our observations where possible. Several useful insights emerge when we apply these questions to Pam's narrative.

Interpreting the Quality of Dialogue and Negotiation

In some ways, Pam's narrative creates a sense that the conflict is both inevitable and necessary in her relationship with Jon. It is inevitable in that she describes the experience with Jon as the only major conflict the couple ever had. Because conflict is such an integral part of relational development, we may infer they were, in a sense, due for a conflict. By avoiding taboo subjects, such as past relationships and sexual history, the couple had not negotiated the dialectic of openness and closedness to reach a mutually acceptable balance. The conflict was also inevitable in that they agreed to play a game involving a great deal of personal risk and self-disclosure. The conflict was necessary so the couple could begin to negotiate the contradiction of openness and closedness together and move the relationship to a different place. In retrospect, the couple's ability to renegotiate the relational definition together, bringing them closer together, was beneficial.

On the other hand, the conflict can be interpreted as damaging to the relationship in two ways. First, what was said in anger can never be taken back. Second, Jon now knows something about Pam she states she never wanted to reveal about herself, which is a very real personal risk for her. However, as she explains, they now laugh about what happened. You can assume they have truly dealt with the experience and have been able to move on together.

There are several myths about relationships and communication at work in Pam's narrative. One is that relationships are built through interaction in the present, that the past is not important. Inappropriate topics from the past should be avoided. Pam explains that they never discussed the taboo topic of past sexual history because she does not believe it would have done any good. She is implying that communication is not just strategic, but should be used for only positive discussions, and not for issues irrelevant to the relationship. This assumption ties into her approach to conflict as a game of "all or nothing." She states she thought their relationship was over after Jon stormed out because trust and respect had been broken. She could not see how the relationship would recover from such an event. She also sees communication as a very serious process where you do not ask questions when you are not prepared to hear the answer. Her understanding of Jon and the situation led her to decide the answer to his question would not be well received. Her all-or-nothing approach to both conflict and communication, however, limited her options. She could have lied, not answered the question, or distorted the truth. However, from her perspective, the only possible response was what she calls "a very honest answer." In turn, Jon chose to interpret her answer as an act of aggression.

What Pam and Jon may learn from this conflict narrative is that there are multiple interpretations available. If you accept that you are responsible for your own experiences, you can begin to make wise choices as to what interpretations you want to use. In essence, Jon chose to feel threatened, just as Pam chose to feel required to answer, although they may not have seen it that way at all. For example, another interpretation of Pam's disclosure is that she is proud of how many people she slept with, but because of cultural constraints, it is not acceptable for her to openly announce how sexually desirable she can be. As a result, she is "pressured" into disclosing the truth. You could construct her as a woman of the world, a woman who is highly desired and in a position of power. Jon could have decided what was important was that regardless of who she could have, Pam had decided to be with him. The partners in this conflict can learn a great deal by studying this narrative and expanding their possible alternatives by explicating multiple interpretations.

Pam and Jon effectively negotiated this relational conflict by renegotiating their relationship's rules and boundaries. They decided together that this episode was not important enough to end their relationship. They listened to each other's point of view and decided to put the past behind them. This happened after Jon ran around Pam's house yelling and stormed out. It is not until they have both had a chance to come to terms with their anger that they were able to negotiate a new relational reality. Their conflict style at first is very all-or-nothing and heated. However, they confront the conflict directly. They do not avoid and repress it. They talked through the conflict together once their initial anger had subsided. They are direct and the conflict ends up being handled constructively. Ultimately, they appear to take each other's perspectives, engage one another, and reach a mutually satisfying decision about their relationship.

Interpreting Narrative and Conflict Dynamics

The nature of Pam and Jon's relationship is crucial to understanding her conflict narrative. They are a young, dating couple. Their relationship is very exclusive. They see each other every day and spend most nights together. Perhaps it is their exclusivity, in part, that incites their conflict. Pam's unwillingness to discuss the past and Jon's need for reassurance that he is special to Pam provides the backdrop for their conflict. Her narrative works because we understand the nature of their relationship and their relational communication behavior, as well as the significance of the topic.

Pam structures her story to bring to life the motives of the participants in a way that makes the story meaningful. By paraphrasing the development of the narrative, you can see how she achieves this. The structure of the story unfolds as follows:

1. Pam provides the background of the context and the nature of the relationship. You learn they have a close relationship that is very exclusive. She provides clues about their relational communication, especially as it relates to the conflict.

2. You move to the beginning of the actual conflict episode. Pam reflects on how she felt and provides details that set the scene.

3. They play the truth or dare game and Jon asks her a question she does not want to answer. They continue and Pam describes how she felt and that Jon continues to press her to disclose information she does not want to.

4. The climax of the story occurs when Pam answers Jon's question. She recounts his reaction and the events that lead to his exit.

5. Pam reflects on the event and explains that the relationship is over. She goes through the process of perception checking with her friends.

6. Jon calls her and they agree to meet to talk. Pam describes what was going through her mind. Pam makes a decision as to what she is going to tell Jon.

7. The resolution process is explained. Pam tells you how they worked through the conflict. She leaves you with their agreement to stay together, and tells you the episode was not important enough to end the relationship.

Pam wants to avoid discussing a topic she knows to be risky. She attempts to persuade Jon not to enter into a conversation she does not wish to have. However, she portrays Jon as forcing her into a position where she is required to answer. In a way, she constructs the conflict episode as out of her control, thus minimizing her sense of responsibility. She answered the question only because he kept nagging her. She appears powerless to stop him from making her answer. They had tried to set boundaries for the game. However, the story is constructed so you are given to believe alcohol is the reason—that is, through no fault of their own, the boundaries were crossed.

You can imagine what the participants might learn from this conflict story. They can learn the issues important to the relationship. They may have a deeper understanding of the other person, their desires, what they want from the relationship and from each other. They have shared a new experience that has moved their relationship to a different place. They may have learned what they want to change about how they approach conflict or the filters they use to interpret communication events.

Telling and listening to this story creates new opportunities for interpretation. At first, the conflict appears to be a simple, topic-specific issue. However, a closer reading reveals there are deeper relational issues at work as well. This is not just about how many people Pam has slept with, but about trust, being open, being with someone who makes you feel special, setting acceptable boundaries, and so on. There are numerous interpretations. It is by being open to this multiplicity of opportunities that interpersonal partners can truly learn from each other and their experiences.

Interpreting Representations of Self, Other, and Context

In her narrative Pam constructs herself in multiple ways. She appears wiser or superior to Jon in some ways and powerless in others. She is wiser in that she knows they should not discuss her past sexual history. She seems to have an idea as to the outcome of her disclosure and she wants to avoid it. She also thinks she knows the outcome of the conflict once it has occurred, deciding the relationship must be over and going so far as to collect all of Jon's belongings to return them. Pam also portrays herself as avoiding this topic because she is a caring individual. She states there is no use in discussing topics when they can hurt someone. However, she also portrays herself as powerless when she describes that she only answered because she was forced to. To use her words, "he would not leave it alone." She describes herself as pressured into answering the question, even though she admits this is something she never intended to reveal to anyone. Pam portrays herself as not responsible for the conflict because all she did was tell the truth. She refuses to feel guilty about things that happened in the past that she cannot change. Conflict is very all-or-nothing for Pam and this seems to guide her actions. By "all or nothing," we mean black or white. She does not see the relationship as a flexible, ongoing system that can withstand bad situations and still continue.

Jon is portrayed as the other in Pam's narrative. Although it is clear she cares about him very much, he is portrayed as forcing her to disclose. He asks an inappropriate question and then yells and runs around when he hears the answer. He is constructed as being responsible for the conflict because he is the one who would not leave the subject alone. He was warned not to ask anything he did not really want to know and yet he continued. He is the one who apologizes, who shows up with roses and a card, reinforcing this construction of him as the instigator.

Important to the context of the conflict is the nature of the relationship. Pam and Jon are dating and are very exclusive. Their relational communication, although deep and fulfilling, does not include certain taboo topics. Although they agree to take part in a risky game, they set boundaries that end up being broken. The context partly helps to create the conflict itself. There are also very important cultural values about sex and men and women at work in this narrative.

Pam's disclosure may make Jon feel "inadequate." Jon did not want to know that he was not "the first." These are cultural myths about appropriate and inappropriate sexual activity. In some cultures (including the United States), although it is acceptable, even expected, for men to have a keen understanding of how to have sex, women should not have as great an understanding and certainly not a great many sexual partners. Although these stereotypes are changing, they still exist. For example, women are still far more likely to be called "sluts" than men. Society does not typically construct men in that way. Myths about "good girls" and "bad boys" play an important role in this conflict. The ideal is a virgin woman and a man of the world. The conflict happens when reality does not match the fairy tale ideal. This context plays an important role in how Pam constructs herself, Jon, and their motives. This conflict is also about relational ideals and learning the skills necessary to one day be a part of the ultimate relational ideal in our culture, marriage.

Learning From the Dynamics of Interpersonal Conflicts

Learning from Pam's conflict experience can help you think about your various interpersonal conflicts. You can learn there are multiple interpretations of each side of a story, and some interpretations are very helpful to you. You can also learn bad things can happen in a relationship, people can argue and say hurtful things, but that does not necessarily mean the relationship is over. Sometimes conflict has to occur for people in interpersonal relationships to realize it is time to redefine the rules or renegotiate a dialectical balance. Sometimes it takes conflict to illustrate to those involved just how important and strong their relationship is.

Some Final Reflective Questions on Pam's Narrative

1. How can alcohol and other drugs affect the process and outcome of a conflict?

2. How do you typically engage in self-disclosure when you are building a new romantic relationship?

3. How might Pam and her boyfriend retell this story as a good "getting to know you" tale?

4. What good conflict stories have brought you closer to your significant other?

5. How would you have handled the conflict situation that Pam found herself in? What, if anything, would you have done differently from Pam or her boyfriend?

Exercises and Dialogue About Interpersonal Conflicts

Interpersonal Conflict Exercise: Working With Friends and Romantic Partners

Read Shelly's narrative and work through these questions:

1. How do the participants negotiate their roles within the conflict?

2. How does the blurring of lines between friends and family complicate the conflict?

3. What impact does the conflict have on the interpersonal relationships of the participants?

4. What seem to be the rules or expectations of these interpersonal relationships?

5. What rules or expectations of these relationships are violated or threatened?

6. How do you think they can constructively work through this conflict?

7. What can the participants learn from this conflict?

(continued)

(*continued*)

Knowing what you do about dialogue and narrative approaches to conflict, write a paper explaining how you would approach this conflict. Describe what you would say and how you would negotiate the situation from Shelly's perspective.

Interpersonal Conflict Exercise: The Other's Perspective

Using Shelly's narrative, write the story of the conflict experience from Dave's perspective. Then reflect on these questions:

1. What can we learn by taking the perspective of the other people in our conflict experiences?

2. How does this exercise facilitate dialogue?

3. Was this exercise difficult? Why? What elements were challenging to you?

4. Can you apply this exercise to a conflict experience in your own life?

Exemplar Narrative: We Can't Get Away From Our Shadow

—SHELLY

My fiancé Paul and I just recently became engaged after having dated for eight years. We have our share of conflicts, but we have always been successful at working through them. However, there is one conflict we cannot seem to overcome. It does not involve and Paul and me directly, but rather a third person. This person is Paul's cousin Dave. Dave is one year older than Paul and ever since they were infants, they have grown up together. They are best friends. They both went to the same high school and the same church and enjoy the same activities. This may sound like the ideal friendship so far, but things aren't always what they seem.

The problem is, Dave is a copycat. Everything Paul and I do, we can be sure that Dave is right behind attempting to do the exact same thing. When Paul and I went off to college in Virginia, Dave decided that would be a good place to go as well. When Paul and I decided to get married last May, Dave also decided to ask his girlfriend to marry him. While this may all sound like coincidence, Paul and I know better. For years, we have been walking around on eggshells, careful not to mention our next move to Dave because, as soon as we do, it will be mimicked.

Dave is a very good friend to us, and we do things together all the time. When we first realized he was doing everything we did, we felt a little flattered, but it didn't take long to realize that it was getting out of hand.

Since we all went to college together, things have only been worse. Last Valentine's Day Dave asked me, "Shelly, what are you and Paul doing tonight?" I thought it would be okay to tell him because we had made reservations out of town at a very nice lodge. I told him where we were going and, at that time, he still didn't have plans. As Paul and I walked into the restaurant that evening, there sat Dave and his girlfriend. I was so angry I could not even enjoy myself. It seemed too blatant to me, but Dave acted as if nothing was out of the ordinary.

Another incident that really infuriated me happened just months ago when Paul and I were deciding where we would live once we were married. After much thought, we decided to fix up his grandmother's house and live in it for a few years. One day Dave, in his roundabout way, asked Paul what our plans were after we were married. Although Paul knew better, he confided in him. It didn't even take Dave one week to act on that information and he is presently living in that old house, and plans to once he is married. I believe he honestly thinks it was his original idea.

This incident made me so angry. Paul begged me not to say anything because he didn't want me to do anything that would wedge any barriers in the family. One side of Paul's family refuses to be around the other because of past conflict, and Paul does not want the same thing to happen to us. Although he didn't want me to say anything, I couldn't just let it pass without a word. So, I rehearsed what I would say and I hoped I would be very forceful. When the time came, however, I was much less forceful and effective than I had hoped. It is during times like these that I can feel my temperature rising, my hands sweat, and my blood boil. I feel like any moment I could just snap. However, I guess Dave just really knows how to push my buttons. I view myself as the victim because it seems that I can't get away from his childish actions.

With our wedding only two weeks before that of Dave and his fiancé, I can only imagine the conflicts that lie ahead. Already he is asking me what caterer and florist I am using. I conveniently avoid the answer. He asked me where we were going on our honeymoon and I purposely denied that I knew. The most recent thing that happened has still got me fired up. Paul and I have a horse farm, so our wedding is going to have a western theme. Dave knows we are going to hold our rehearsal dinner at our barn, and we are going to have a bluegrass band come in and play for us. Last Wednesday night Dave said, "I've been thinking that it would be neat to have my rehearsal dinner at a barn and maybe have a bluegrass band come in and play." I thought I was going to blow my top but, before I could, Paul responded. I could hear the frustration and disbelief in his voice as he said, "Dave, why don't you just walk down the aisle right behind us and it would save everybody a whole lot of money?" I thought Dave might get the picture or be offended or something, but all he did was chuckle and say, "Yeah, that's the truth."

This is starting to take its toll on me and I don't know how much I can take. Recently, I've started feeling very bitter toward Dave and staying away from him. Paul can tell it is really getting to me, but just wants to keep the peace in the family, and I understand. Is it possible that Dave is living out his life through Paul? Is Dave really not aware that he is our shadow? Should I say something or should I try to maintain peace? Should I risk causing this generation of the family to split? What is the real reason behind Dave's actions? I'm worried about the consequences if I say something, but I know for myself that I need to find a productive way to deal with this conflict. We hate that we have to sneak around and avoid telling Dave our plans for fear that he will copy us. Now, when he asks us a question we avoid a direct answer. This keeps him probing more and more but, for the meantime, Paul and I have agreed that this is the best way to keep peace and avoid the risk of being copied.

The above conflict is certainly a strange one, and probably one few of you have experienced. It is, however, symbolic of more typical relational concerns such as how to create space and privacy to have an intimate relationship, how to negotiate relationships with friends and relatives, and how to have difficult conversations with those who violate your relational expectations. There are lessons for us all in her experience.

CONCLUSION

As Bochner explains in the quotation at the beginning of this chapter, negotiating interpersonal relationships is an extremely complex and difficult process requiring skill, sensitivity, and an investment of time and energy. Managing conflict in friendships and romantic relationships further complicates the process. Such friendships can often be perceived by us as fragile and vulnerable. We often avoid conflicts with friends and lovers just to keep things normal and to avoid losing a person we feel so strongly about. Our hearts can be a powerful force in guiding our behavior. We also often think close relationships should not have conflicts, and may even view conflict as a sign of failure in a relationship.

However, we can learn to view conflict as a positive force necessary for the development and maintenance of a worthwhile and fulfilling relationship. This chapter should challenge you to examine your own interpersonal conflicts for opportunities to learn, grow, and change. You should also challenge yourselves to search for the multiple voices and multiple interpretations of those voices that occur in your conflict experiences and strive to learn from them.

In this book you have worked through the development of interpretive skills that help you better understand the conflict that surrounds you. You have learned how to talk about your experiences through personal narratives. You have learned to ask questions of your conflicts from examining those narratives. And, you have learned to look for opportunities to take the answers to those questions back to your lives so you can better manage your conflicts. Specifically, you should become more attuned to the possibilities that conflict situations embody for improving dialogue between people and for opportunities to change your everyday reality, of which conflict is an important part. As a final thought in this book, we simply challenge you to continue developing your interpretive skills and your communication, as you both create and find yourselves in conflict.

Continue to recognize the importance of conflict in your life and in the world. Work to sharpen your conflict management skills, build your negotiation skills, broaden your dialogue skills, and learn from your conflict experiences. Set goals for working on conflicts in particular aspects of your lives and recognize when you are making progress. Do what you can in your conflicts to bring peace to your relationships, families, workplaces, and communities. Take what you can from your conflicts to build the life narrative that brings peace to you.

References

Agar, M. H. (1996). *The professional stranger: An informal introduction to ethnography.* New York: Academic Press.

Albrecht T. L., & Hall, B. J. (1991). Facilitating talk about new ideas: The role of personal relationships in organizational innovation. *Communication Monographs, 58,* 273-288.

Allison, D. (1996). *Two or three things I know for sure.* New York: Penguin.

Anderson, P. A. (1993). Cognitive schemata in personal relationships. In S. Duck (Ed.), *Individuals in relationships* (pp. 1-29). Newbury Park, CA: Sage.

Applegate, J. L., & Delia, J. G. (1980). Person centered speech, psychological development, and contexts of language use. In R. N. St. Clair & H. Giles (Eds.), *The social and psychological contexts of language* (pp. 245-314). Hillsdale, NJ: Lawrence Erlbaum.

Arnett, R. C. (1980). *Dwell in peace: Applying nonviolence to everyday relationships.* Elgin, IL: Brethren Press.

Arnett, R. C. (1986). *Communication and community: Implications of Martin Buber's dialogue.* Carbondale: Southern Illinois University Press.

Arnett, R. C. (1997). Communication and community in an age of diversity. In J. M. Makau & R. C. Arnett (Eds.), *Communication ethics in an age of diversity* (pp. 27-47). Urbana: University of Illinois Press.

Atkinson, P. (1990). *The ethnographic imagination: Textual constructions of reality.* London: Routledge.

Atkinson, P. (1992). *Understanding ethnographic texts.* Newbury Park, CA: Sage.

Austin, D. A. (1996). Kaleidoscope: The same and different. In C. Ellis & A. P. Bochner (Eds.), *Composing ethnography: Alternative forms of qualitative writing* (pp. 206-230). Walnut Creek, CA: AltaMira.

Banks, A., & Banks, S. P. (Eds.) (1998). *Fiction and social research: By ice or fire.* Walnut Creek, CA: AltaMira.

Baron, R. A. (1984). Reducing organizational conflict: An incompatible response approach. *Journal of Applied Psychology, 69,* 272-279.

Barrett, M., & McIntosh, M. (1982). *The anti-social family.* London: Verso.

Barry, W. A. (1970). Marriage research and conflict: An integrative review. *Psychological Bulletin, 73,* 849-857.

Bateson, G. (1972). *Steps to an ecology of the mind.* New York: Ballantine Books.

Bateson, G. (1980). *Mind and nature: A necessary unity.* New York: Bantam Books.

Bauman, R. (1986). *Story, performance and event: Contextual studies of oral narrative.* Cambridge: Cambridge University Press.

Baxter, L. A. (1988). A dialectical perspective on communication strategies in relationship development. In S. Duck (Ed.), *Handbook of personal relationships* (pp. 257-273). Chichester, UK: Wiley.

Baxter, L. A., & Montgomery, B. M. (1996). *Relating: Dialogues & dialectics.* New York: Guilford.

Bedard, M. E. (1992). *Breaking with tradition: Diversity, conflict, and change in contemporary American families.* New York: General Hall.

Bell, E. C., & Blakeney, R. N. (1977). Personality correlates of conflict resolution modes. *Human Relations, 30,* 849-857.

Benhabib, S., & Dallmayr, F. (1990). *The communicative ethics.* Cambridge: MIT Press.

Bennett, S., & Brown, J. (1995). Mindshift: Strategic dialogue for breakthrough thinking. In S. Chawla & J. Renesch (Eds.), *Learning organizations: Developing cultures for tomorrow's workplace* (pp. 185-196). Portland, OR: Productivity Press.

Benoit, P. J. (1997). *Telling the success story: Acclaiming and disclaiming discourse.* Albany: State University of New York Press.

Berger, A. A. (1997). *Narratives in popular culture, media, and everyday life.* Thousand Oaks, CA: Sage.

Berger, C. R. (1987). Communicating under uncertainty. In M. E. Roloff & G. R. Miller (Eds.), *Interpersonal process: New directions in communication research* (pp. 39-62). Newbury Park, CA: Sage.

Berger, P. L. (1998). *The limits of social cohesion: Conflict and mediation in pluralistic societies.* Boulder, CO: Westview.

Bethanis, S. J. (1995). Language as action: Linking metaphors with organizational transformation. In S. Chawla & J. Renesch (Eds.), *Learning organizations: Developing cultures for tomorrow's workplace* (pp. 185-196). Portland OR: Productivity Press.

Blake, R. R., & Mouton, J. S. (1970). The fifth achievement. *Journal of Applied Behavioral Science, 6,* 413-418.

Blakely, E. J. (1979). Toward a science of community development. In E. J. Blakely (Ed.), *Community development research: Concepts, issues, and strategies* (pp. 15-24). New York: Human Science Press.

Bochner, A. P. (1976). Conceptual frontiers in the study of communication in families: An introduction to the literature. *Human Communication Research, 2,* 381-397.

Bochner, A. P. (1984). The functions of communication in interpersonal bonding. In C. Arnold & J. Bowers (Eds.), *Handbook of rhetorical and communication theory* (pp. 544-621). Boston: Allyn & Bacon.

Bochner, A. P., & Eisenberg, E. (1987). Family process: Systems perspectives. In C. R. Berger & S. Chaffee (Eds.), *Handbook of communication science* (pp. 540-563). Newbury Park, CA: Sage.

Bochner, A. P., & Eisenberg, E. (1994). Perspectives on inquiry: II. Theories and stories. In M. Knapp & G. Miller (Eds.), *Handbook of interpersonal communication* (2nd ed., pp. 21-41). Thousand Oaks, CA: Sage.

Bochner, A. P., & Eisenberg, E. (1997). It's about time: Narrative and the divided self. *Qualitative Inquiry, 3,* 418-439.

Boje, D. M. (1991). The storytelling organization: A study of story performance in an office-supply firm. *Administrative Science Quarterly, 36,* 106-126.

Bowen, M. (1978). *Family therapy in clinical practice.* New York: Jason Aronson.

Braiker, H. B., & Kelley, H. H. (1979). Conflict in the development of close relationships. In R. L. Burgess & T. L. Huston (Eds.), *Social exchange in developing relationships* (pp. 135-168). New York: Academic Press.

Brettell, C. B. (1996). *When they read what we write: The politics of ethnography.* Westport, CT: Bergin & Garvey.

Broderick, C. B. (1993). *Understanding family process: Basics of family systems theory.* Newbury Park, CA: Sage.

Brown, J. (1995). Dialogue: Capacities and stories. In S. Chawla & J. Renesch (Eds.), *Learning organizations: Developing cultures for tomorrow's workplace* (pp. 153-166). Portland, OR: Productivity Press.

Brown, J. D., Childers, K. W., Bauman, K. E., & Koch, G. G. (1990). The influence of new media and family structure on young adolescents' television and radio use. *Communication Research, 17,* 65-82.

Browne, S. H. (1996). Encountering Angelina Grimke: Violence, identity, and the creation of radical community. *Quarterly Journal of Speech, 82,* 55-73.

Buber, M. (1972). *Between man and man.* New York: Macmillan.

Bruner, J. S. (1986). *Actual minds, possible worlds.* Cambridge, MA: Harvard University Press.

Burke, K. (1966). *Language as symbolic interaction.* Berkeley: University of California Press.

Burrell, G., & Morgan, G. (1979). *Sociological paradigms and organizational analysis.* London: Heinemann.

Burrell, N. A., & Fitzpatrick, M. A. (1994). The psychological reality of marital conflict. In D. Cahn (Ed.), *Intimates in conflict: A communication perspective* (pp. 167-185). Hillsdale, NJ: Lawrence Erlbaum.

Cahn, D. (1990a). Confrontation behaviors, perceived understanding, and relational growth. In D. Cahn (Ed.), *Intimates in conflict: A communication perspective* (pp. 153-165). Hillsdale, NJ: Lawrence Erlbaum.

Cahn, D. (1990b). Intimates in conflict: A research review. In D. Cahn (Ed.), *Intimates in conflict: A communication perspective* (pp. 1-22). Hillsdale, NJ: Lawrence Erlbaum.

Cahn, D. (1992). *Conflict in intimate relationships.* New York: Guilford.

Cahn, D. (1997). Conflict communication: An emerging communication theory of interpersonal conflict. In B. Kovacic (Ed.), *Emerging theories of human communication* (pp. 45-64). Albany: State University of New York Press.

Campbell, K. K. (1998). The power of hegemony: Capitalism and racism in the "nadir of Negro history." In J. M. Hogan (Ed.), *Rhetoric and community: Studies in unity and fragmentation* (pp. 36-61). Columbia: University of South Carolina Press.

Canary, D. J., & Cupach, W. R. (1988). Relational and episodic characteristics associated with conflict tactics. *Journal of Social and Personal Relationships, 5,* 305-325.

Canary, D. J., Cupach, W. R., & Messman, S. J. (1995). *Relationship conflict: Conflict in parent-child, friendship, and romantic relationships.* Thousand Oaks, CA: Sage.

Cantor, M. G., & Cantor, J. M. (1992). *Prime-time television: Content and control.* Newbury Park, CA: Sage.

Carbaugh, D. A. (1996). *Situating selves: The communication of social identity in American scenes.* Albany: State University of New York Press.

Carter, B., & McGoldrick, M. (1988). Overview: The changing family cycle: A framework for family therapy. In B. Carter & M. McGoldrick, *The changing family cycle: A framework for family therapy* (2nd ed., pp. 3-28). New York: Gardner.

Cate, R. M., Lloyd, S. A., & Henton, J. M. (1988). Courtship. In S. Duck, D. Hay, S. Hobfoll, W. Ickes, & B. Montgomery (Eds.), *Handbook of personal relationships: Theory, research, and interventions* (pp. 409-427). Chichester, UK: Wiley.

Chase, S. E. (1995). Taking narrative seriously: Consequences for method and theory in interview studies. In R. Josselson & A. Lieblich (Eds.), *Interpreting experience: The narrative study of lives* (Vol. 3, pp. 1-26). Thousand Oaks, CA: Sage.

Chase, S. E. (1996). Personal vulnerability and interpretive authority in narrative research. In R. Josselson (Ed.), *Ethics and process in the narrative study of lives* (pp. 45-59). Thousand Oaks, CA: Sage.

Chawla, S., & Renesch, J. (Eds.). (1995). *Learning organizations: Developing cultures for tomorrow's workplace.* Portland, OR: Productivity Press.

Cheney, G. (1995). Democracy in the workplace: Theory and practice from the perspective of communication. *Journal of Applied Communication Research 23,* 167-200.

Cissna, K. N., Cox, D. E., & Bochner, A. P. (1990). The dialectic of marital and parental relationships within the stepfamily. *Communication Monographs, 57,* 44-61.

Cissna, K. N., Cox, D. E., Bochner, A. P., & Anderson, R. (1998). Theorizing about dialogic moments: The Buber-Rogers position and postmodern themes. *Communication Theory, 8,* 63-104.

Clemens, A. W., & Axelson, L. J. (1985). The not-so-empty nest: The return of the fledgling adult. *Family Relations, 34,* 259-264.

Cohen, A. P. (1985). *The symbolic construction of community.* New York: Tavistock.

Condit, C. M., & Greer, A. M. (1998). The particular aesthetics of Winston Churchill's "War situation I." In J. M. Hogan (Ed.), *Rhetoric and community: Studies in unity and fragmentation* (pp. 167-203). Columbia: University of South Carolina Press.

Conquergood, D. (1983). Homeboys and hoods: Gang communication and cultural space. In L. Frey (Ed.), *Communication in context: Studies of naturalistic groups.* Hillsdale, NJ: Lawrence Erlbaum.

Conrad, C. (1990). *Strategic organizational communication* (2nd ed.). New York: Holt, Reinhart & Winston.

Coser, L. (1956). *The functions of social conflict.* New York: Free Press.

Cushman, D., & Cahn, D. (1985). Communication competence in the resolution of intercultural conflict. *World Communication, 14,* 85-94.

Davis, J. E. (1991). *Contested ground: Collective action and the urban neighborhood.* Ithaca, NY: Cornell University Press.

Denzin, N. K. (1997). *Interpretive ethnography.* Thousand Oaks, CA: Sage.

Deutsch, M. (1973). Conflicts: Productive and destructive. In F. E. Jandt (Ed.), *Conflict resolution through communication* (pp. 27-48). New York: Harper & Row.

Dobson, J. E., & Dobson, R. L. (1985). The sandwich generation: Dealing with aging parents. *Journal of Counseling and Development, 63*, 572-574.

Donohue, W. A. (1997). An interactionist framework for peace. In B. Kovacic (Ed.), *Emerging theories of human communication* (pp. 65-87). Albany: State University of New York Press.

Douglas, W., & Olson, B. M. (1995). Beyond family structure: The family in domestic comedy. *Journal of Broadcasting & Electronic Media, 39*, 236-261.

Duck, S. (1988). *Relating to others.* Chicago: Dorsey.

Earnest, W. R. (1992). Ideology criticism and life-history research. In G. C. Rosenwald & R. L. Ochberg (Eds.), *Storied lives: The cultural politics of self-understanding* (pp. 250-264). New Haven, CT: Yale University Press.

Eisenberg, E. M. (1998). From anxiety to possibility: Poems 1987-1997. In A. Banks & S. P. Banks (Eds.), *Fiction and social research* (pp. 195-202). Walnut Creek, CA: AltaMira.

Eisenberg, E. M., & Goodall, H. L. (1997). *Organizational communication: Balancing creativity and constraint.* New York: St. Martin's.

Ellis, C. (1997, November). [Notes from seminar on narrative ethnography.] Seminar presentation at the National Communication Association Annual Convention, Chicago.

Ellis, C., & Bochner, A. P. (1996a). *Composing ethnography: Alternative forms of qualitative writing.* Walnut Creek, CA: AltaMira.

Ellis, C., & Bochner, A. P. (1996b). Introduction: Talking over ethnography. In C. Ellis & A. Bochner (Eds.), *Composing ethnography: Alternative forms of qualitative writing* (pp. 13-48). Walnut Creek, CA: AltaMira.

Emerson, R. M., Fretz, R. I., & Shaw, L. L. (1995). *Writing ethnographic fieldnotes.* Chicago: University of Chicago Press.

Etzioni, A. (1993). *The spirit of community: Rights, responsibilities and the communitarian agenda.* New York: Crown.

Farmer, J. D. (1998). Scholarly communities and the discipline of the communication discipline. *The Southern Communication Journal, 63,* 169-172.

Fetterman, D. M. (1989). *Ethnography: Step by step.* Newbury Park, CA: Sage.

Fisher, R., & Ertel, D. (1995). *Getting ready to negotiate: A step by step guide to preparing for any negotiation.* New York: Penguin.

Fisher, R., & Ury, W. (1981). *Getting to yes.* New York: Penguin.

Fisher, W. R. (1984). Narration as a human communication paradigm: The case of public moral argument. *Communication Monographs, 51,* 1-22.

Fisher, W. R. (1987). *Human communication as narration: Toward a philosophy of reason, value, and action.* Columbia: University of South Carolina Press.

Fisher, W. R. (1989). Clarifying the narrative paradigm. *Communication Monographs, 56,* 55-58.

Folger, J. P., & Poole, M. S. (1984). *Working through conflict: A communication perspective.* Glenview, IL: Scott, Foresman.

Folger, J. P., Poole, M. S., & Stutman, R. K. (1997). *Working through conflict: Strategies for relationships, groups and organizations* (3rd ed.). New York: Addison-Wesley.

Ford, J. D., & Ford, L. W. (1995). The role of conversation in producing intentional change in organizations. *Academy of Management Review, 20,* 541-570.

Fry, D. P., & Bjorkqvist, K. (1997). *Cultural variation in conflict resolution: Alternatives to violence.* Mahwah, NJ: Lawrence Erlbaum.

Galtung, J., & Ruge, P. (1965). The structure of foreign news. *Journal of Peace Research, 1,* 64-90.

Galvin, K. M., & Brommel, B. (1982). *Family communication: Cohesion and change.* Glenview, IL: Scott, Foresman.

Galvin, K. M., & Brommel, B. (1986). *Family communication: Cohesion and change* (2nd ed.). Glenview, IL: Scott, Foresman.

Geertz, C. (1973). Thick description: Toward an interpretive theory of culture. In C. Geertz (Ed.), *The interpretation of cultures* (pp. 3-30). New York: Basic books.

Geertz, C. (1988). *Works and lives: The anthropologist as author.* Stanford, CA: Stanford University Press.

Gergen, M. (1992). Life-stories: Pieces of a dream. In G. C. Rosenwald & R. L. Ochberg (Eds.), *Storied lives: The cultural politics of self-understanding* (pp. 127-144). New Haven, CT: Yale University Press.

Goodall, H. L. (1989). *Casing a promised land.* Carbondale: Southern Illinois University Press.

Goodall, H. L. (1991). *Living in the rock 'n' roll mystery.* Carbondale: Southern Illinois University Press.

Goodall, H. L. (1994). *Casing a promised land: The autobiography of an organizational detective as cultural ethnographer* (Expanded ed.). Carbondale: Southern Illinois University Press.

Goodall, H. L. (1995). Work hate: Narratives of mismanaged transitions in times of organizational transformation and change. In R. K. Whillock & D. Slayden (Eds.), *Hate speech* (pp. 80-121). Thousand Oaks, CA: Sage.

Goodall, H. L. (1996). *Divine signs: Connecting spirit to community.* Carbondale: Southern Illinois University Press.

Gottmann, J. M., Markman, H., & Notarius, C. (1977). The topography of marital conflict: A sequential analysis of verbal and nonverbal behavior. *Journal of Marriage and the Family, 39,* 461-477.

Gottmann, J. M., Markman, H., & Notarius, C. (1990). Finding the laws of personal relationships. In I. E. Sigel & G. H. Brody (Eds.), *Methods of family research: Biographies of research projects I: Normal families* (pp. 249-263). Hillsdale, NJ: Lawrence Erlbaum.

Greenberg, B. S., Hines, N., Buerkel-Rothfuss, N. L., & Akin, C. K. (1980). Family role structures and interactions on commercial television. In B. S. Greenberg (Ed.), *Life on television: Content analysis of U.S. TV drama* (pp. 149-160). Norwood, NJ: Ablex.

Gresson, A. D. (1992). African Americans and the pursuit of wider identities: Self-other understandings in black family narratives. In G. C. Rosenwald & R. L. Ochberg (Eds.), *Storied lives: The cultural politics of self-understanding* (pp. 165-177). New Haven, CT: Yale University Press.

Gudykunst, W. B., & Ting-Toomey, S. (1988). *Culture and interpersonal communication.* Newbury Park, CA: Sage.

Halpern, J. (1994). The sandwich generation: Conflicts between adult children and their aging parents. In D. Cahn (Ed.), *Conflict in interpersonal relationships* (pp. 143-160). Hillsdale, NJ: Lawrence Erlbaum.

Hammersley, M. (1990). *Reading ethnographic research: A critical guide.* London: Longman.

Handy, C. (1995). Managing the dream. In S. Chawla & J. Renesch (Eds.), *Learning organizations: Developing cultures for tomorrow's workplace* (pp. 45-56). Portland, OR: Productivity Press.

Hart, R. P. (1985). The politics of communication studies: An address to undergraduates. *Communication Education, 34,* 162-165.

Hart, R. P. (1998). Introduction: Community by negation—An agenda for rhetorical inquiry. In J. M. Hogan (Ed.), *Rhetoric and community: Studies in unity and fragmentation* (pp. xxv-xxxviii). Columbia: University of South Carolina Press.

Hays, R. B. (1985). A longitudinal study of friendship development. *Journal of Personality and Social Psychology, 48,* 909-924.

Healy, J. G., & Bell, R. A. (1990). Assessing alternative responses to conflicts in friendships. In D. Cahn (Ed.), *Intimates in conflict: A communication perspective* (pp. 25-48). Hillsdale, NJ: Lawrence Erlbaum.

Heisey, D. R. (1991). Defining peace communication. In R. Troester & C. Kelley (Eds.), *Peacemaking through communication* (pp. 19-20). Annandale, VA: Speech Communication Association.

Hocker, J. L., & Wilmot, W. W. (1995). *Interpersonal conflict* (4th ed). Madison, WI: Brown & Benchmark.

Hogan, J. M. (1998). Conclusion: Rhetoric and the restoration of community. In J. M. Hogan (Ed.), *Rhetoric and community: Studies in unity and fragmentation* (pp. 292-302). Columbia: University of South Carolina Press.

Hogan, M. J., & Williams, G. L. (1996). Defining "the enemy" in revolutionary America: From the rhetoric of protest to the rhetoric of war. *The Southern Communication Journal, 61,* 272-288.

Hyde, B. I., & Bineham, J. L. (2000). From debate to dialogue: Toward a pedagogy of non-polarized discourse. *The Southern Communication Journal, 65,* 208-228.

Jacobson, D. (1991). *Reading ethnography.* Albany: State University of New York Press.

Jackson, M. (1995). *At home in the world.* Durham, NC: Duke University Press.

Jackson, M. (1998). *Minima ethnographica: Intersubjectivity and the anthropological project.* Chicago: University of Chicago Press.

James, J. (1996). *Thinking in the future tense: Leadership skills for a new age.* New York: Simon & Schuster.

Jensen, J. V. (1997). *Ethical issues in the communication process.* Mahwah, NJ: Lawrence Erlbaum.

Johannesen, R. L. (1981). *Ethics in human communication.* Prospect Heights, IL: Waveland.

Johnson, B. (1977). *Communication: The process of organizing.* Boston: Allyn & Bacon.

Jones, G. R. (1983). Life history methodology. In G. Morgan (Ed.), *Beyond method: Strategies for social research.* Beverley Hills, CA: Sage.

Josselson, R. (1995). Imagining the real: Empathy, narrative, and the dialogic self. In R. Josselson & A. Lieblich (Eds.), *The narrative study of lives* (Vol. 3, pp. 27-44). Thousand Oaks, CA: Sage.

Josselson, R., & Lieblich, A. (Eds.) (1992). *The narrative study of lives.* Newbury Park, CA: Sage.

Josselson, R., & Lieblich, A. (1996). On writing other people's lives: Self-analytic reflections on narrative research. In R. Josselson (Ed.), *Ethics and process in the narrative study of lives* (pp. 60-71). Thousand Oaks, CA: Sage.

Kahn, L. S., & Landau, J. H. (1988). *Peacemaking: A systems approach to conflict management.* Lanham, MD: University Press of America.

Kellett, P. M. (1987). The function of metaphors in discourse dynamics: A case study of metaphor in the dynamics and resolution of conflict interaction. *Belfast Working Papers in Language and Linguistics, 9,* 118-139.

Kellett, P. M. (1995). Acts of power, control, and resistance: Narrative accounts of convicted rapists. In R. K. Whillock & D. Slayden (Eds.), *Hate speech* (pp. 142-162). Thousand Oaks, CA: Sage.

Kellett, P. M. (1999). Dialogue and dialectics in organizational change: The case of a mission-based transformation. *The Southern Communication Journal, 64,* 211-231.

Keltner, J. S. (1991). The role of dispute resolution professionals in the peacemaking process. In R. Troester & C. Kelley (Eds.), *Peacemaking through communication* (pp. 77-82). Annandale, VA: Speech Communication Association.

Kiesinger, C. E. (1998). Portrait of an anorexic life. In A. Banks & S. P. Banks (Eds.), *Fiction and social research: By ice or fire* (pp. 115-135). Walnut Creek, CA: AltaMira.

Kirkwood, W. G. (1992). Narrative and the rhetoric of possibility. *Communication Monographs, 59,* 30-47.

Kofman, F., & Senge, P. (1995). Communities of commitment: The heart of learning organizations. In S. Chawla & J. Renesch (Eds.), *Learning organizations: Developing cultures for tomorrow's workplace* (pp. 15-44). Portland, OR: Productivity Press.

Kohler-Reissman, C. (1992). Making sense of marital violence: One woman's narrative. In G. C. Rosenwald & R. L. Ochberg (Eds.), *Storied lives: The cultural politics of self-understanding* (pp. 231-249). New Haven, CT: Yale University Press.

Knudson, R., Sommers, A., & Golding, S. (1980). Interpersonal perception in mode of resolution in marital conflict. *Journal of Personality and Social Psychology, 38,* 751-763.

Kriesberg, L. (1998). *Constructive conflicts: From escalation to resolution.* Lanham, MD: Rowan & Littlefield.

Krisek, R. L. (1998). Lessons: What the hell are we teaching the next generation anyway? In A. Banks & S. P. Banks (Eds.), *Fiction and social research: By ice or fire* (pp. 89-114). Walnut Creek, CA: Altamira.

Lakoff, G., & Johnson, M. (1980). *Metaphors we live by.* Chicago: University of Chicago Press.

Lang, A., & Brody, E. (1983). Characteristics of middle-aged daughters and help to their elderly mothers. *Journal of Marriage and the Family, 45,* 193-202.

Langellier, K. M. (1989). Personal narratives: Perspectives on theory and research. *Text and Performance Quarterly, 9,* 243-276.

Langellier, K. M. (1999). Personal narrative, performance, performivity: Two or three things I know for sure. *Text and Performance Quarterly, 19,* 125-144.

Langellier, K. M., & Peterson, E. E. (1993). Family storytelling as a strategy of social control. In D. K. Mumby (Ed.), *Narrative and social control: Critical perspectives* (pp. 49-76). Newbury Park, CA: Sage.

Lanigan, R. L. (1988). *Phenomenology of communication: Merleau-Ponty's thematics in communicology and semiology.* Pittsburgh: Duquesne University Press.

Lay, M. M., Wahlstrom, B. J., & Brown, C. (1996). The rhetoric of midwifery: Conflicts and conversations in the Minnesota home birth community in the 1900s. *Quarterly Journal of Speech, 82,* 383-401.

Lloyd, S. A., & Emery, B. C. (1994). Physically aggressive conflict in romantic relationships. In D. Cahn (Ed.), *Conflict in personal relationships* (pp. 27-46). Hillsdale, NJ: Lawrence Erlbaum.

MacCannell, D. (1979). The elementary structure of community: Macrostructural accounting as a methodology for theory building and policy formulation. In E. J. Blakely (Ed.), *Community development research: Concepts, issues, and strategies* (pp. 46-66). New York: Human Science Press.

Mackin, J. A. (1997). *Community over chaos: An ecological perspective on communication ethics.* Tuscaloosa: University of Alabama Press.

Margolin, G., & Wampold, B. (1981). Sequential analysis of conflict and accord in distressed and nondistressed marital partners. *Journal of Consulting and Clinical Psychology, 49,* 554-567.

Marshall, L. J., Mobley, S., & Calvert, G. (1995). Why smart organizations don't learn. In S. Chawla & J. Renesch (Eds.), *Learning organizations: Developing cultures for tomorrow's workplace* (pp. 111-122). Portland, OR: Productivity Press.

Mason, S. A. (1993). Communication processes in the field research interview setting. In S. L. Herndon & G. L. Kreps (Eds.), *Qualitative research: Applications in organizational communication* (pp. 29-38). Cresskill, NJ: Hampton.

McCorckle, S., & Mills, J. (1992). Rowboat in a hurricane: Metaphors of interpersonal conflict management. *Communication Reports, 5* (2), 57-66.

McLain, R., & Weigert, A. (1979). Toward a phenomenological sociology of the family: A programmatic essay. In W. R. Burr, F. I. Nye, & I. L. Reiss (Eds.), *Contemporary theories about the family* (pp. 160-205). New York: Free Press.

Mead, G. H. (1934). *Mind, self, and society.* Chicago: University of Chicago Press.

Meadowcroft, J. J., & Fitzpatrick, M. A. (1988). Theories of family communication: Toward a merger of intersubjectivity and mutual influence process. In R. P. Hawkins, J. M. Weinmann, & S. Pingree (Eds.), *Advancing communication science: Merging mass and interpersonal processes* (pp. 253-275). Newbury Park, CA: Sage.

Miller, M. (1998). (Re)presenting voices in dramatically scripted research. In A. Banks & S. P. Banks (Eds.), *Fiction and social research: By ice or fire* (pp. 67-78). Walnut Creek, CA: AltaMira.

Minuchin, P. (1992). Conflict and child maltreatment. In C. U. Shantz & W. W. Hartup (Eds.), *Conflict in child and adolescent development* (pp. 380-401). New York: Cambridge University Press.

Minuchin, S. (1974). *Families and family therapy.* Cambridge, MA: Harvard University Press.

Morgan, G. (1983). Research as engagement: A personal view. In G. Morgan (Ed.), *Beyond method: Strategies for social research.* Beverley Hills, CA: Sage.

Morgan, G. (1989). *Creative organizational theory: A resource book.* Newbury Park, CA: Sage.

Moritz, M. J. (1995). The gay agenda: Marketing hate speech to mainstream media. In R. K. Whillock & D. Slayden (Eds.), *Hate speech* (pp. 55-79). Thousand Oaks, CA: Sage.

Morris, L. E. (1995). Development strategies for the knowledge era. In S. Chawla & J. Renesch (Eds.), *Learning organizations: Developing cultures for tomorrow's workplace* (pp. 323-336). Portland, OR: Productivity Press.

Morse, S. W. (1998). Five building blocks for successful communities. In F. Hesselbein, M. Goldsmith, R. Beckhard, & R. F. Schubert (Eds.), *The community of the future* (pp. 229-236). San Francisco: Jossey-Bass.

Mumby, D. K. (1987). The political function of narratives in organizations, *Communication Monographs, 54,* 113-127.

Mumby, D. K. (1993). *Narrative and social control.* Newbury Park, CA: Sage.

Nierenberg, G. I. (1973). *Fundamentals of negotiating.* New York: Hawthorne Books.

Okely, J., & Callaway, H. (Eds.) (1992). *Anthropology and autobiography.* London: Routledge.

Ochberg, R. L. (1992). Social insight and psychological liberation. In G. C. Rosenwald & R. L. Ochberg (Eds.), *Storied lives: The cultural politics of self-understanding* (pp. 214-230). New Haven, CT: Yale University Press.

Osborne, L. N., & Fincham, F. D. (1994). Conflict between parents and their children. In D. Cahn (Ed.), *Conflict in interpersonal relationships* (pp. 117-141). Hillsdale, NJ: Lawrence Erlbaum.

Osborne, M., & Bakke, J. (1998). The melodramas of Memphis: Contending narratives during the sanitation strike of 1968. *The Southern Communication Journal, 63,* 220-234.

Osmond, M. W. (1987). Radical-critical theories. In M. B. Sussman & S. K. Steinmetz (Eds.), *Handbook of marriage and the family* (pp. 103-124). New York: Plenum.

Pedersen, P. B., & Jandt, F. E. (1996). *Constructive conflict management: Asia-Pacific cases.* Thousand Oaks, CA: Sage.

Pelias, R. J., & VanOosting, J. E. (1987). A paradigm for performance studies. *Quarterly Journal of Speech, 73,* 219-231.

Peterson, E., & Langellier, K. M. (1997). The politics of personal narrative methodology. *Text and Performance Quarterly, 17,* 135-152.

Piore, M. J. (1995). *Beyond individualism.* Cambridge, MA: Harvard University Press.

Polkinghorne, D. E. (1983). *Methodology for the human sciences: Systems of inquiry.* Albany: State University of New York Press.

Polkinghorne, D. E. (1988). *Narrative knowing and the human sciences.* Albany: State University of New York Press.

Poole, M. S. (1985). Communication and organizational climates. In R. D. McPhee & P. Tompkins (Eds.), *Organizational communication: Traditional themes and new directions* (pp. 79-108). Beverly Hills, CA: Sage.

Putnam, R. W. (1996). Creating reflective dialogue. In S. Toulmin & B. Gustavsen (Eds.), *Beyond theory: Changing organizations through participation* (pp. 41-52). Philadelphia: John Benjamins.

Rabinow, P. (1977). *Reflections on fieldwork in Morocco.* Berkeley: University of California Press.

Rapoport, A. (1992). *Peace: An idea whose time has come.* Ann Arbor: University of Michigan Press.

Rawlins, W. K. (1994). Being there and growing apart: Sustaining friendships during adulthood. In D. J. Canary & L. Stafford (Eds.), *Communication and relational maintenance* (pp. 275-296). San Diego, CA: Academic Press.

Resick, P. A., Barr, P. K., Sweet, J. J., Kieffer, D. M., Rudy, N. L., & Spiegel, D. K. (1981). Perceived and actual discriminators of conflict from accord in marital communication. *The American Journal of Family Therapy, 9,* 58-68.

Retzinger, S. M. (1991). *Violent emotions.* Newbury Park, CA: Sage.

Richardson, L. (1995). Narrative and sociology. In J. Van Maanen (Ed.), *Representation in ethnography* (pp. 198-221). Thousand Oaks, CA: Sage.

Roloff, M. E. (1976). Communication strategies, relationships, and relational change. In G. R. Miller (Ed.), *Explorations in interpersonal communication* (pp. 173-195). Beverly Hills, CA: Sage.

Roloff, M. E., & Cloven, D. H. (1990). The chilling effect in interpersonal relationships: The reluctance to speak one's mind. In D. Cahn (Ed.), *Intimates in conflict: A communication perspective* (pp. 49-76). Hillsdale, NJ: Lawrence Erlbaum.

Rosenwald, G. C. (1992). Conclusion: Reflections on narrative self-understanding. In G. C. Rosenwald & R. L. Ochberg (Eds.), *Storied lives: The cultural politics of self-understanding* (pp. 265-290). New Haven, CT: Yale University Press.

Rosenwald, G. C., & Ochberg, R.L. (1992). Introduction: Life stories, cultural politics, and self-understanding. In G. C. Rosenwald & R. L. Ochberg (Eds.), *Storied lives: The cultural politics of self-understanding* (pp. 1-18). New Haven, CT: Yale University Press.

Rusbult, C. E. (1987). Responses to dissatisfaction in close relationships: The exit-voice-loyalty-neglect model. In D. Perlman & S. Duck (Eds.), *Intimate relationships: Development, dynamics, and deterioration* (pp. 209-237). Newbury Park, CA: Sage.

Schindler-Rainman, E., & Lippitt, R. (1992). Building collaborative communities. In M. R. Weisbord (Ed.), *Discovering common ground: How future search conferences bring people together to achieve breakthrough innovation, empowerment, shared vision, and collaborative action* (pp. 35-44). San Francisco: Berrett-Koehler.

Schwass, R. (1992). A conservation strategy for Pakistan. In M. R. Weisbord (Ed.), *Discovering common ground: How future search conferences bring people together to achieve breakthrough innovation, empowerment, shared vision, and collaborative action* (pp. 159-170). San Francisco: Berrett-Koehler.

Seibold, D. R., Cantrill, J. G., & Meyers, R. A. (1985). Communication and interpersonal influence. In M. L. Knapp & G. R. Miller (Eds.), *Handbook of interpersonal communication* (pp. 551-611). Beverly Hills, CA: Sage.

Senge, P. M., Kleiner, A., Roberts, C., Ross, R. B., & Smith, B. J. (1994). *The fifth discipline fieldbook: Strategies and tools for building a learning organization.* New York: Currency Doubleday.

Shanas, E. (1979). Social myth as hypothesis: The case of family relations of old people. *The Gerontologist, 19,* 3-9.

Shehan, C., Berado, D., & Berado, F. (1984). The empty nest is filling again. *Parenting Studies, 1,* 67-73.

Shipka, B. (1995). The seventh story: Extending learning organizations far beyond the business. In S. Chawla & J. Renesch (Eds.), *Learning organizations: Developing cultures for tomorrow's workplace* (pp. 143-152). Portland, OR: Productivity Press.

Shotter, J., & Gergen, K. J. (Eds.) (1989). *Texts of identity.* Newbury Park, CA: Sage.

Shupe, A., Stacey, W. A., & Hazlewood, L. R. (1987). *Violent men, violent couples.* Lexington, MA: Lexington Books.

Sillars, A. L. (1980). Attributions and communication in roommate conflicts. *Communication Monographs, 47,* 180-200.

Smith, R., & Eisenberg, E. M. (1987). Conflict at Disneyland: A root metaphor analysis. *Communication Monographs, 54,* 367-380.

Stafford, L., & Dainton, M. (1995). Parent-child communication within the family system. In T. J. Socha & G. H. Stamp (Eds.), *Parents, children, and communication* (pp. 3-22). Hillsdale, NJ: Lawrence Erlbaum.

Stewart, J. (1978). Foundations for dialogic communication. *The Quarterly Journal of Speech, 64,* 183-201.

Stone, E. (1988). *Black sheep and kissing cousins: How our family stories shape us.* New York: Time Books.

Stueve, C. A., & Gerson, K. (1977). Personal relations across the life-cycle. In C. S. Fischer (Ed.), *Networks and places: Social relations in the urban setting* (pp. 79-98). New York: Free Press.

Tannen, D. (1990). *You just don't understand: Women and men in conversation.* New York: William Morrow.

Tannen, D. (1998). *The argument culture: Moving from debate to dialogue.* New York: Random House.

Thorne, B., & Yalom, M. (1981). *Rethinking the family: Some feminist questions.* New York: Longman.

Tillmann-Healy, L. (1996). A secret life in a culture of thinness: Reflections on body, food, and bulimia. In C. Ellis & A. P. Bochner (Eds.), *Composing ethnography: Alternative forms of qualitative writing* (pp. 76-108). Walnut Creek, CA: AltaMira.

Ting-Toomey, S. (1994). Managing conflict in intimate intercultural relationships. In D. Cahn (Ed.), *Conflict in personal relationships* (pp. 47-77). Hillsdale, NJ: Lawrence Erlbaum.

Troester, R., & Dowlin, S. S. (1991). Reconciliation and community building: New metaphors for conceptualizing peace and the role of communication studies in peace education. In R. Troester & C. Kelley (Eds.), *Peacemaking through communication* (pp. 37-43). Annandale, VA: Speech Communication Association.

Trujillo, N. (1998). In search of Naunny's grave. *Text and Performance Quarterly, 18,* 344-368.

Ulrich, D. (1998). Six practices for creating communities of value, not proximity. In F. Hesselbein, M. Goldsmith, R. Beckhard, & R. F. Schubert (Eds.), *The community of the future* (pp. 155-166). San Francisco: Jossey-Bass.

van Dijk, T. A. (1987). *Managing conflict: Interpersonal dialogues and third-party roles.* Reading, MA: Addison-Wesley.

van Dijk, T. A. (1995). Elite discourse and the reproduction of racism. In R. K. Whillock & D. Slayden (Eds.), *Hate speech* (p. 1-27). Thousand Oaks, CA: Sage.

Walton, R. E. (1969). *Interpersonal peacemaking: Confrontations and third part consultations.* Reading, MA: Addison-Wesley.

Weick, K. E. (1979). *The social psychology of organizing* (2nd ed.). Reading, MA: Addison-Wesley.

Weick, K. E. (1995). *Sensemaking in organizations.* Thousand Oaks, CA: Sage.

Weisbord, M. R. (Ed.) (1992). *Discovering common ground: How future search conferences bring people together to achieve breakthrough innovation, empowerment, shared vision, and collaborative action.* San Francisco: Berrett-Koehler.

Weiss, R. L., & Dehle, C. (1994). Cognitive behavioral perspectives on marital conflict. In D. Cahn (Ed.), *Conflict in personal relationships* (pp. 95-115). Hillsdale, NJ: Lawrence Erlbaum.

Welker, L. S., & Goodall, H. L., Jr. (1997). Representation, interpretation, and performance opening the text of Casing a Promised Land. *Text and Performance Quarterly, 17,* 109-122.

Wetherell, M., & Potter, J. (1980). Narrative characters and accounting for violence. In J. Shotter & K. J. Gergen (Eds.), *Texts of identity. Inquiries in social construction series* (Vol. 2, pp. 206-219). London: Sage.

Wheatley, M. J., & Kellner-Rogers, M. (1998). The paradox and promise of community. In F. Hesselbein, M. Goldsmith, R. Beckhard, & R. F. Schubert (Eds.), *The community of the future* (pp. 9-18). San Francisco: Jossey-Bass.

Whillock, R. K. (1995). The use of hate as a stratagem for achieving political and social goals. In R. K. Whillock & D. Slayden (Eds.), *Hate speech* (pp. 28-54). Thousand Oaks, CA: Sage.

White, L. P., & Wooten, K. C. (1986). *Professional ethics and practice in organizational development: A systematic analysis of issues, alternatives, and approaches.* New York: Praeger.

Whyte, D. (1994). *The heart aroused: Poetry and the preservation of soul in corporate America.* New York: Currency Doubleday.

Wills, T. A., Weiss, R. L., & Patterson, G. R. (1974). A behavioral analysis of the determinants of marital satisfaction. *Journal of Consulting and Clinical Psychology, 42,* 802-811.

Wilson, G. L., Hantz, A. M., & Hanna, D. (1995). *Interpersonal growth through communication.* Madison, WI: Brown & Benchmark.

Wolcott, H. F. (1995). Making a study "More ethnographic." In J. Van Maanen (Ed.), *Representation in ethnography.* Thousand Oaks, CA: Sage.

Wood, J. T. (1992). *Gendered lives: Communication, gender, and culture.* Belmont, CA: Wadsworth.

Wood, J. T. (1997). *Gendered lives: Communication, gender, and culture* (2nd ed.). Belmont, CA: Wadsworth.

Yerby, J., Buerkel-Rothfuss, N., & Bochner, A. P. (1990). *Understanding family communication.* Scottsdale, AZ: Gorsuch Scarisbrick.

Zillmann, D. (1990). The interplay of cognition and excitation in aggravated conflict among intimates. In D. Cahn (Ed.), *Intimates in conflict: A communication perspective* (pp. 187-208). Hillsdale, NJ: Lawrence Erlbaum.

Index

About the Authors

Peter M. Kellett is Associate Professor and Director of Graduate Studies in Communication at the University of North Carolina at Greensboro. He received his PhD in 1990 from Southern Illinois University. His research, teaching, and consulting interests concern the development of dialogue, particularly in organizations. He has written numerous book chapters and articles exploring strategies for developing dialogic communication. His most recent publication is "Dialogue and Dialectics in Managing Organizational Change: The Case of a Mission-Based Transformation," *Southern Communication Journal* (1999).

Diana G. Dalton is a member of the Change Leadership Team at VF Corporation in Greensboro, North Carolina. Her professional duties include assessing the impacts of potential changes on the organization, developing strategies to manage the change process, and creating strategic interactions to support change initiatives within the corporation. She also works in leadership alignment and organizational development, and provides the organization with education and information on communication, team building, and conflict management. She received her MA in 1998 from the University of North Carolina at Greensboro.